SEX APPEAL

*the art and science
of sexual attraction*

**'An actress with sex appeal is
four times out of five a more
effective actress.'**

*AMERICAN MERCURY, FEBRUARY 1924 – THE FIRST KNOWN
INSTANCE OF THE TERM 'SEX APPEAL'*

SEX APPEAL

*the art and science
of sexual attraction*

**KATE AND
DOUGLAS BOTTING**

St. Martin's Press ❦ New York

Every effort has been made by the authors
to trace the holders of copyright material
included in this work; following
notification, any errors or omissions will
be corrected in subsequent editions. For a
list of picture credits, please see page 190.

Quote page 102 © 1993 by Maureen
Orth. Permission granted by
International Creative Management, Inc.

Library of Congress Cataloging-in-
Publication Data

Botting, Kate.
    Sex appeal : the art and science of
sexual attraction / by Kate Botting and
Douglas Botting.
        p.   cm.
    ISBN 0-312-14412-1
    1. Sexual attraction.   I. Botting,
Douglas.
HQ23.B68   1996
155.3 — dc20   96-617
                                CIP

First published in Great Britain by
Boxtree Limited

First U.S. Edition: May 1996

10 9 8 7 6 5 4 3 2 1

For Anna with love

contents

preface

'Sex appeal is what life on earth is all about.'

LIONEL TIGER AND ROBIN FOX

A hot Greek beach on a high summer noon. The taverna hi-fi is playing a sultry number sung by Charis Alexiou, one of the modern Greek greats. Her voice is vibrant, earthy, deeply charged with sexual emotion, longing, lust, agony and ecstasy. Love goddess, sex kitten and earth mother rolled into one, she sings her heart out, till her voice is unceremoniously drowned by a deep-throated throbbing roar. Tarzan has arrived in his speedboat, zooming like a latter-day Ulysses out of the glittering sea. Huge, bronzed, muscular and V-shaped, built like a heavyweight boxing champion and decked out like an Athenian rock star with gold chain, black shades and shoulder-length hair, he stands at the wheel of an enormous and very pricey power-boat called *Tiger*, bumping and boring among the lesser fishing-boats as he approaches the little jetty. Beside him is a pretty, diminutive, bikini-clad young woman, a stereotypical Jane with blonde hair and exquisite physique. Tarzan ties up and jumps off; Jane leaps into his arms. He carries her ashore, tip-toeing muscularly over the scorching pebbles – a perfect metaphor for the classic sexual attraction equation: youth and fertility in the arms of wealth and status.

It was hereabouts that *Sex Appeal* had its genesis. Explain the comings and goings, the postures and preenings, the signallings and fondlings of the little bunch of itinerant human beings temporarily inhabiting this one spot, and we reckoned we would be some way towards discovering the lodestone, the alchemist's secret that would make both instant sense of the bewildering permutations of human sex appeal and explain at a stroke the mysteries of sexual attraction – who is attracted to whom and why. At least this is what we thought.

In fact, writing a book about sex appeal is like sharing the fate of Captain Bligh after the mutiny on the *Bounty*, cast adrift in the middle of the Pacific without compass or stars to steer by, bobbing about across a vast, largely unmapped ocean. We found ourselves driven hither and thither by contrary winds and currents, hauling up strange and exotic creatures of the deep, running aground on uncharted reefs, and exploring untrodden atolls. There we ran the gauntlet of hostile tribes who resented our intrusion in their midst, dodging and ducking the slings and arrows of outraged romantics, fundamentalists, optimists, politically correctists, feminists, post-feminists, anti-feminists, iron johns, new men, and all the anthropophagi who inhabit the confused and confusing archipelago where sex, sex appeal and mating strategies have their dominion.

What began as an engaging bagatelle about one of life's more attractive baubles soon spread its tentacles into every aspect of existence, so that by the end it almost seemed we were writing an alternative history of life on earth. As challenges go it has proved an obdurate one. The popular view is that it is mission impossible, for sex appeal is seen as entirely subjective, entirely in the eye of the beholder – and therefore infinite in its variety. Charles Darwin, who started the ball rolling with his discovery that sexual selection was the key to the evolution of species, concluded that sex appeal was as varied as all the cultures that nurtured it, devoid of any common single denominator. Since then psychologists, sexologists, anthropologists, neurologists, ethologists, behaviourists, biochemists, geneticists and medics of all sorts have swung into action. Like naturalists in the Amazon they have swatted, pickled, pinned, measured, labelled and described a whole museum-load of sex appeal specimens, from the tattooed penises of Japan and the elongated breasts of West Africa to the Jack the Zipper syndrome and the sex kitten's wiggle-walk of the West. They have meticulously listed the who, what, when and where of human sexual attraction, but until recently the how and the why have remained obscure.

Sex Appeal is intended as an authoritative, enlightening, diverting, dazzling – yet practical – guide through the jungle of sexual attraction encounters. *Sex Appeal* is not so much about sex itself as sex's interface – sexual attraction, its secrets and the part it plays in our lives. With an ancestry stretching back to the primordial soup we are each a walking embodiment of its effectiveness; with billions of us packed into six continents around the globe, the whole human race is a living testimony to its pleasures and potency .

Modern man's sexual attraction mechanism evolved in the dawn of humankind, so today we have a 40,000BC boy-meets-girl system in a 2,000AD set-up. Has anything changed? If a woman uses just 400 eggs in a lifetime and a man produces 12 million sperm in an hour, does that affect sexual attraction? Why should a woman who wants to attract a man never walk with a stride longer than three to five inches? What faces will we pick from the morgue when cosmetic whole-face transplant surgery comes along in the next few years? Just why exactly do men's heads turn when they pass a blonde in the street – and why do so many of the great male romantic heroes have dark hair? And as sex in the twenty-first century looms like an uncharted planet – birth without sex, sex as sport, sex as god, in this the end of sexual civilization as we know it?

It is impossible to please everyone and offend no one – and we have not tried. We have surveyed the ground, identified the building blocks and put together, as frankly and honestly as we can, an edifice for which no previous architect's plan existed. The few precedents are mostly academic, or go to the opposite extreme. We aim to be seriously entertaining, incorporating new research and the latest shifts in scientific and social perspective. It is, we believe, the first book to look at total sex appeal in the round, incorporating the glitz and the glamour as well as the genetic imperatives, supermodels as well as evolutionary biology, the folklore of love as well as sexual body chemistry, pheromones and smell science. In fact, experts in multifarious aspects of the subject – from cosmetic surgery and hormonal care to voice and body language training and fragrance use – have provided invaluable advice, not to mention a sequence of master classes, insiders' insights into their arcane science or art. Structured like an onion, *Sex Appeal* passes from the outer skin to the inner core of the mystery.

We have also been won over to the evolutionary psychology school of thought. Over the last decade or so a small group of psychologists and sociobiologists in America have worked out a unified theory of human mating behaviour which amounts to a grand theoretical principle for dealing with sexual attraction and mating strategies. The bedrock of this theory is that inside the skull of every modern man and woman is a Stone Age mind responding to residual behaviour patterns formed by the pressures of life that impacted on our distant ancestors hundreds of thousands of years ago. The light that evolutionary psychology casts is a penetrating one; the behaviour it illuminates is often unflattering. Romantic love, religious scruples and personal niceties are cast aside to reveal sexual attraction as a blatant form of advertising and sexual mating – a calculated form of barter transaction between males and females with different, sometimes competing and sometimes co-operating, agendas. The fact is, there is no right and wrong in the evolutionary process, only the plain facts of evolutionary life. Even though the goalposts are being shifted here and there, and the game plan may well undergo fundamental revision in the future, the evolutionary psychology paradigm nevertheless presents an uncomfortably persuasive explanation of the true nature of sexual attraction and human mating strategy.

It has been an enormous help that we are that relatively rare combination, a father and daughter team. This has had two crucial advantages for a subject like this, for we not only represent two sexes but span two generations as well.

KATE AND DOUGLAS BOTTING, LONDON 1995

acknowledgements

A subject so all-embracing required multi-source research. We buttonholed contacts in the glamour and fashion industry, ransacked private memories of personal experience, quizzed friends and strangers in bars and at parties, fired off questionnaires by the hundreds and resorted to the latest research tool of the global villager and cyberspace explorer, the Internet. Our thanks go to all those who contributed to these sex appeal surveys who wish to remain anonymous.

This book could not have been written without the help and advice of a large number of people from various countries and walks of life to whom we extend our unstinted gratitude. In particular, we would like to thank the following:

Michael Alcock; Bush Boake Allen Ltd; Christine Appleyard, Deputy Editor, *Daily Mail*;

Dr John Bancroft, MRC, Edinburgh; Mike Bate; Professor Jay Belsky, Pennsylvania State University; Anna Botting; Louise Botting; Stephen Boxer; Laurence Bradbury; British Library and Science Library; British Psychological Society; British Sociological Association; Errol Bryant; Professor Ray Bull, University of Portsmouth; Arthur Burnham; John and Viv Burton; Professor David Buss, University of Chicago; Pofessor Laura Betzig, University of Michigan;

Dr Malcolm Carruthers, Andrology Centre, London; Dr P. L. Carter; Professor Elizabeth Cashdan, University of Utah; Professor Graham Chapman, School of Oriental and African Studies, London; Dave Crooks; Robin and Trish Crichton; James Cronin, Ceroc, London; Joseph Cymrank;

Roja Dove, *Professeur de Parfum*, Guerlain; Peter Duffin, Gallup; Professor Robin Dunbar, University College London; Professor Donald G. Dutton, University of British Columbia, Vancouver;

Frank Edwards, TCAS; Erox Corporation, USA;

Tony Garnett and all the staff at Island World Productions; Linda Gibson; Yvonne Gilan; John and Carol Gleeson; Professor Heidi Greiling, University of Michigan;

Bill and Penrose Halson; Mark Hayes, Vidal Sassoon; Andrew and Margaret Hewson; David Hopper; Valerie Hoskins; Fiona Houston, Washington DC; Peter Hutton, Mori;

Interactive Fragrance Technologies Ltd, London; Dr Andrew Ionnides, Open University;

Cindy Jackson, The Cosmetic Surgery Network;

Dr Akko Kalma, University of Utrecht; Marie Louise Solarris Kantaris; Professor Douglas T. Kenrick, Arizona State University; Dr M. Kirk-Smith, University of Ulster; Dr Chris Knight, University of East London;

Ann Lawton, Wellington Hospital, London; Professor Bobbi Low, University of Michigan; Adrian Lyne;

Sarah Mahaffy; Eric Massey; Jane Mays, Literary Editor, *Daily Mail*; Bill Miller; Sylvia Milton; Michael John Agency;

Virginia Nichols;

Lindsay O'Hagan;

Philipp Panni; James Partridge, Changing Faces; Liz Poole; Professor Stephen Pope, Boston College, Massachusetts; Dr. Camilla Power, University College London; Dr George Prati, Monell Chemical Senses Centre, Philadelphia; Psychology Library, University of London; Public Libraries, Fulham and Kingston; Jane Russell;

Dr Joanna E. Scheib, McMaster University, Ontario;

Roy Shackleton, Lasercare Clinic, London; Linda Silverman; Professor Devendra Singh, University of Texas at Austin; Professor Meredith Small, Cornell University; Kate Smart, Lucie Clayton Grooming and Modelling School; Anthony Smith; Mary Spillane, Colour Me Beautiful; Professor Donald Symons, University of California at Santa Barbara;

Professor Robert Trivers, University of California at Santa Cruz;

U.S. Embassy Reference Centre, London;

Dr David Veale, Grovelands Priory Hospital; Virtual S, London;

Professor Kevin Warwick, University of Reading; Gordon Scott Wise; Mr Norman Waterhouse, Wellington Hospital, London;

Dr Ken Zucker, International Academy of Sex Research, Toronto.

sex appeal makes the world go round

'The heart has its reasons that reason does not know'

BLAISE PASCAL

sex's interface

Sex appeal is sex's outrider, scouting ahead, Cupid's Kalashnikov in hand, cruising for targets, hunting for love. Or put it another way. Sex appeal is the interface – the crucial, electric, mysterious interface – between the humdrum neuter everyday and the explosive sexual life of the individual and the species.

Without sex appeal there would be no sex – and without sex there would be no life. On the barely rational allure of a curve of the body, a look in an eye, the timbre of a voice, the toss of a head – the impulse of a micro-second, perhaps – depends the continuance of the human species.

'The final aim of all love intrigues,' wrote that devastating Victorian, Charles Darwin, 'is nothing less than the composition of the next generation.'

But sex appeal isn't just a physical thing. Nor is it just a matter of simple good looks – otherwise how could American comedian Woody Allen, or rock 'n' roll icon Mick Jagger be said to have it? ('Jagger,' observed a bitchy Truman Capote, 'is about as sexy as a pissing toad.')

It involves a whole complex of reactions – vision, sound, touch, smell, mind, body chemistry and group psychology, the conscious and the unconscious, the known and the unknown. Essentially sex appeal is a matter of transmitting (and receiving) a multiple coded message that signals a man's or a woman's sexual desirability.

'We are transmitters,' wrote D.H. Lawrence. 'That is part of the mystery of sex, it is flow onwards. Sexless people transmit nothing.'

the lover with a thousand faces

The differences in ideals of beauty and sexual attraction among peoples, declared Charles Darwin, as he sailed round a still largely unwesternized world, are cultural and not genetic in origin.

In some Arab countries, for instance, the perfect woman is still one who, 'looked at sitting, is like a round dome', and though the Sumo wrestlers of Japan are considered enormous in the West, girl groupies mob them on their home patch – one 574 lbs. superstar called Konishiki boasted a geisha girlfriend who was slimmer than either of his legs. Some differences are purely physiological (as in the steatopygia, from the Greek meaning fat-rumped, of the females of certain southern African tribes); other differences are cosmetic (such as filing of teeth, cicatricing of cheeks, pluggling of lips, ringing of noses); others a matter of custom and traditional taste (explaining why whiskered women find favour in the Ukraine, depilated women in the Arab world, and furry people in the Kuril Islands).

'Hearts have as many changing moods as the face has expressions. To capture a thousand hearts demands a thousand faces.'

OVID

'This is the woman I've been looking for all my life' – Richard Burton of Elizabeth Taylor (left). Giant sumo wrestlers like Konishiki (below) may not be everybody's idea of the body beautiful – but to their groupies they are the acme of male sex appeal

Charles Darwin was the first to look at sexual attraction from an evolutionary viewpoint – a mechanism of sexual selection for the reproduction of the fittest

In spite of such variations, however, there is still only a single family of modern man. A great many people in one culture can happily respond to the sex appeal of a great many people from a wide spectrum of other cultures. Time has not changed the ways in which human beings can be sexually attractive, only the fashions by which they are judged. 'The same thing a thousand years ago; ten thousand years ago!' observed D.H. Lawrence in *Lady Chatterley's Lover*. 'The same on the Greek vases, everywhere! The refinements of passion, the extravagances of sensuality!'

Amongst Neolithic peoples female beauty tended to revolve around fertility, much as it does today. A figure found in Japan dating from the Jomon period (10,000 – 200BC) displays a vast pelvis, tiny pointed breasts, slant eyes made with a quick stab of a knife, and a very big bottom – not quite the contemporary Western sex kitten, but obviously a sex icon for the ancient Japanese.

More accessible to today's male in the West are the dancing girls of ancient Egypt and the bullfight girls of the Knossos frescoes of ancient Crete, who would grace any fashion show or beauty contest in Europe or America.

sex appeal in evolution

But the key to unlocking the secrets of sex appeal and human mating strategy in our modern world is not to be found solely in the myriad of human cultures, but in the evolution of the human mind in its response to the needs of a human society struggling to propagate and survive in a world long gone.

Man is an animal, a part of nature. In the natural world, as in the world of man, the creatures of the land, sea and air – and for that matter the plants of the forests, plains and hills – resort to the same dazzling mechanics and paraphernalia, the same exorbitant behavioural somersaults and loop-the-loops of sexual display, as all the variants of the human species. Like the celestial bodies of the cosmos, the outward manifestations of the sex appeal of living things glitter, orbit, parabolate, wax, explode and wane. For many living organisms (though not all) sex exists and sex appeal facilitates its purposes. Man is part of that gigantic organic circus, one among many gifted performers, though not necessarily the star turn.

Technology and genetic engineering have modified but not yet obliterated man's animality, his place in nature. Modern man's sexuality evolved biologically among his animal ancestors in the very distant past. To fully comprehend human sexual attraction we need to put it in this unbelievably ancient context. For what we have inherited from this primordial biochemical, physical and behavioural mix, combined with the prehistoric imperatives of mate selection, still determines the laws of sexual attraction today.

Just as our bodies have evolved specialized organs to deal with the intricate mechanics of sex, so our minds have evolved to cope with this fundamental aspect of our existence. Beneath the dazzling veneer of cultural variation lies an overriding behavioural logic that is common to every man and woman in every part of the world and every period of the past.

If the ultimate purpose of human sexual attraction and mating is (in evolutionary terms) reproduction and the rearing of offspring, then the male and female are confronted with very different scenarios which totally affect their sexual preferences and priorities.

In other words, traditionally a man has valued those qualities in a woman which best enabled her to cope as efficiently as possible with the taxing tasks of reproduction and child rearing, while a woman has valued those attributes in a man which indicated his willingness and ability to care and provide for both the woman and her offspring during the long period required for the children's nurturing and upbringing – the longest of any animal on earth.

From these different evolutionary roles springs everything else – the whole shooting match of sexual passion, preening, posing, makeup, so-called love, so-called romance, the shape of your boobs, the size of your wallet, the cut of your jib, jealousy, betrayal and *crime passionnel.*

Because of the continuity of evolutionary programming, this logic still applies inexorably, even in our highly modified modern world, where men and women who are attracted to, and go to bed with, each other may have no intention of having children or of caring and providing for anybody or anything. This evolutionary perspective on contemporary man, which throws a remarkable light on such hitherto mysterious human behaviour patterns as sexual attraction and mating strategies, stems from the work of a new group of researchers, based mainly at American universities, who call themselves evolutionary psychologists. Their premise is that within the modern human skull is an age-old mind shaped by the mating priorities of our ancient ancestors which continues to exert a compelling influence on our sexual behaviour even today.

Evolutionary psychology is a harsh, unblinking, unflattering credo. In the evolutionary world sex is red in tooth and claw. Men and women are there to do the business and get what they can out of it – at each other's expense if need be.

'Let's hope that it's not true, and if it is true, let's hope that it does not become widely known.'

LADY ASHLEY ON LEARNING OF DARWIN'S THEORY OF EVOLUTION, 1859

'Much of what I discovered about human mating is not nice,' writes David Buss, a leading proponent in the field. 'In the ruthless pursuit of sexual goals, for example, men and women derogate their rivals, deceive members of the opposite sex, and even subvert their own mates.'

In this throwback, twilight world, still reeking of the brutal, barbarous life of the primordial savannahs from which we come, infidelity is a common strategic option and divorce an adaptive response. It is rough out there – conflict, competition and manipulation, fancy and being fancied, bang and being banged.

Evolutionary psychology shows how the implications of our actions for the future have their origins in the very necessary and sensible actions of our ancestors, and how a knowledge of those distant brethren and their world can make sense of so much of the magnificent chaos, galactic brilliance and the weird, barmy, cruel and beautiful phenomena of sexual attraction and everything it leads to.

'Sex appeal? A brilliant mind with a terrific sense of humour - outrageous at times, articulate, caring, very protective and cuddly, a man who loves the piano as much as I do and can play for me and to me. A tallish man, not too skinny, twinkly alive eyes. A man who enjoys a drinking session occasionally and Thai food or curries. A scruffy man but one who smells clean and masculine. A fairly organised man, so I can play daffy. A hard man to the rest of the world, but soppy to me. An amusing man above all. A man who finds me sexually attractive can be a turn on, but of course not always! A man with strong handwriting. A well-read man. A tactile man, a sexy best friend.'

ANONYMOUS FEMALE INTERNET SURVEY RESPONSE

'All our pet theories fall to the ground in the presence of forces coming to us from a past more ancient than the race,' wrote Ralcy Husted Bell, a literary-minded pre-war American medic years ahead of his time on the subject of sex and evolution. 'We are the victim and beneficiary of inheritance, environment and the combination of chance and fate, as we call the unknown. Our behaviour is the result of innumerable factors (over the majority of which we have no control whatsoever).

'Biological influences dominate our ideals; and back further than we can go in any direction looms a mysterious shadow, and from its depth arises a cry, and the cry is sex. Whence came it? No man knows. We only know that sex manifests itself in some form in all life – perhaps in all chemistry – maybe in all celestial phenomena.'

great sex appeal icons

A sex appeal idol is a sex appeal superstar of the here and now – here today and maybe gone tomorrow. A sex appeal icon, by contrast, is a sex appeal idol who has stood the test of time – be it a generation, a century, or even a millennium. The sex appeal icon is more than a superstar. The icon is a sex appeal supernova – still burning bright in the collective memory long after the one-time beauty has faded and even the body beautiful turned to dust.

Nefertiti *d. circa 1350BC*

An ancient queen of Egypt, wife of the Pharoah Akhanaten, 'Mistress of Sweetness' and 'Lady of the Two Lands', her serene, elegant, unnervingly contemporary, *Vogue*-cover beauty is preserved in a priceless painted bust now in the Berlin Museum and in an unfinished head with dreaming eyes and a ravishing profile dug up from the studio of the court artist of the time.

Though Nefertiti lived over three millenia ago in a world that bore little relation to our own, so vivid is her likeness and so modern her looks that she wouldn't seem a month or an inch out of place if she were to glide into the bar of the Paris Ritz and order a damiana cocktail – alive, cool, classy, *soignée*, not a day past 3,000 and as ravishing as ever. What her body looked like, whether she was tall and slim, whether she had good legs and a neat behind, we will never know. Nefertiti stands as a metaphor for a timeless continuity of female beauty, and her charisma leaps across the ages.

Cleopatra *69 – 30 BC*

Cleopatra, one of the most renowned female sex appeal icons of all time, was part Greek and part Persian by blood, Egyptian by nationality, Roman by citizenship and queen by vocation. A famous lover of men, she practised erotic secrets she had picked up in a bordello in Alexandria, later bedding the two most powerful men of her world and time – the Roman statesmen Julius Caesar and Mark Antony. To look at, though, it seems she was no great shakes. As her biographer, Petrarch, wrote: 'Cleopatra was not incomparably beautiful.' But she was bright – and she had terrific style and charisma. 'The contact of her presence, if you lived with her, was irresistible,' Petrarch recounted, 'the attraction of her person, joining with the charm of her conversation, and the character that attended all she said and did, was something bewitching. It was a pleasure to hear the sound of her voice, with which, like an instrument of many strings, she could pass from

one language to another; so that there were few of the barbarian nations she answered by an interpreter. She was the only human being except Hannibal who ever struck fear into Rome.' In the end it was all down to sex appeal. 'If Cleopatra had had a different nose,' wrote Pascal, 'the whole face of the earth would have changed.'

Marilyn Monroe *1926 – 1962*

Beauty, curves, enigma, charisma, flirtatiousness, vulnerability, unattainability – Marilyn was the embodiment of sex appeal. Despite, or maybe because of her tragic suicide (like Cleopatra she killed herself through poisoning), she has remained the most enduring and frequently imitated sex appeal icon there has ever been in modern times. 'I got a chill,' recalled the cameraman at her first screen test. 'Every frame of that film radiated sex.' But not everyone was so overwhelmed. 'Necking with Marilyn Monroe is like kissing Hitler,' complained Tony Curtis (a future paramour). 'Her face was as wooden as a ventriloquist's dummy,' commented drama coach Natasha Lytess on meeting Monroe for the first time. 'I saw that her nose had a lump on its tip, which she had tried to disguise with heavy make-up. Her voice was like a knife clattering on a plate. She was a vacuous girl dressed like

a trollop.' Marilyn may have appeared the archetypal dumb blonde bimbo, but she was no bimbo, nor was she dumb nor particularly blonde (she bleached her hair). Her on-screen sexuality and sensuality, her natural, unreconstructed beauty, her direct, unrestrained appeal to all men, including the President of the USA and his brother, as the incarnation of their dreams, were and remain anything but false.

Marlon Brando *1924 –*

'Ballet-like,' was how actor John Malkovich described Marlon Brando. 'He had presence, and people wanted to fuck him, which in movies is a thing of paramount importance.' 'There was something almost sexually ambivalent about him,' says fellow actor Anthony Hopkins. His sexual ambivalence has intrigued biographers and critics alike. To writer Truman Capote he revealed he had had sexual experiences with men, to others he described himself as 'trisexual'. For the millions of women who were his steadfast fans he was simply 'sexual' – 'a different girl in my bed every night' was his battle cry. Reputed to pace around his dressing room with a copy of Freud in one hand and Charles Atlas's *You Too Can Have a Body Like Mine* in the other, the young Brando was what every young man has ever wanted to be and every young girl has ever wanted to have – male sex appeal incarnate.

Brigitte Bardot *1934 –*

'God Created Woman but the Devil Created Bardot!' cried the headlines as the ultimate sex symbol burst upon the world's film screens, tanned, pouting and

blatantly wanton. As with so many of the great sexual icons, it was the ambiguity of her sex appeal that helped to create it. 'What bowled me over when I saw her naked was the extraordinary mixture of innocence and femininity, modesty and timidity,' says her first husband and the creator of 'BB', Roger Vadim. Wide-eyed innocence perhaps, unabashed sexuality undoubtedly. 'Even without a French accent, Brigitte would be too much for British studios to handle,' commented Dirk Bogarde. 'You see, Brigitte takes the trouble to put across sex as an art. With many of our girls, it's farce.' With a pout to die for and a body to yearn for, Brigitte Bardot was every schoolboy's and every grown man's fantasy babe.

Richard Burton *1925 – 1984* and Elizabeth Taylor *1932 –*

Twice married to each other, and twice divorced, this tempestuous pair were for a long time synonymous with sex, glamour and high living, both on and off the screen. Both had their ups and downs. Burton nearly boozed himself to death. Taylor once grew so fat it was claimed that 'she puts mayonnaise on an aspirin'.

Burton's soaring sex appeal was based on a dashing but sensitively masculine variety of male beauty, a wry, reckless, iconoclastic intelligence, a charismatic presence of the wilder sort, and a voice that was the wonder of the age – a beautiful musical instrument in its own right, strong, versatile, sexy, Welshly harmonized, hypnotically modulated. If Burton did not always fulfil his immense promise as an actor, he more than fulfilled it as a man, for though in the end he may

have had an eye for only one woman, many women had eyes for him.

Richard Burton's own account of his first encounter with 19-year old Elizabeth Taylor round a swimming pool in California reveals a lot about the appearance of the woman – and a lot about the persona of the man:

'A girl on the other side of the pool lowered her book, took off her sunglasses and looked at me. She was so extraordinarily beautiful that I nearly laughed out loud. She was, I decided, the most astonishingly self-contained, pulchritudinous, removed, inaccessible woman I have ever seen. She was the Mona Lisa type, I thought. She is older than the deck chair on which she sits, and she is famine, fire, destruction and plague, she is the dark lady of the sonnets, she is the only true begetter. Her breasts were apocalyptic, they would topple empires before they withered.

Indeed her body was a miracle of construction, the work of an engineer of genius. She was unquestionably gorgeous. She was lavish. She was a dark unyielding largesse. She was, in short, too bloody much. There was no question about it. She was female. Those huge violet-blue eyes (the biggest I've seen outside those who have glandular trouble) had an odd glint in them. You couldn't describe it as a twinkle. Searchlights cannot twinkle. Aeons passed, civilizations came and went while these cosmic headlights examined my flawed personality. Every pockmark on my face became a crater of the moon... I went home and somebody asked, when I told them where I'd been, what she was like. "Dark. Dark. Dark. She probably," I said, "shaves."'

'It is better to be beautiful than good, but it is better to be good than ugly.'

Oscar Wilde

come on baby, light my fire

What are the forces that attract one to another? Can they be explained? Or must they remain forever a mystery? Ask anyone, male or female, in any street, on any train, at any airport, and they will come up with a pandemonium of responses. Sexual attraction is about 'the whole' or 'curves' or 'big ones' or 'the back of someone' or 'the bottom of someone' or 'a lot of smiles' or someone who is 'very clever' and 'amusing' or 'extrovert' and 'fancies me' – and so on *ad infinitum*.

In fact the most secret mechanisms of sexual attraction occur in the very first stages of purely physical attraction. This is nearly always a visual encounter – particularly for the male – though other senses may rapidly, sometimes almost simultaneously, become involved. Voice, touch, smell and perhaps pheromones all come rushing in pell-mell, with secondary visual interpretations involving personality, status and age in hot pursuit. A complete set of cerebral computer print-outs with relevant memory and association data bring up the rear.

The whole physical attraction process may take only a second or two, though its consequences – desire, passion, obsession, erotomania, love, true love, turn-off, break-up, crack-up, murder, suicide – may take anything from a few minutes to half a lifetime.

Physical attraction is not by any means the whole of sex appeal (though it can be), any more than sex appeal is the whole of love (though it can be). It is the spark that lights the fuel that fires the rocket that bears us away to an unknown heaven. Physical attraction is the Law of Gravity of the sexual cosmos, the bio-gravitational pull that keeps the myriad of carnal and celestial bodies of the human species drawn to each other like the stardust of galaxies. You cannot ignore it. It cannot ignore you.

the halo effect

It's a harsh fact, but physical attractiveness ranks at least as high as intelligence and personality – some would say higher – in determining what kind of life we will lead and what kind of love life we will enjoy.

In virtually every aspect of life people who are physically attractive generally fare better than people who are not. Physically attractive people get better jobs, higher marks in class, more votes in elections, lighter sentences in court, and better-looking mates. They are responded to more favourably, and perceived more favourably, in both their personal and professional life. 'Nothing,' wrote Tolstoy,

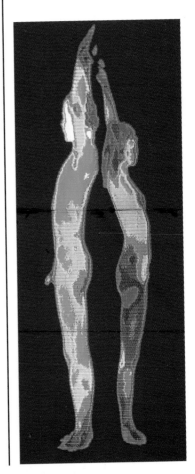

Love can go by many other names, depending on whether cupid (left) fires an arrow, a cross-bow bolt or a .350 magnum parabellum. But seen in a thermograph (below), the body's heat patterns can be a giveaway. Colours run from white (hottest) to blue (coolest); this man's face is boiling hot, while his partner is icy cold from the waist down

'has so marked an influence on the direction of a man's mind as his appearance, and not his appearance itself, so much as his conviction that it is attractive or unattractive.'

A massive national survey carried out in the United States a few years ago revealed that physically attractive people are widely assumed to be more sensitive, kind, interesting, intelligent, independent, strong, poised, modest, sociable, outgoing, creative and motivated. It is generally understood that they will live more socially exciting and active lives, have more sex, receive greater respect, make better dates, more competent spouses and happier marriages (but lousier parents).

This 'Halo Effect' seems to involve an instinctive but systematic manipulation of evidence and suspension of belief and comes into its own in the area of sexual relations. Good-looking people are universally believed to be sexually warmer and more responsive, even though they may be no such thing.

A test using a telephone pinpointed this massaging of reality, this involuntary corruption of the critical faculty. Male volunteers were asked to speak to various women, some of whom they were advised were attractive and others not. When a man spoke on the phone to a woman he believed was attractive, his manner was observed to be much more sociable and outgoing than when he spoke to a woman he believed to be unattractive, irrespective of the warmth or sexiness of her voice. The women, too, were observed to be more sociable and outgoing when they talked to men who believed they were attractive, even though the women knew nothing about the trick that was being played.

The Halo Effect can work at one step removed, by reflection or attribution. If you are not an attractive man to start with, for instance, you can easily end up as one if you start to go out with an attractive woman on your arm. Her high level of attractiveness will raise your own low level in the eyes of others, if only by enhancing your status and hence your desirability. The closely related 'Hang Around Effect' works in much the same way – average-looking women appear to look more attractive when they hang around with other, more attractive women.

But while physical attractiveness is important to both sexes – both to judge and be judged by – it is important in different ways for a man and a woman and on balance to the disadvantage of the woman. For a man to be physically attractive is a bonus. It will help him in his work life and love life but it is not absolutely vital to his success in either, as many arguably ugly men, like Aristotle Onassis, Benito Mussolini,

Mick Jagger and many others, have demonstrated. For a woman though, her physical attractiveness plays a vital role. A long series of polls and studies indicate conclusively that men rate the physical attractiveness of a woman as her most important attribute, playing a crucial part in partner preference at the first-impact and short-term sex stage – but a lesser part in permanent mate selection and marriage, for which a different set of values applies. The nature and degree of this attractiveness the average man can determine in approximately seven seconds.

This emphasis on a woman's physical attractiveness is constant around the world and seems to have been constant throughout the ages. In an unusual study conducted in the USA over a period of 50 years the values that men and women placed on various characteristics in a mate remained unchanged over the generations. Men saw physical attractiveness as crucial in a woman, women saw it as desirable but not essential in a man. 'Regardless of the location, habitat, marriage system, or cultural living arrangement,' says evolutionary psychologist Dr David Buss, 'men value physical appearance in a potential mate more than women.'

Physical attractiveness alone can blind its beholder not only to other positive qualities, but to profoundly negative ones as well, as this case from the psychotherapy files of an American clinic dramatically demonstrates. The patient in question, driven to distraction by his pain-in-the-neck girlfriend, described her to his psychotherapist as 'a chronic alcoholic, a castrating bitch and a psychotic – but she was extraordinarily physically attractive.' Noted the therapist (Dr R. Robertiello): 'Though he was a very intelligent, sophisticated man, he felt his attraction to her should override his cognitive appraisal of her and he was irresistibly fated to persist in a relationship with her.'

'When a man sits with a pretty girl for an hour, it seems like a minute. But let him sit on a hot stove for a minute – and it's longer than any hour. That's relativity!'

ALBERT EINSTEIN

Miss Isle of Man wins a kiss and a prize in the 1960s. Forced to bend with the times, the beauty contest survives around the world as a public exhibition of the valued evolutionary qualities of youth, health and good looks

the burden
of beauty

To be good looking is one thing, to be outstandingly beautiful (whether male or female) is another. The truly beautiful are both blessed and cursed. In ordinary social life extreme beauty can be a handicap. As one American batchelor once put it: 'I have an attractiveness range. That is, a certain range of physical good looks appeal to me. But if I see an extremely attractive woman it's a turn-off to me, because I'd figure I didn't have a prayer and wouldn't try, there's nowhere to go with it.'

Robert Redford has related how he has suffered because of his good looks, often being cast as the male equivalent of the dumb blonde when he would prefer to have been a villain or a psychopath. His beauty, he sighs, has been a burden as far as his acting aspirations are concerned. Even now, approaching 60, the papers ask: 'Is Redford too beautiful to be true?' The same question is now being asked about another actor cast in the same mould: 'Can Ralph Fiennes be good

THE WONDERFUL WORLD OF THE BEAUTY PAGEANT

Specialist beauty pageant film maker, Bill Miller, describes how American pageant judges assess female sex appeal in the context of the running battles between local beauties and pageant pros:

Some of the girls in the beauty pageants really are beautiful, but unfortunately it's the actresses who seem to win more often than the true beauties.

In particular states for example, such as Texas, California and Florida, they dump hundreds of thousands of dollars into the pageant system. For eight hours a day for a whole year they'll teach the girls how to walk, how to stick their butts up the right way, how to give a good interview, what the judges want to hear them say.

There are a lot of Barbies in the pageant system, but they don't always win. In California, for instance, it's the physically attractive, dark-skinned blonde who'll win. In North Dakota dark-haired girls stand a better chance, while in some south-eastern states you can be a lot shorter than in North Carolina or Virginia and still do well.

The judges always say: 'Before I even talked to her I thought she was the one. She had the look.' There's always 'The Look' at every pageant. It's more than physical appearance, it's comfort within yourself, the comfort of someone who walks into a room and the room brightens not because she's gorgeous necessarily, but because she's confident. The younger girls don't have that confidence yet, they haven't quite realised what a body they've got and how they can get doors opened just by winking. By twenty or twenty-two they know. They know how to manipulate and they work it.

Having said that, it's very common for the girls to have plastic surgery to help them win. A very good friend of mine has just had breast enlargement. She decided she was going to dedicate herself to pageants for the next five years and she wants to win Miss Hawaiian Tropic Swimsuit – so she had the operation. The young ones tend to starve themselves.

looking and a great actor?'

How people react to the physical attractiveness of someone else depends in part on how they estimate that someone else will react to them. Fear of rejection is rife and is the tripwire that foils many a first contact or amorous ambuscade. While most people prefer attractive partners, they also take into account their own attractiveness. Various experiments have revealed what many of us already know – in ordinary life, people choose partners who have similar looks. In this sense a close encounter of the physical attraction kind depends as much on a person's own self-perception and self-esteem as on his or her perception and esteem of the other.

In an experiment that tested this thesis, a selection of wedding photos were cut up and the images of the brides and bridegrooms shuffled like cards. Volunteers were then asked to reassemble the photos according to who they thought was married to whom. In the main they were paired on the basis of similar attractiveness ratings.

pressure

Part of the pressure to look good comes from the mass media. This has been true for the last hundred years or more. Back in 1899 a certain Mrs Humphry, better known to her readers as Madge of the periodical *Truth*, wrote:

'There is every excuse for a girl to wish to be pretty. If she opens a book of poems, or a novel, she finds beauty being praised and ugliness condemned. If she looks in at a picture gallery, or gazes at the photographs in a shop window, she finds the handsomest faces selected to be hung on the line. At the opera or theatre she sees the attention excited by a lovely face. In the park she watches with appreciation the pretty faces and observes that others do as well. Wherever she goes, in fact, the great truth, that the pretty are among the most sought after things on earth, is made patent for her.'

The daily barrage of media images of physical perfection (often computer enhanced to remove every blemish and imperfection or even alter the very structure of the face) is beginning to distort our individual perception of attractiveness. In one experiment it was found that men subjected to images of stunning women then rated their own partners as less attractive afterwards.

No wonder a pretty rich woman like Ivana Trump felt compelled to admit: 'I once said I'm never going to be older than 28. I watch my weight and do exercise. And yes, I've had a bit of a nick and tuck. If you can do something to help yourself and feel better about yourself, that's good. Life isn't a dress rehearsal. You've only got this one shot.'

Ivana Trump, ex-wife of American tycoon Donald Trump, has few illusions about the importance of physical attractiveness. Eternal youth by any means, in her view, is one never-failing secret of eternal sex appeal

everyone has sex appeal for someone

THE FAT, THE BLACK AND THE FRIZZY

From an Englishman who was won over by the natural, unpretentious charms of two volumetrically enhanced belles laides from the South Seas:

The prevailing beauty industry ideal of a woman – someone with a schoolgirl's build and damn nearly a schoolgirl's age – was not something I subscribed to. One night when I was in New York I had dinner at the apartment of an American woman friend. The two other guests at dinner were two Papuan ladies hot foot (and barefoot) from New Guinea. What a surprise! What a relief! Here were two natural, uninhibited, jolly, responsive, affectionate, feminine, comfortable, comforting, cuddly, terribly nice women who had never read Vogue or Marie Claire, and weighed about a ton each. I loved them. I loved their shining rich blue-black purpley plum skin, their rippling flesh, their ample pneumatic bodies, their ready laughter, their gentleness, their total, unabashed womanliness that broke every rule in the western beauty and fashion canon. They were scrumptious, they were women – and they were real.

Few of us are born beautiful, though, and even fewer have beauty thrust upon us later. Few of us are born ugly either, though we often, usually wrongly, think we are. Most of us, the great majority of the five or more billion of our species, are born ordinary, physically speaking – somewhere between plain, average and so-so. We must assume that Nature wants us in the safest place, slap in the middle of the gene pool, not bucking the system at either extreme.

And it has been proved that there is no such thing as physical perfection. A mathemetician musing on what might constitute the perfect woman postulated 12 required features with ten degrees of perfection for each, and found that it would take ten to the thirteenth power of woman to find a perfect one, or one in one hundred billion. But sex appeal is not just about physical appearance: it is about mental and emotional attitudes as well. At the end of the day sex appeal is brain sex – tune your mind in to it. Everyone has sex appeal for someone. Usually, in the first instance, it is for yourself. To be sexy you must think yourself sexy. To love and be loved you must first develop self-love, self-regard and self-esteem.

gay rites

Broadly speaking homosexual men and heterosexual men share the same pronounced preference for physically attractive people, while homosexual women and heterosexual women both place less importance on physical attractiveness in others.

Using 800 ads from several American East Coast and West Coast papers, Kay Deaux and Randel Hanna carried out one of the most systematic studies of homosexual mate preferences to date. They found that 53.5 per cent of gay men and 42.5 per cent of heterosexual men stressed their own physical attractiveness in personal ads, and 29 per cent of homosexual men and 48 per cent of heterosexual men spelled out they were looking for attractive partners.

By comparison only 19.5 per cent of heterosexual women and 18 per cent of gay women placed any emphasis on physical attractiveness in the partners they were seeking, though 69.5 per cent of heterosexual women stressed their own physical attractiveness, while only a very small percentage of homosexual women did the same.

In a separate survey it was found that 57 per cent of gay men and 59 percent of male heterosexuals felt it was important that their partner should be sexy looking. Sexual orientation apart, therefore, there appears to be almost no difference between homosexual and heterosexual male preferences; both consider youth and physical appearance to be of paramount importance.

SEX, NATURE AND OUR GENES

'Nature, Mr Allnutt, is what we're put in this world to rise above.'

KATHARINE HEPBURN TO HUMPHREY BOGART IN THE AFRICAN QUEEN

Human beings are not alone in placing great emphasis on the importance of sexual attraction. This is hardly surprising. Man is part of nature, one of the five species of the superfamily of apes. 99 per cent of our genetic material we share with the chimpanzee. But, unlike most apes, we are generally choosy about the mates we mate with.

Sex appeal in the natural world is as varied and dazzling as it is in the human species, and the rituals of courtship behaviour no less complex and diverse. Birds, fishes, reptiles, mammals, insects and even plants all display attractant features of one sort or another in order to attract a mate or fertilizing agent and pass on their genes to the next generation. Part of the competition for suitable mates entails displaying features that are indicators of parental qualities valued by the opposite sex. Human beings are attracted to other human beings of high reproductive and genetic potential – the healthy and the fit, the powerful (male) and the beautiful (female). Survival of the fittest is only a back-up to the main business of life, which is reproduction of the fittest. The great majority of us are examples of the success of the system.

Birds especially are noted for the magnificence of their sex attractant plumage and colour patterns, and their almost infinite variety. As one biologist noted: 'Crests, wattles, ruffs, collars, tippets, trains, spurs, excrescences on wings and bills, tails of weird or exquisite form, bladders, highly coloured patches of bare skin, elongated plumes, brightly hued feet and legs... The display is nearly always beautiful.' Few human beings in all their costumed glory can match the blue bird of paradise or African wydah bird in full display, or the peacock displaying in its full panoply.

But sexual attraction is not common to all forms of living things, for there are ways of reproducing other than by sexual means. Even in the sexually reproductive world, the familiar pattern of two genders practising fusion sex in order to pass on their genes to the next generation is not the only pattern. Mushrooms, for example, have 10,000 sexes on average, while mould slime has 13 genders. Even among animals with the conventional number of genders – like your average rat, rabbit and chimpanzee – sex appeal may be given short shrift, by-passed rapidly in favour of getting on with the business of sex itself as quickly as possible, as often as possible, and with as many partners as possible – irrespective of their sexual attraction qualities.

So why do we have sex appeal? Why two genders, why men and women, why sex at all? Sure, we are driven to it by obscure urges, it can be fun, as a form of stimulation of the pleasure centre of the brain, it can even be addictive. But that, in terms of our overall role on earth, our principal function in life, is beside the point, more a matter of carrot and stick. Sex is central to the human species and sexual reproduction is the only purpose for which we are designed. Our bodies are evolutionary vehicles for our genes and it is to our mother's ovary that we owe our descent, not her body or her mind.

From the biological point of view the only aim of the human species (and every other species that reproduces sexually) is for its individual members to pass on their genes. The exchange of DNA sequences is the central sexual event. Sexual attraction facilitates that event and sexual selection modifies it. Sex appeal and courtship behaviour can be explained only in terms of the selective competition of the genes. Sexual reproduction ensures the uniqueness of the individual and all the potential for evolution and change that that entails.

The joy of sex is fun. The point of sex is reproduction. The price of sex is death. It follows from this that individuals are the important elements in life, not societies, for individuals are the vehicles for the genes. But sex leads to society, for sex is a collective enterprise. Every new being has two parents of different genders and therefore different aims and strategies. Though sex also engenders conflict it must also involve co-operation, caring and loving – of parents for children, of couples for each other. Love is not universal among sexual creatures, but even dung beetles appear to display it. For every creature that plays a part in protecting and bringing up the young there is thus life after sex. Sex appeal, sex, love and all the conflict, co-operation and creativity that are entailed, form a major part of the brilliance and drama of life on earth.

3

object of desire - the human body

'Love's mysteries in souls do grow But yet the body is his book.'

JOHN DONNE

in the beginning was the body, and the body was good

Sex appeal in the first instance is what happens between one body and another, as is sex itself. Bodies are what we lust after, yearn for, dream of, drool over, admire, adore, love and love with. At their best, bodies are among the most beautiful and marvellous artifacts of creation, the gravitational pull between them as powerful and irresistible as the centrifugal force which binds moon to earth and planet to sun.

In the eyes of most men and women who have ever lived, a beautiful woman or a beautiful man is one of the wonders of creation. So powerful is the allure of beauty that the nature of it, the components of it, the relationship between beauty and sexual attraction, and the relationship between beauty and less physical attributes like personality, intelligence, and above all inner fire, have been a matter of conjecture and analysis since ancient times.

Are beauty and sexual attractiveness one and the same? Freud was adamant that the answer was yes. 'There is to my mind no doubt,' he wrote in 1905, 'that the concept of "beautiful" has its roots in sexual excitation and its original meaning was "sexually stimulating."' D.H. Lawrence felt much the same. 'Sex and beauty are inseparable,' he declared, 'like life and consciousness.' The English scholar Sir Kenneth Dover went even further. 'To praise someone's beauty,' he pronounced, 'is (whether we like it or not) a sexual act.'

'I'd like to be beautiful,' sighed one who was not. 'It'd be a big kick. It'd be great. It'd be wonderful because of all the compliments you'd get, being pampered and fussed over.' The idea that the beautiful princess lives happily ever after is one of the most abiding myths, the most precious fantasies in the lives of many. It is a fantasy that can lead to disappointment and distress on the one hand and rebellion and outrage on the other, especially for women.

An Arizona State University survey has spelled out the cost. Three minutes spent flicking through a glossy women's magazine plunges many women, who have no hope of matching up to the impossibly stunning, lissom and youthful supermodels they see in the ads and articles, into a trauma which can manifest itself as depression, stress, guilt, shame, eating disorders, even suicide.

The human form (left) – to many the embodiment of sex appeal. With her blonde hair, Zeppelin breasts and pouting lips, Baywatch's *Pamela Anderson (above) has transformed herself into an evolutionary babe*

'Ask a toad what is beauty and he will answer that it is his female with two huge round black eyes coming out of her tiny head, large flat mouth, yellow belly and brown back.'

VOLTAIRE

RODIN ON BEAUTY

I can only grasp the beauty of the soul by the beauty of the body, but some day someone will come along and explain what I can only catch a glimpse of and will declare how the whole earth is beautiful, and all human beings beautiful. I have never been able to say this in sculpture as well as I wish. For poets Beauty has always been some particular landscape, some particular woman; but it should be all women, all landscapes. A Negro or a Mongol has his beauty, however remote from ours, and it must be the same with their characters. There is no ugliness.

When I was young I made that mistake; I could not undertake a woman's bust unless I thought her pretty; today I would do a bust of any woman, and it would be just as beautiful. And however ugly a woman may look, when she is with her lover she becomes beautiful; there is beauty in her character, in her passions. Beauty exists as soon as character or passion becomes visible, for the body is a casting on which passions are imprinted. And even without that, there is always the blood that flows in the veins and the air that fills the lungs.

AUGUSTE RODIN, 1840 – 1917

'I am the plain Jane of the family and just long for beauty,' went one typical cri de coeur in a letter to a women's magazine. 'When I go to the pictures and see beautiful girls it makes me nearly cry to think I'm so unattractive.' Not even top fashion models are exempt. 'I believed I was totally plain, if not on the ugly side,' recalled the stunning Paulina. 'I've always felt like an imposter the whole way. I was always grateful for anyone who thought I was attractive.'

theories of beauty

What makes a person beautiful has taxed the mind of man since man first began to pile one thought on top of another. From Socrates through to Hollywood, great and little minds alike have wrestled to unlock the secrets of physical attraction. From the Stone Age to the 1990s most of the men and women who have taken part in the Long March of Everyman have known whom and what they fancied; but, with the exception of a handful of sexual visionaries, shining like guttering torches in the all-enveloping dark, next to none of them have had the slightest idea why.

In the early days of classical Greece, beauty was considered the jewel in the crown of the human condition. Greek art celebrated the beauty of the naked human body, both male and female, in sculptures which set the benchmark for the ideal form for centuries to come in the West. But some of the towering minds of Western civilization plunged into confusion whenever they tried to analyse the exact nature of that ideal form.

Socrates, for example, took an ergonomic standpoint and proclaimed that the beautiful, the useful and the good were all part of the same package. In his view, if a humble dung-basket did its job properly it was beautiful, whereas a golden shield, however magnificent, was ugly if it failed to serve its purpose. By extrapolation, a woman and a man who perfectly fulfil their biological role must be beautiful, though there are enough exceptions to invalidate the premise.

Aristotle, by contrast, looked at beauty from a structural angle. The beauty of men, women, animals, wooden boats, chariot wheels or anything else composed of a number of parts, depended on the orderly arrangement and proportion of those parts, as well as a certain magnitude. So a bug might be too small to be beautiful and an elephant might be too big to take in as a whole.

Theory after theory followed as centuries of widespread rampant sexual attraction went by in a state of glorious ignorance and bliss. By the eighteenth century the theorists were tackling the problem from the standpoint of art aesthetics. In the eyes of the London portrait painter Hogarth, a body was a work of art, and to be beautiful it had to contain six elements: variety, symmetry, simplicity, intricacy, magnitude, and the fitness of the parts for the design.

Victorian art critic John Ruskin agreed, and also came up with six elements: infinity, unity, repose, symmetry, purity, moderation. Ruskin's credentials for commenting on female beauty were less than adequate, however – on his wedding night he was so dismayed to find that his wife's body sported pubic hair, unlike any Victorian portrait of a nude he had ever seen, that he never consummated his marriage.

The theorists got nearer to grips with the problem when they turned from abstract notions to naked flesh. None was better placed to study the ins and outs of bare bodies than Dr Thomas Bell, a nineteenth-century London physician who seems to have specialized in the treatment of the fairer sex. He came up with three principal laws or types of female beauty – the Mechanical, the Vital and the Intellectual. All women were one of these three.

The Mechanical Woman sounded fun: 'The whole figure is precise, striking and brilliant. From its proportions, it seems almost aerial; and you would imagine that if your hands were placed under the lateral parts of her tapering waist, the slightest pressure would suffice to throw her in the air.'

The Vital Woman came nearest to the contemporary male ideal. 'A figure soft and voluptuous in the extreme; a luxuriant profusion of flaxen or auburn hair; eyes of the softest azure; complexion of rose and lily; shoulders softly rounded; luxuriant bosom; waist encroached on by the voluptuous *embonpoint* of all the contiguous parts; haunches greatly expanded...'

The Intellectual Woman, by contrast, was the Georgian thinking man's crumpet – an acquired taste which the good doctor himself seems to have preferred. Such a woman was a walking parable of virtues, characterized by admirable but sexually unharassable qualities such as sensibility, modesty, dignity, elegance, grace – and a brain.

'The superiority of feminine beauty has one unique cause: unity of line. What makes women more beautiful is the invisibility of her genital organs. With the human male, and precisely because of his upright posture, the sex organs are the most noticeable and visible feature, an obstacle to the eye, like a break in a smooth line. The harmony of the feminine body is therefore geometrically much more perfect, above all if one considers the male and female at the height of sexual desire.'

RÉMY DE GOURMONT, 1858 – 1915

Lucas Cranach's Venus and Love,
*1509. Youth and fertility are constant
attractants in any century*

The French writer Rémy de Gourmont was preoccupied with the realities of naked flesh and used it to approach the geometry of beauty from a novel angle. In his turn of the century essay, *The Nature of Love*, he argued that it was the sexual organs that got in the way of perfect sexual beauty. Paradoxically, it took a man who hated women to see the nature of female beauty clearly. The German metaphysical philosopher, Arthur Schopenhauer, a life-long misogynist, wrote an essay entitled *On Women* in which he set down for the first time the essential ingredients of female sexual attraction as he saw them. He wrote:

'The most important attribute of Beauty, in the lover's eye, is youth. Health ranks next in importance. A fine framework or skeleton is the third desideratum. A certain plumpness or fullness of flesh is the next thing considered in sexual selection. Excessive leanness is repulsive, and so is excessive stoutness. Facial beauty ranks last.'

Either Schopenhauer was prescient, or he had a gift of seeing the obvious in a world where the obvious was not obvious at all. With a little tweak here and there, this long-dead metaphysical misogynist's critique could have come straight out of the psychology department of any of a number of American universities today. For it spelled out many of the key features (youth, health, fecundity) that have emerged from the theory of evolutionary psychology as it relates to sexual attraction and mating strategies.

birds of paradise: what men like most

According to recent psychological studies in the UK the qualities that men cherish most in women are (in descending order): physical desirability, erotic capability, affectionate nature, social skill and domestic aptitude. In other words, even in the Nineties a woman's body (and what she can do with it) still counts for a great deal more among a majority of men than either her brains or her bank balance. Commented comedian Bernard Manning: 'Nineties men are after a nice-looking slender woman with high cheekbones, a glamorous girl. I think whether she's intellectual or not is secondary. They don't want to come home to someone working a computer, fetching in more money than they are. There are a few pansies around who'll stay at home while their wife is out playing darts. But they're not proper men.'

An American survey that ran between 1939 and 1989 monitored the different sex appeal characteristics men and women preferred in each other. The preferences remained the same from generation to generation for the entire 50 years. In every generation the men rated physical attractiveness more highly than the women and they continued to rate it more highly year after year.

In fact the importance attached to good looks has gone up over the decades among both men and women as a result of the impact of TV, advertising and the fashion magazines, but the ratio of preference between the two sexes has remained the same. It's the same around the world, irrespective of race, religion, politics, culture, marriage system or whatever. 'Men's preference for physically attractive mates,' reports one university psychologist who has conducted a systematic study into the subject, 'is a species-wide psychology mechanism that transcends culture'.

Like it or not, a woman's body and all its parts remain among her most valued assets in men's eyes. To some modern women, trying to break away from the destiny their evolutionary past seems to have dictated for them, all this is irksome. 'Is it too much to ask,' asked Germaine Greer, 'to be spared the daily struggle for super human beauty in order to offer it to the caresses of a sub-humanly ugly mate?'

But if the body's the thing, what kind of body? In a recent survey of female lonelyheart ads, it was the traditionally curvaceous Goldie Hawn lookalike that rated highest among men.

'The Goldie Hawn type coming first doesn't surprise me,' commented Jackie Collins. 'I've mixed with some very sophisticated men but if a girl with big bosoms comes along their mouths drop

---

A PROFILE OF BEAUTY IN EIGHTEENTH CENTURY LONDON

In John Cleland's late eighteenth century blue romance, *Fanny Hill – Memoirs of a Woman of Pleasure*, the young heroine gives a rundown of her physical attributes which reveals a far more classically natural female form than the conventional fashion of the time would suggest:

I was tall, yet not too tall for my age; my shape perfectly straight, thin waisted, and light and free, without owing anything to stays; my hair was a glossy auburn, and as soft as silk, flowing down my neck in natural buckles, and did not a little set off the whiteness of my skin; my face was rather too ruddy, though its features were delicate, and the shape a roundish oval, except where a pit on my chin had far from a disagreeable affect; my eyes were as black as can be imagin'd, and rather languishing than sparkling, except on certain occasions, when I have been told they struck fire fast enough; my teeth, which I ever carefully preserv'd, were small, even and white; my bosom was finely rais'd, and one might discern the round, firm breasts. In short, all the points of beauty that are most universally in request, I had.

open and they turn into little boys.'

As long ago as the 1860s a certain straight-laced Victorian academic with a naughty but studiously lidded twinkle in his eye sought to describe the phenomenon in terms of geometric mechanics. 'The curvature of the outline in the ideal feminine figure,' wrote Dr Alexander Bain, Professor of Logic at Aberdeen University, 'is continuous and varying, passing through points of contrary flexure, from convex to concave, and again resuming the convex.'

There are good evolutionary reasons for this, child bearing and

VOLUMETRICALLY ENHANCED OF THE WORLD UNITE!

No aspect of beauty in the West is more contentious than that of fatness and thinness. It has become a credo that thin is good and fat is bad. Novelist Fay Weldon spelled out the truth as she saw it: 'Thin feels healthier, looks better, has a better sex life, more boyfriends, a bigger house, a higher income – more choice in life, in fact – than fat, and statistics prove it. None of this is fair, it's just true.' As one

headline about farming ambiguously put it: 'Slim chicks lay better'.

It was not always thus. Stone Age chicks like the Venus of Willendorf were fat in all the wrong places and desired by all. Rubens and Renoir celebrated the beauty of plump women; Renoir's fat girls are still as sexy and lovely in our eyes as they were in his. Comparisons with other societies show that where food resources are scarce, plumper people are judged more attractive; if food resources are abundant to the point of excess (as in Europe and the US), thinness is favoured.

A recent survey by two Finnish doctors studied the shapes and sizes of shop-window mannequins from the 1920s to the present day. The 1920s mannequin is not very different from the Renaissance ideal as depicted in Botticelli's Venus. Even into the 1950s it had not greatly changed, fuller than the Italian ideal of 400 years before, but still archetypally female, with broad hips and a wasp waist like Marilyn Monroe (who was a size 16). The radical shrinkage begins in the Sixties, culminating in the 'superwaif' of the Nineties, Kate Moss, posters of whom were defaced by radical protesters (left).

The hips of the typical mannequin of the Sixties and beyond are 6 inches smaller and the thighs 4 inches smaller than those of a typical real-life woman in good shape. If such slender mannequins had been real women, the Finnish doctors pointed out, they would not have enough body fat to be able to menstruate or reproduce, and they would probably fail to achieve a proper bone mass. In terms of normal biological function, such women would not be female at all. Contemporary fashion designer Jasper Conran sums it up thus: 'Women have bellies and hips, a womb and breasts. I have never met a woman, however perfect her figure, who is happy with her body. I think women subscribe to an ideal too much, they do themselves a disservice. The idea you should be thin is cruel.'

PACIFIC ISLAND BELLES

Vigour, vitality and strength, a well proportioned body, a smooth and properly pigmented, but not too dark skin are the basis of physical beauty for the native... It is notable that their main erotic interest is focused on the human head and face. For the rest of the body, the breasts in the woman and the build and size in the man are most important, with the colour and the quality of their skins... A slim, straight, tall body is much admired in a man. In women, also, a slim body without excessive abdominal development is considered desirable. Slim, small-bellied are words of praise. A woman's breasts are of special importance. Nutaviya describes a full, round, firm formation. Nupisiga is applied to small, undeveloped, girlish breasts, which are considered less attractive than the first category. Smoothness of skin and a full brown colour are much sought after. Dark brown is decidedly a disadvantage. In the magic of washing and in other beauty formulae, a desirable skin is compared with white flowers, moonlight and the morning star... They always told me that I looked much more like a Melanesian than like an ordinary white man. They even fortified this compliment by specific documentation: thick lips, small eyes, absence of any sharp outline in the nose, were credited to me as assets. I am afraid, however, that the Trobrianders are more polite than truthful...

BRONISLAW MALINOWSKI, ROBERT MOND EXPEDITION TO NEW GUINEA
1914 – 18

rearing being the principal one. The general curvaceousness of a woman's body as a whole is a sexual attractant in its own right. With the onset of puberty the body outline of the boy-like girl is transformed into the unmistakable shape of the sexually mature woman – a shape which, with its elongated legs, full breasts, large hips and noticeably hourglass waist, boldly proclaims her new-found, sexually receptive, biologically reproductive condition. The body of a woman contains almost twice as much fat as that of a man and thus presents a more voluptuously fleshed appearance in comparison with the lean, angular, jutting, sinewy, muscular frame of the fit young male.

the human envelope

The smoothness of the skin is a powerful erotic attractant for the male. So is the colour of the skin, though the signals on this score are more confused than they have ever been. In general the paler version of the regional or ethnic norm seems to be preferred. This is true among the Indians, the Arabs, the Chinese, the Japanese, the Brazilians, the people of South-east Asia and the island groups of the

The respectable Victorian woman was not only a captive wife but a captive body, rarely seeing the light of either day or gaslamp. But for the gentleman's entertainment, there were those who did linger saucily on the paler side of blue

> ## THE MEDIEVAL CONCEPT OF BEAUTY:
> ## SEX APPEAL IN CHAUCER'S TIME
>
> *The type of feminine beauty praised by the poets in the catalogues of charm is, without an exception, a blonde, whose hair is golden or like gold wire, eyes sparkling bright and light blue in colour, cheeks lily-white or rose-red, white evenly set teeth, long, snow-white arms, and white hands with long slender fingers. Her figure is small, well-rounded, slender and graceful, with a small willowy waist as a prime standard of excellence. The skin is everywhere of dazzling whiteness, rivalling the finest silk in softness; and the lower limbs are well-formed and white as milk, with small white and shapely feet.*
>
> Walter C. Curry

Pacific. It used to be true among people of Caucasian or white origin as well, before Coco Chanel took up sunbathing on the French Riviera in the 1920s and the beautiful people followed suit. In the post-war West the suntan rapidly caught on as the badge of sexy, jet-setting, well-heeled chic. White people with a tan not only felt better but were popularly judged to look better.

But more even than its smoothness or coloration, the condition of the skin is of vital importance for both sexes. A clean, clear skin is a measure of a person's sex appeal in virtually every culture in the world. A poor complexion, dirty, pimply skin, skin blemishes and skin infections are universally shunned. The reasons have their origins in our evolution. The young bloods among our primordial ancestors – thanks to whose sexual attractiveness and unfettered libido we are here today – knew instinctively that it was bad news to mate with someone who carried a serious disease or affliction. The condition of the skin was one indicator of health or infection, rough and ready though it may have been, and lack of wrinkles was an index of youthfulness and child-bearing age. The girl with the smooth, unblemished, unwrinkled, glowing with health and vitality outer wrapping was the girl who got the Prince Charming of the primordial savannahs and lived happily ever after – or at least until she died of old age at 25. Upon this simple perception, as valid today as it was around the time man discovered fire, alcohol and sex appeal, is based the world-wide, mega-money cosmetics industry that recycles the dreams of millions into a dividend of millions.

the naming of parts

the bottom line

When we learned to stand on two legs our perspective changed. To keep us upright all day we had to develop strong muscles on our backsides, and this led to a physical feature unique among primates – full, rounded buttocks. These buttocks were the number one source of visual sex signals among human beings, particularly the female, whose buttocks were larger than the males due to the widening of the pelvic girdle and heavier fat deposits required for the demands of child-bearing. Since the human female is sexually receptive at all times, unlike other primates, there was never any diminishing in the fullness and roundness of the buttocks with which she had been endowed.

Though man's biological evolution to a two-legged posture led to the genitalia being more usually viewed and accessed from the front than the rear, the buttocks continued to serve as a primary sexual attractant, and everything was done, by man and nature alike, to accentuate its allure. Judging from the enormous buttock dimensions of prehistoric female figurines, it is possible that at one time the majority of our female ancestors were endowed with a natural physiological condition known as steatopygia – though it is also possible that our male ancestors were so obsessed with the sexual promise of their prehistoric womenfolk's bums that they projected their fantasies into their sculptures.

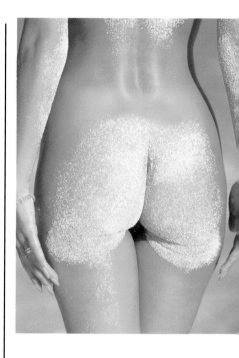

'Men don't make passes at girls with no arses'
BRIGITTE BARDOT

THE AMERINDIAN CONCEPT OF BEAUTY

The people of the Siriono tribe in Eastern Bolivia have a very different ideal of female beauty. For them, the desiderata are firmly fixed on a woman's sexual and procreative functions.

Besides being young, a desirable sex partner should also be fat. She should have big hips, good-sized but firm breasts, and a deposit of fat on her sexual organs. Fat women are referred to by the men with obvious pride as 'fat vulvas' and are thought to be much more satisfying sexually than thin women, who are summarily dismissed as being 'bony'. In fact, so desirable is corpulence as a sexual trait that I have frequently heard men make up songs about the merits of a fat vulva... In addition, certain other signs of erotic beauty are recognized. A tall person is preferred to a short one; facial features should be regular; eyes should be large. Little attention is paid to the ears, the nose, or the lips, unless they are obviously deformed. Pubic hair is undesirable and is therefore depilated, although a certain amount of pubic hair is believed to add zest to intercourse. A woman's vulva should be small and fat, while a man's penis should be as large as possible.

A.R.HOLMBERG, 1946

'What's she like? Thin, pretty, big tits – your basic nightmare!'

WHEN HARRY MET SALLY

The form of the classic hourglass is often taken as the touchstone of female bodily beauty

---

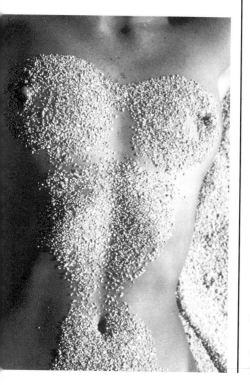

Though the exaggerated behind made a kind of comeback in the artifical guise of the Victorian bustle, the genuine article survives today only amongst certain minority cultures, most notably the San (formerly known as the Bushmen) of Southern Africa, among whom it is more likely that the woman's exaggerated buttocks are a vestigial sex signal system from an earlier era, representing the sex appeal ideal of the Stone Age.

But steatopygia is a question of degree rather than kind. Today, when a girl walks down a street in a pair of tightly-fitting jeans or clinging cat-suit, she is basically emphasizing the same come-on contours of her behind, the attractiveness of which she can increase dynamically by adopting an undulating form of walk.

When standing still a woman differs in posture from a man, for her back is more arched and as a result her behind sticks further out than the male's. Full, rounded and voluptuous, protrusive and undulatory – it is hardly surprising that a woman's bottom transmits an unmistakeable, and sometimes unforgettable, erotic message to the male and that it is still the favoured target for a pat or a pinch by that demonized phantom of the contemporary sex scene, the male sexual harasser.

So powerful is the buttock as a sexual display system that it has even been suggested that the universal symbol of love – the stylized human heart, which in fact does not really resemble the human heart at all – is in fact based on the female buttocks seen from behind, complete with the little cleft at the top.

busted

Breasts play a key role in signalling a woman's sexual attractiveness. Some psychologists have even theorized that a man's interest in a woman's breasts is basically an infantile reaction, a harking back to the comfort, security and oral pleasure of the maternal breasts at which he once sucked. Few men, though, can be in any doubt that their interest in the female breast stems almost entirely from their sexual interest in the girl in front of them rather than any hankering for the mother in their past.

What kind of breast is another matter. 'How do you like them?' the Parisian author Colette once asked, teasingly running through the options. 'Like a pear, a lemon, *à la* Montgolfière, half an apple, or a cantaloupe. Go on, choose, don't be embarrassed.'

Research has shown that a repressed individual, shocked or confused by the 'brazen' signalling of the full-blown breasts of the full-grown woman, may favour the small, pointed, coyer and less threatening breasts that are typical of the immature, virginal juvenile. A mother-fixated or daughter-orientated individual, by contrast, or a matriarchal society of the West African or Southern European variety, might plump for the overblown, drooping breasts more typical of the matron approaching middle age.

The majority of men in the majority of cultures are somewhere in the middle of these two extremes. In one survey of reaction to different female body shapes carried out by a national newspaper, it was reported that 'if a girl isn't skinny with breasts the size of melons, men don't want to know about her.'

Of one girl (a size 10) all the men's comments revolved around her breasts. 'She has a very good figure,' went one typical response. 'Everything's there. Her breasts are a good size and her thighs are nice and round.' Perhaps the reason why Charles liked Camilla, apart from her 'vivacious, witty, friendly and intelligent' personality, is that reputedly she has 'wonderful boobs'.

The most prized of breasts are those breasts which are typical of the young woman at her reproductive and sexual optimum in her late teens and early twenties – breasts that are full but not yet at their fullest. These are the breasts of the pin-up, the cover girl, the centrefold, the floor show, the beauty contest, the superstar and the supermodel – and for that matter, of the statues of classical Greece like the Venus de Milo and the beauties of the Renaissance like Botticelli's model, Simonetta Vespucci.

To the Western male, such fine, pert, upstanding, fully rounded breasts signal youthful maturity and vitality, much sought after sex appeal characteristics in a woman. A woman is at her physical peak around her mid-twenties, when all the growth processes of maturation have been completed and her breasts have achieved their maximum fullness and roundness. 'Her breasts were like full moons, and the nipples like sugar-loaf jewels of the flesh,' wrote Ralcy Husted Bell, an American writer-physician much dedicated to the love of women. 'You must understand, there is as much to the slant of a nipple as there is to its size and shape; and a courtesan's breasts, when beautiful, are dearer to her than jewels.'

showing a leg

The legs in particular have at different times and in different climes exerted an enormous sexual pull for some males, though not always for the same reasons. For many men a long-legged woman is attractive, the reason being that the lengthening of the limbs is a feature of sexual maturing, which is one reason why women wear

Two young jungle Eves from opposite ends of the Amazon Basin (Suya woman, Brazil, top, Guiaca girl, Venezuela, bottom), exhibiting widely appreciated features of the female body beautiful: trim, curvaceaous figure, small hip-waist ratio, full pert breasts, long legs and rounded behind

Banned as indecent in Victorian times, long legs signify maturity, and hence sexiness and fecundity

high-heeled shoes, enhancing the length and also the shape of the leg. For some men a round-legged woman is attractive, the curvaceous contours and proportions of calf and thigh being the attractant signal. For other men in other periods a fatter kind of leg has proved attractive, especially around the thighs, where woman have greater deposits of fat than men.

From a historical perspective the degree of exposure of the female leg has been the key to its sexual attractiveness. In the depths of the Victorian age, when women's legs were normally completely hidden from view, a momentary glimpse of a naked ankle could send a man into a swoon of frustrated desire, so legs (table legs and piano legs as well the human female kind) were kept under wraps and the very word 'leg' was banned in polite society.

In the post-war Twenties, when the skirt-length shot up along with the champagne corks and testosterone levels, the legs for a while usurped the role of the buttocks and breasts and became the man's chief focus of desire. 'What undoubtedly attracted young men of the period was legs!' wrote one social historian of the time. 'Far from looking male, girls with that daring length of limb on show appeared

SEX APPEAL AT THE COURT OF HARUN AL-RASHID

In order that a woman may be relished by men, she must have a perfect waist, and must be plump and lusty. Her hair will be black, her forehead wide, she will have eyebrows of Ethiopian blackness, large black eyes, with the whites in them very limpid. With cheek of a perfect oval, she will have an elegant nose and a graceful mouth, lips and tongue vermilion; her breath will be of pleasant odour, her throat long, her neck firm; her breasts must be full and firm, her belly in good proportions, and her navel well-developed and marked; she must have the thighs and buttocks hard, the hips large and full, a waist of fine shape, hands and feet of striking elegance, plump arms and well-developed shoulders. If one looks at a woman with those qualities in front, one is fascinated; if from behind, one dies of pleasure. Looked at sitting, she is a rounded dome; lying, a soft bed; standing, the staff of a standard. She hides her secret parts, is always elegantly attired, perfumes herself with scents, uses antimony for her toilet, and cleans her teeth with souak [bark of the walnut tree, which reddens the lips and gums and well as cleans the teeth].

Such a woman is cherished by all men.

CHEIKH NEFZAOUI, C. 600AD

**WHO LIKES WHAT -
THE LATEST
FIGURES**

*According to a 1995
survey in Germany,
what people like about
each other's bodies is
changing – the genitalia
are now acknowledge
to score higher than
they did before*

[Source: *Fit for Fun*]

*Full hair
49%*

what men find sexy in a woman's body

Almond-shaped oriental eyes 51%

Sensuous, erotic mouth 83%

*Below 50%
come trim arms,
small breasts
and large
nipples*

*Full, firm breasts
80%*

*Athletic body
53%*

*Slim figure
73%*

*Rounded hips
64%*

*Nicely arched
vulva 54%*

*Shaved pubis
67%*

*Womanly thighs
62%*

*Long legs
77%*

CARTOON APPEAL

Jessica Rabbit was the cartoon heroine of the animation and live action movie *Who Framed Roger Rabbit?* 100 per cent pure sex appeal, Jessica was created by male animators to conform to the stereotype of the female sex bomb, and though she was only a paint-and-trace fantasy she had audiences gasping. These are the carefully crafted components of her cartoon sex appeal:

Husky voice
Hooded eyes
Projecting lips
Luscious long hair
Pneumatic breasts
Very long legs
High heels
Neat, melon-like behind
Tight red dress, slashed down the back
Confident, sexy personality
Unambiguous sexual signalling

not less but more delightfully feminine than ever. Young men in dance halls, talked "legs" – ankles, calves, shapes.' Some citizens of the time retreated in outrage and confusion. 'The provocation of a silken leg and half-naked thigh,' protested one distinguished lawyer, 'was devastating and overwhelming.'

In the 'Swinging Sixties' skirts went almost as high as they have ever been, leaving the thigh more exposed than ever before, and the sexual stimulation of the female leg more intense than ever before. Now the secret, sacred portals where the legs joined – the basic subtext of the legs' erotic signal – was but a twitch or a gust of wind away.

These key parts of a woman's body – buttocks, breasts and legs – form a major part of the vocabulary of her sexual body language. These prime parts (along with the back, another zone of intermittent erotic interest, offering a broad expanse of bare flesh but no specific sexual object) are also the main areas of the body that are exposed, consciously or unconsciously, in certain socio-sexual contexts, such as nightclub and cabaret leg shows, topless bars and beaches, even formal functions where the *décolleté* or off-the-shoulder dress is an accepted norm.

Partial flesh exposure can be an automatic, unconscious sexual response in women. In a recent research programme the sexual cycles of women out for an evening's dancing in night clubs were analysed and the data compared with the degree of flesh exposed by their clothing. The results showed that maximum exposure took place at the time of ovulation, the peak of sexual display coinciding (totally unconsciously) with the peak of fertility and sexual receptivity.

bellies, bull's eyes and other spare parts

There was a time when a pot belly in a woman was considered fashionable and attractive. That passing fad for blatant fertility symbolism has long gone, and most women today are as anxious as their menfolk to present a trim, flat stomach to the world at large.

But it is neither easy nor natural to attain such a state, as body image consultant Sondra Howell points out: 'We each of us has a uterus and 27 feet of intestines. It is absurd to expect to have a flat belly.'

In women it is not so much the belly itself as the belly's reticent little appurtenance, the belly button, that concentrates male sexual interest. According to a theory posited by research zoologists in Germany in the Sixties, the belly button is an example of what is called a 'genital echo'.

As proselytized by Desmond Morris, any part of the body that bears a passing resemblance to a genital, and might conciously or unconsciously serve as a sexual double entendre inside a man or woman's mind, is a genital echo. As it happens, all the plausible genital echoes are female-related ones, in that they are all orifices, or vagina look-alikes.

The two most effective genital echoes are the mouth and the belly button. The belly button is the body's most unlikely candidate as a genital substitute. For one thing it is tiny and intrinsically insignificant, for another it goes nowhere, does nothing and permits little to be done to it. But it has a strategic location slap in the middle of the naked belly, and enjoys certain discreet cameo versatility much appreciated by connoisseurs of the female body. The male navel on the other hand is curiously neuter and mute, sending no sexual signal and receiving no sexual interest in return.

By rights the crotch or genital area of the human body ought to be the prime focus for human physical attractiveness par excellence. But is it? In their classic study of sexual behaviour in non-Western society, Ford and Beach could find no example of any society in which the female genitals were regularly exposed. As a visual signal in physical attraction the female genitals may well be too powerful to serve much use in ordinary situations.

By contrast, there are still many societies in which the male penis remains fully exposed. Evolutionary pressures towards pair-bonding by the human female, it seems, may have programmed her not to be sexually aroused by the sight of the male genitalia in general. In spite of beliefs to the contrary, the penis is not seen as a sex-attractant by women, but rather an instrument of sexual pleasure designed to reinforce their pair-bond with an individual male.

This does not mean that the genitals play no role in sexual attraction. The Japanese, for example, tend to see the body as a mere assemblage of different functional parts, and for them the genitals are the most intrinsically relevant parts when it comes to eroticism and arousal. Probably no nation on earth has such a rich and extensive vocabulary of genital euphemisms – so many, in fact, that sexologist Nakano Eizo felt obliged to publish a popular *Genital Glossary* listing such erotic metaphors as 'scallop', 'octopus', 'snapping turtle', 'middle leg', 'teapot' and 'honourable little tinkle-tinkle'.

THE HINDU CONCEPT OF BEAUTY: A SUBTLE COMBINATION OF THE EROTIC AND PLATONIC, NOT TO SAY THE BOTANIC.

Her face is pleasing as the full moon; her body, well clothed with flesh, is as soft as the mustard flower; her skin is fine, tender, and fair as the yellow lotus, never dark colored. Her eyes are bright and beautiful as the orbs of the fawn, well cut and with reddish corners. Her bosom is firm, full, and high; she has a good neck; her nose is straight and lovely; and three folds or wrinkles cross her middle – about the umbilical region. Her vulva resembles the opening lotus bud, and her love-seed is perfumed like the lily that has newly burst. She walks with flamingo-like gait, and her voice is low and as musical as the Kokila bird.

QUOTED BY HAVELOCK ELLIS

waist not, want not: the waist-hip ratio

Professor Devendra Singh, an Indian psychologist working at the University of Texas in Austin, has applied scientific analysis to the matter of the female figure.

As an evolutionary psychologist, Singh was looking for sexually attractive features that were common to every woman in every society and every epoch. He began by studying the so-called vital statistics of the women in *Playboy* centrefolds from 1955 to 1990 and the Miss America beauty contests between 1923 and 1987 and found that the measurements had changed during these periods.

Miss America's vital statistics, for example, had shrunk from 35-24.5-35 in 1940 to 35-23.5-34.5 in 1987, while her weight had gone down by by between 11 and 16 pounds. The ideal Western woman, it seemed, was becoming lighter and slenderer, with a smaller upper torso, especially around the bust.

But Singh's calculations showed that, though the female figure had been shifting from relatively full and heavy to relatively slim and light, the ratio of waist measurements to hip measurements (calculated by dividing the waist measurement by the hip size, counting the buttocks in with the hip) remained remarkably constant. It was this waist-hip ratio, in Singh's view, that was the crucial indicator of the sexual attractiveness of a woman's body.

'She was beautiful beyond description, and nothing she could have uttered might have enhanced the magic of that perfection. I remember thinking, "Well, at least she has big hips... she's human."'

SHIRLEY MacLAINE ON AVA GARDNER

Women who are perfectly healthy always have a waist-hip ratio below .80, regardless of their whole body weight. The ideal range for pre-menopausal women is between .67 and .80 (which works out at between 24- and 28-inch waists with 36-inch hips, and 27-inch to 31-inch waists with 40-inch hips). The lower the waist-hip ratio, the more sexually attractive the woman becomes.

Other features of a woman's body, such as bustline, physique and body weight, have had their importance over the years in Western society, but none of them have displayed the same consistency. The ideals of feminine beauty in nineteenth century Britain and America were big bosomed and comfortably built. By contrast, the most sought-after fashion models of the 1960s took after Twiggy, and were slender and flat-chested. The one thing these two extremes of female attractiveness had in common was a low waist-hip ratio. At 31-24-33 in her flatchested heyday, Twiggy still had a low average waist-hip ratio of .73.

But was it the waist-hip ratio that enabled Miss Americas to win the beauty titles or Playboy Playmates to secure coveted centrefolds?

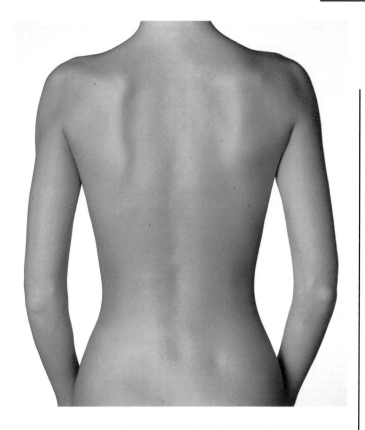

Waist measurement ÷ hip size (including buttocks) = waist-hip ratio. The smaller the ratio the sexier the figure

Or was it the shape of the breasts, the length of their legs, the promise of the smile, the pout of the lips?

To find out Professor Singh asked 580 men and women of different ethnic groups and educational backgrounds between the ages of 18 and 86 to rate drawings of twelve female figures on the basis of their good health, youthful looks, attractiveness, sexiness, and desire and capability for having children. The faces and breasts of the women in the drawings remained the same, only their weights and hip-waist ratios were different. So four of the women were normal weight, four were overweight and four underweight, and in each group the waist-hip ratios ranged from low to high.

Among both the men and the women the favourite figure of all – the sexiest, most attractive woman with the best health and the greatest desire and capability for having children – was judged to be the normal weight woman with the low waist-hip ratio. Out of the overweight and underweight groups the favourite figure was invariably the woman with the narrowest waist.

The men did not appear to equate plumpness with fertility or thinness with beauty. This last finding (a by-product of the test) was a surprise, given the current shibboleth in America and the West that thin is beautiful.

Why do men react in this way? Devendra Singh believes the male

STONE AGE WAIST-HIP RATIO DISCOVERED IN PAPUAN JUNGLE

Until now it has been widely assumed that the ideal of female beauty in Stone Age times was the rotund Earth Mother figure of the Venus of Willendorf figurine – an idealized woman with enormous buttocks and breasts and tremendously thickened waist, a symbol of fertility and motherhood. At first it seemed the present-day Stone Age women of the Papua interior were little different. Explorer David M. Davies reported:

'Their weak points are their unusually short waists (if they have waists at all), their big bellies, short, fat thighs and bulging buttocks.'

At one remote village, however, Davies made an amazing discovery. When he arrived two girls emerged from a hut.

'One girl had a waist and was the prettiest I had seen so far; her lips were painted with red clay, and altogether she looked very seductive. She had all the temperament of a glamour girl, flinging her hands above her head and wriggling like an eastern dancer. I was quite taken aback, for she was the first grown-up girl I had seen that resembled the European idea of a woman. The other girl was good-looking too, but she didn't have a waist, so she didn't have quite the same amount of sex appeal.'

reaction amounts to an unconscious assessment of the female's sexual and reproductive capabilities, based on clues provided by the dimensions of the woman's waist, and that these clues have their origins in man's deep past.

Waist-hip ratio is to do with the distribution of body fat, a great signifier of a person's age and sex, rather than the amount of fat. At ten years old, for example, a girl has much the same figure as she will have around the age of forty. On reaching puberty, she will begin to deposit more fat on her hips, which not only gives her her classic female shape, but also a waist-hip ratio that is much lower than the males. This remains the case until the female menopause, when the female waist-hip ratio becomes similar to that of the male.

A recent report has found a direct link between waist-hip ratio and fertility. Married women who have a high waist-hip ratio experience greater difficulty in becoming pregnant and also have their first live birth at a later age.

The human male, concludes Professor Singh, has learnt to use the waist-hip ratio as the most important bodily clue to a woman's reproductive capability and health status.

male beauty in perspective: what women like most

More than twenty years back a poll of the physical preferences of 100 men and 100 women in a New York newspaper, *Village Voice*, revealed that only 2 per cent of the women voted a big penis as their favourite attribute in the male anatomy, and only 1 per cent voted for muscular chest and shoulders, and none at all voted for muscular arms. The inordinately well hung and muscle-bound did not find much favour. In fact most of the women did not view men as sex objects at all. When pressed, however, they gave an overwhelming vote in favour of the buttocks as the most attractive part of a man's body – though even then the buttocks had to be 'small and sexy', not pumped-up globes of muscle. Some good way behind came slimness, a flat stomach and expressive eyes as other attributes which achieved double figures in the poll, followed by tallness and long legs.

It would seem that in the days of 'Flower Power' and 'Unisex' women tended to weigh up a man's bum even before they looked into his eyes let alone at his crotch. All that has changed it seems. According to a current survey in Germany a new generation of women has radically revised its preferences (or admitted to them!) when it comes to the male body beautiful. Attention has shifted towards the genitalia, and a big penis now appears to be third in the top ten most desirable features, behind broad shoulders and a muscular body. In evolutionary terms such features signal not only male gender, but strength, power, and the youthful muscular athleticism of the runner, the hunter and the provider of the ancient savannah.

head and shoulders above the rest –
the importance of height

Research in America in the early 1990s shows that American women consistently prefer men of average or greater than average height as their ideal marriage partner. In an ideal world it seems that men below 5 feet 11 inches are deemed to be less desirable as dates or permanent mates. In this respect human females have something in common with the females of other animal species.

The classical Greeks' fascination with harmony and proportion, as seen in this early marble figure of the male, set the benchmark for the ideal human form for centuries to come

A female gladiator frog will strike a male gladiator frog a mighty blow when courting to see if he falls over or runs away; if he stands his ground without flinching he is judged suitable mate material with the physical potential to protect her offspring against male aggressors. Similarly, female baboons will trade sex for protection with males who are prepared to defend both the female and her young against other males. The same is true in human society. The size, strength and physical prowess of a man are ancient indicators of his ability to protect a woman and her children in a society where women can often find themselves on the receiving end of male physical and sexual aggression, sometimes of a violent kind.

In our ancient past and among hunter-gatherer societies today, the big men in the tribe, the men who call the shots, are literally the big men, the men who walk tall, physically speaking. In contemporary Western society, men of stature also tend to be men of status. In evolutionary terms their advantages in height and physical prowess have been redeployed from hunting and wrestling power to executive and earning power, but the principle remains the same. Taller men get better jobs, earn more money, are promoted sooner and more often – and walk off with the best-looking women. A survey in the *Wall Street Journal* revealed that brokers who were 6 feet 2 inches or more earned an average of 12.5 per cent more than men who were less than 6 feet in height (every inch worth an extra $6,000 in salary), while men who have sexual partners who are more physically attractive than themselves tend to be more than two and a half inches taller than males whose partners are less attractive. One commentator has gone so far as to claim that 'American society is a society with a heightist premise: to be tall is to be good and to be short is to be stigmatized.'

THE IMPORTANCE OF BEING TALLER?

On the banks of an unexplored tributary of the Upper Orinoco, Venezuela, expeditionary Douglas Botting poses with a diminutive Guiaca warrior, on leave from a tribal war raging in the surrounding forest. The warrior is armed to the teeth with spear, bow and a deadly curare poison that can kill a man in seconds. Douglas Botting, by contrast, has nothing but a useless cigarette—and his height, nearly 6 feet 2 inches of it.

In our ancient past and among hunter-gatherer societies today, the big men in the tribe, the men who call the shots, are literally the big men, the men who walk tall. In contemporary Western society, men of stature also tend to

be men of status (with some notable exceptions). In the United States, for example, almost every president since 1900 has been the tallest candidate in the presidential election, and on average every inch of height is worth an extra $6,000 in income. So although the Guiaca warrior has superior weaponry, his power/status advantage is balanced out by the explorer's superior stature (always assuming that the curare is aimed in a different direction).

**what women find sexy
in a man's body**

Full hair 55%

Long hair 41%

Broad shoulders 72%

Sensual mouth 37%

Muscular arms 64%

Imposing body proportions 80%

Muscular athletic body 76%

**WHO LIKES WHAT –
THE LATEST
FIGURES**

*Earlier polls played
down the role of brawn
and bigness in male
beauty. But a 1995
survey has put them
firmly near the top of
contemporary female
preferences*

[Source: *Fit for Fun*]

Narrow hips 34%

Small bottom 60%

Large penis 65%

Muscular legs 31%

*At 30% or less come the
following (in descending order):
slim build
three-day beard
striking nose
soft skin*

A MID-CENTURY VIEW FROM 007

In the days before AIDS and political correctness James Bond had a different girl every adventure. Black hair, brown hair, blonde hair—it didn't bother Special Agent 007. Blue eyes, a pouting mouth, a tiny nose, high cheekbones and a cracking pair of boobs and she was all right for Bond. But the man with the license to thrill wasn't immune to the idea of marriage. And he had a clear

idea of what his ideal wife would be like, as he explained to Tiffany Case in *Diamonds Are Forever*:

He lit a cigarette thoughtfully. "Somebody who can make sauce Béarnaise as well as love," he said. "Holy mackerel! Just any old dumb hag who can cook and lie on her back?" "Oh no. She's got to have all the usual things." Bond examined her. "Gold hair, Grey eyes. A sinful mouth. Perfect figure. And of course she's got to be witty and poised and know how to dress and play cards and so forth. The usual things." "And you'd marry this person if you found her?" "Not necessarily," said Bond.

Heightism works two ways – the taller a man the higher his status is perceived to be, the higher his status is the greater his height is perceived to be (even when he's short). For nearly 200 years now the members of the American Senate have been taller than the American male average, and few American presidents have stood much below six feet in their socks.

There are always exceptions of course. Deng Xiaoping of China (5 feet), Attila the Hun (4 feet something), Napoleon Bonaparte and Emperor Haile Selassie were all short men who enjoyed absolute power. Hollywood is full of little sawn-off male stars who have played romantic roles as well as tough-guy action parts, from Mickey Rooney (who managed to land some of Hollywood's most beautiful women) and Alan Ladd (who wore built-up boots on camera) to Mel Gibson and Tom Cruise. Ex-Oxford organ scholar and Hollywood movie comedian Dudley Moore is pushing 60 and only 5 feet 2 inches; a former so-called 'sex thimble' now unkindly described as an 'ageing miniature', he can still pull the odd young giantess now and then.

According to Californian engineer and author Thomas T. Samaras, short people have a lot more going for them. They are less likely to fall over. They produce less sewage and so present less of a threat to the biosphere. And they are really more attractive to women than tall men because they are less complacent and more giving. French women, says Samaras, especially young ones, equate short men with 'virility, power and sexual experimentation', and he cites the Catalan painter Pablo Picasso (French by domicile) as a noted lothario who was only 5 feet 4 inches. Not everyone would agree though. Columnist Catherine Bennett declared that it was even worse to be small than it was to be fat, because if you were fat you could always stop eating. Short men made a woman look silly and had no appeal at all. Unless, of course, they happen to be rich, powerful, famous, funny, intelligent, sexy... and good-looking – like Robert Redford.

incredible hulks

A man's shape is almost as important as his height. The trouble is that what a man likes and thinks a woman likes is often a far cry from what a woman really likes. For example, 84 per cent of German men today believe that the ideal male shape is that of the broad-shouldered cowboy figure and that such a figure is magically attractive to women, just as they did 600 years ago, when the ideal Englishman was described as a man who had 'great stature, enormous strength, long sinewy arms, broad square breast and shoulders, small waist and

retreating stomach. His legs are long, with thighs thick and strong, and in general appearance he is more like a giant than a mere knight'.

But times have changed. The Western world no longer has any real socio-biological need for incredible hulks of aurochs-wrestling strength. According to psychosexual physician Dr Andrew Stamway, the Chippendale type of male is too narcissitic for most women. The cuddly sort of man is more attractive because he is more accepting and doesn't pressurize the woman with any quest for perfection. By contrast, women feel excluded by men who pump iron all day, 'guzzle high-calorie food and take drugs to develop their frames'. Such men are deemed to be too self-centred, too preoccupied with their own physicality to share their lives in a satisfactory way.

Research at the Loyola University of Chicago has shown that only 1 per cent of women favoured the 'He-Man' type (only the 'Pear-shaped Man' fared worse). The 'Muscle Man' was widely regarded as a kind of freak. 'He looks abnormal,' was a typical reaction, 'like someone's head on an ape's body.' Muscle Man was seen as vain, inadequate and unnatural. 'He looks like he wants to beat a lady to death,' commented one woman.

However, what women look for in male body shape seems to depend to some extent on their own personality type. The Loyola research revealed that clean living, sporty women preferred muscular men; neurotic, radical women liked thinner, more linear shapes; maturer women opted for men with broader figures; while most women tended to feel more comfortable with men whose figures were a little like their own – so overweight women favoured men with broad figures (and vice versa).

The majority female preference, however, appears to be for the 'V-shaped Man', with slim legs, middling-thin lower trunk, and middling-broad upper trunk. Perhaps Olympic champion sprinter and record-breaker Linford Christie embodies one kind of ideal for one large category of women. Columnist Louise France believes that if God ever has another crack at making man, he could do worse than use athlete Linford Christie, with his perfect proportions, muscular torso, powerful legs and fine bone structure, as a prototype.

While surveys differ in their estimations of whether Tarzan-like iron-pumping muscle men – here acted by Johnny Weissmuller – find favour, tall guys still win in the sex appeal stakes

'I don't go to the movies where the hero's bust is bigger than the heroine's.'

Groucho Marx

How to Approach Cosmetic Surgery

Reconstructive plastic surgery involves trying to make the abnormal normal. Cosmetic plastic surgery uses the same principles to make the normal better. The last ten years have seen an exponential growth in the number of people requesting cosmetic procedures. This may be due to better information about what is available or perhaps, as a society, we are simply more open about trying to improve appearance.

Cosmetic surgical procedures are directed towards improving attractiveness or restoring a more youthful appearance. All of these procedures impact on self-image. Occasionally, a single procedure may produce a dramatic improvement in a patient's quality of life. Following breast reduction, for example, the ability to wear different clothes, to participate in sports, to become more confident in personal and professional relationships is often described as life changing. Liposuction to hips, thighs, abdomen and legs is probably the most commonly requested procedure and is clearly directed to improving body contour. Associated with the physical changes comes greater confidence and a sense of well-being with one's own self-image.

Few patients actually talk about sexual attractiveness as a motivation for surgery, although breast surgery is an exception. Patients requesting implant surgery will often talk of lacking in confidence and feeling less feminine because of small breasts. Following childbirth and breast feeding, the breasts often droop and lose the shape and volume of a young breast, and in seeking breast lift procedures many women state that the surgery helps them to maintain their identity in terms of attractiveness and desirability. Men seeking penis enlargement clearly view this in terms of sexual confidence and attractiveness.

Most people requesting surgery do so to counter the ageing process. Face lifts, eyelid surgery and hair transplantation are good examples. But it should be remembered that these procedures by themselves do not confer attractiveness *per se*. If one is old and unattractive, a face lift will only make you look younger. However, the sophistication of modern plastic surgery is such that many procedures can, and do, enhance appearance.

Rhinoplasty, chin reduction and augmentation, cheek implants, lip augmentation can all be used, where appropriate, to improve appearance.

The vast majority of people seeking surgery are normal, sensible, well-balanced individuals who are looking to make the best of themselves or to correct a perceived problem. Occasionally, requests for cosmetic surgery are inappropriate – usually when a patient has completely unreal expectations about what can be achieved. A patient who puts a photograph of Cher or Richard Gere on the desk with a view to looking like them, is usually a bad candidate for any form of surgery.

Another difficult area is anyone looking to change ethnic features which are normal, such as the Westernization of oriental eyes. At the extreme end of the spectrum is the use of skin lightening agents in dark-skinned peoples.

It is the responsibility of the surgeon to explain what can and can't be achieved through surgery. The use of photographs to illustrate typical results should be part of any consultation. Potential complications, scars and recovery time should also be thoroughly discussed. Choosing a surgeon can be a difficult process for potential patients. Unfortunately, many surgeons perform cosmetic surgery and there is a wide range of training and experience. One of the best ways to find a good surgeon is by word of mouth from other patients, and it is often useful to see two or three different surgeons before making a final decision.

As we approach the next century, plastic surgery continues to evolve and become more sophisticated. The emphasis is now on the reduction of scars and the development of 'keyhole techniques' is making this a reality. But the decision to have surgery is still a serious one and should be properly researched by the potential patient.

Norman Waterhouse, MbChB, FRCS, FRCS (Plastic Surgery), consultant plastic surgeon, Harley Street, London

a private viewing - what people really think

Sexual attraction is one of those confusing emotions - the more you analyse it, the more baffling it becomes. It's exciting, consuming and makes you feel alive! Unfortunately you never know when it will happen, you can't control it when it does happen and nor can you choose who you'll be attracted to. It could be someone you normally wouldn't look at twice. Someone who you don't even like or even find positively repulsive. Sexual attraction has a lot to answer for.
ALISON, 20s, BRISTOL

The attraction men feel toward the typical feminine woman is heavily based on the DIFFERENCES between the sexes. Around the age of 10 or 11 I remember becoming aware of the shape of a woman. Specifically breasts, the vaginal gap and, as time went on, the DYNAMIC CURVE!
MARKETING CONSULTANT, MALE, 30

The most sexually attractive part of a person's body is in the curve of the neck where the neck joins the shoulder.
VIETNAMESE WOMAN, 35

I would say a physically attractive woman is one with two arms and two legs but I recently dated a wonderful lady who had less than the full complement.
SIMON, COMPUTER EXPERT, UK

IN PRAISE OF SHORTER MEN

For some reason I always seem to be attracted to short men. Where other people scan a room for the tall, god-like creatures they can't fail to miss my attention is almost always focused nearer floor level. I can spot a short person even when you can't tell he's short - sitting across a table from a man I'm attracted to I know that when we stand up to say our goodbyes his head will reach no higher than my shoulders. Maybe it's got something to do with their personalities. Short men seem to smile more, they're funnier, they seem less fettered by all the boring laws of machismo, they listen and they're interested in what you have to say, their lives aren't focused just on themselves. Maybe it's because I once went out with a short man who was very kind and always made me smile and so now I'm prepared to give all short men the benefit of the doubt.
ANON, FEMALE, 28

The most sexually attractive part of my boyfriend's body is the small of his back and his smooth stomach where it descends into his pants.
FEMALE, 20s, KOREA

From the physical point of view I suppose you could say I'm a tits and bum man. I'm into nuances, clefts and cleavages. Small breasts and tiny nipples do nothing for me intellectually.
LIBRARIAN, SUFFOLK

For some reason I find I am attracted to men who are crippled in some way. Maybe that's why I became a nurse.
ACTRESS, 50, LONDON

I've always been attracted to men with one foot that turned in slightly. Not all the time, necessarily. Just sometimes. It's something they do out of momentary shyness or awkwardness or embarrassment and it's boyish, like hiding one foot behind the other.
PLAYWRIGHT, FEMALE, 30, LONDON

	Length of procedure	Hospital stay	Recovery/ off work	Average cost

Hair

Transplant	2 1/2 hours	-	7 days	$1,700-3,400
Scalp reduction	2 1/2 hours	-	7 days	$1,360-1,700

Upper face

Forehead lines can be reduced with botulin toxin injections; ears can be pinned back (otoplasty); temples, eyes and partial or whole face can be lifted to remove wrinkles and reduce chins.

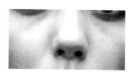

Otoplasty	3/4 hour	0-1 days	1-5 days	$3,060
Temporal lift	1 1/2 hours	1 day	14-21 days	$4,760
Eyebrow lift	1 hour	1-2 days	21 days	$4,590
Upper eye lift	1/2 hour	0-1 day	10 days	$3,060
Lower eye lift	1/2-3/4 hour	1 day	14 days	$3,400
Upper & lower eye	1 hour	1 day	21 days	$4,760
Facelift	2 hours	2 days	21 days	$5,950
with upper or lower eyes	2 1/2 hours	3 days	21 days	$7,650
with upper & lower eyes	3 hours	3 days	21 days	$7,820

Nose, cheeks and skin

The nose can be reshaped, realigned or reduced (rhinoplasty), and cheeks plumped out or smoothed:

Rhinoplasty	1 hour	1 day	14 days	$4,760
Cheek implants	1 hour	1 day	5 days	$4,760
Dermabrasion	1/4-3/4 hour	0-1 day	21 days	$2,550
Mole removal	1/2 hour	-	-	$255
Glycolic acid light peel	1/2 hour	-	-	$85
Chemical peel	1/4 hour	0-1 day	14 days	$850-$1,615

Mouth

Lips can be enlarged, plumped up with collagen, or reduced:

Increase	3/4 hour	0-1 day	10 days	$3,060
Reduction – one lip	1/2 hour	0-1 day	10 days	$3,060
Reduction – both lips	1 hour	1 day	21 days	$3,570
Collagen injections	1/2 hour	-	0-2 days	$255

cosmetic surgery - your options

	Length of procedure	*Hospital stay*	*Recovery/ off work*	*Average cost*

Chin and neck

To avoid a facelift, reduce double chins with liposuction/liposculpture. Receding chins can be augmented with an implant. A fat transfer may improve a lined neck.

Chin implant	3/4 hour	1 day	5 days	$3,570
Chin reduction	1 hour	1 day	10 days	$4,250
Liposuction/sculpture	1/2 hour	-	0-2 days	$2,040
Fat transfer	1/4 hour	-	1-3 days	$1,870

Body

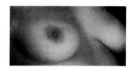

The chest can be adjusted in either direction, and the stomach region improved via abdominal liposuction (or ultrasonic liposculpture, which takes longer in the operating theatre but less time to heal) or a tummy tuck (abdominal lipectomy).

Breast augmentation	1 hour	1 day	5 days	$4,760
Reduction	3 hours	2 days	14 days	$6,290
Uplift	3 hours	2 days	14 days	$6,120
Inverted nipple corrected	1/4 hour	-	-	$1,360
Male breast reduction	1 hour	0-1 day	7 days	$3,400
Pectoral implant	1 hour	1 day	5 days	$4,760
Liposuction/sculpture	1 1/2 hours	1 day	5 days	$3,910
Abdominal lipectomy	2 hours	2 days	21 days	$6,290

Arms

Smooth ageing hands with a fat transplant and have unsightly moles removed; thread or spider veins can also be treated both here and on the legs.

Hips, thighs and legs

Hips, thighs and the bottom can all be reduced with liposuction/sculpture, and the calves and ankles slimmed.

Hip liposuction	1 hour	1 day	5-10 days	$3,400
Inner thigh	1 hour	1 day	5-10 days	$3,400
Outer thigh	1 hour	1 day	5 days	$3,400
Inner & outer	1 1/2 hours	1 day	10-15 days	$3,910
Hips & thighs	1 1/2 hours	1 day	10-15 days	$3,910
Thigh lift	2 hours	1 day	21 days	$5,950
Knee liposuction	1/2 hour	-	-	$2,040
Calf implants	2 hours	1 day	7 days	$4,760
Varicose veins	varies	0-2 days	1-2 days	varies

This list is intended as a guide. Prices may vary from region to region and treatment from hospital to hospital. Information compiled by the Cosmetic Surgery Network, London.

'The cosmetic surgeon is the modern woman's divine sex symbol, claiming for himself the worship that nineteenth century women offered the man of God.'

Naomi Wolf

4

primal impact –
the human face

'You must
think of
nothing...
You are
nothing but a
beautiful
mask.'

MGM DIRECTOR TO
GRETA GARBO DURING
SHOOTING OF THE MOVIE
QUEEN CHRISTINA

about
face

The face is arguably the prime transmitter (and certainly the prime receiver) of sex appeal. The face in general and the eyes in particular are among a person's chief non-vocal means for expressing mood and emotion and communicating messages of various kinds, especially sexual ones. Celebrated by artists and writers from time immemorial, and by photographers and film makers since time more memorial, the beauty of the human face remains elusive. We all recognize a beautiful face when we see one, but why do we think it is beautiful? Is it down to Plato's 'golden section'? Or Hogarth's 'wavy line of beauty'? Or American psychologist Richard Brislin's more prosaically statistical 'Beauty-Score System'?

The mathematical secrets of the human face have yet to be proven. But the more enigmatic the face we look at (Garbo's, for example, or the puzzling *Mona Lisa*) the more its ambiguity seems to rouse the wildest fantasies. In recent years scientists of various persuasions – psychologists, anthropologists, sociologists, biologists – have maintained a continuing interest in trying to lay bare the secrets of the beauty of the human face. Approaching the subject from different directions, their efforts have coincided with those of the plastic surgeons and cosmetic companies.

Until recently, the general consensus was that the beauty – and the sex appeal – of the human face was a subjective matter that lay entirely in the eye of the beholder. Not only did it vary from person to person but from culture to culture around the world and from generation to generation down the ages. In her bestselling book *The Beauty Myth*, Naomi Wolf argues that there is no such thing as a quality called beauty that 'objectively and universally exists'. But now there is a growing belief that perhaps all human beings share the same basic perceptions and standards of human facial beauty.

favourite parts

Various studies in the United States have attempted to pinpoint the most generally admired features of the male and female face. In one study in America the top five favourite components of the face were (in order of preference):

- mouth
- eyes
- facial structure
- hair
- nose

> **'The plainest person can look beautiful, can be beautiful. It only needs the fire of sex to rise delicately to change an ugly face to a lovely one. That is really sex appeal: the communicating of a sense of beauty.'**
>
> D.H. LAWRENCE

> *'Greta Garbo is arguably one of the most beautiful women who has ever lived'*
> KENNETH CLARK

In another study in America the most physically attractive characteristics proved to be:

for females
- frizzy hair texture
- blonde or brunette hair colour
- heart and pear shaped face
- pug nose
- full lips
- fair and rose skin tone

for males
- straight or wavy hair
- dark brown and light brown hair colour
- square shaped face
- Roman nose
- narrow lips
- tan skin tone

A second study tested the same components on an ethnic basis. Ten Asian women and 20 Caucasian women, all American born, were asked to give their ratings. The Asian women valued fair skin and straight, dark-coloured hair more highly than the Caucasian women, while the Caucasian women found Roman and hawk noses in men more attractive than did the Asian women.

Richard R. Brislin has contended that because of the high level of agreement as to what constitutes a beautiful face it is possible to calculate a 'beauty score' for both male and female faces (see left). Brislin also found that the highest beauty score was achieved by faces possessing a proper proportion of the central area of the face in relation to the total face area – that is, a mouth with the width greater than the width of a cheek, and a forehead height greater than the height of the chin.

the gateways of erotic desire – the eyes

The impact a woman's eyes can make and the power they can wield has been known throughout the ages. 'Beautiful women know how to use the look to conquer,' declared the poet Ovid, a notorious Roman authority on the subject; 'it is their first weapon.' Nearly 2,000 years later men were coming up with the same truism. According to a Victorian periodical, the eyes are 'the most formidable part of the feminine artillery', capable of expressing 'all the passions of the soul'. But the sexual power of the eyes is not confined to females alone. Medical records contain several cases where a mere glance from a man has induced orgasm in a woman (stimulation of the earlobes has been known to produce the same result).

Even as far away as the Trobriand Islands of the Western Pacific the eyes have it. Among the Trobriand islanders the eyes are known as 'the gateways of erotic desire' (exactly the same phrase the English

PERFECT FACE

According to Brislin's 'Beauty-Score System' the perfect female face has the following components:

- oval face
- clear complexion
- large blue eyes
- fine eyebrows
- long lashes
- straight, diamond-shaped nose
- moderate-sized mouth
- flat ears
- good-sized earlobes (i.e. not small)

The male face, by contrast, has far fewer criteria to judge by:

- square face
- bushy eyebrows
- Roman nose

sexologist Havelock Ellis had once used). Biting off your lover's eyelashes, a sex act known as *mitakuku*, plays an important part in love-making, and the expression *agu mitakuku* is a term of endearment. The eyes should be bright and shining, but also – and here the Trobrianders seem the exception to the universal rule – small. Large eyes, *puyna-puyna*, are considered ugly. European looks, with their large eyes 'like water puddles', are not highly regarded.

Elsewhere in the world many women use cosmetics to make their eyes look larger. This may enhance a woman's attractiveness by making the lower face look smaller by comparison – an important component of a sexually attractive face. At various times in various cultures women have also attempted to enlarge the pupil of the eye, for it has long been known that when a person of either sex is emotionally excited, usually at the sight of someone they find sexually attractive, the pupil can enlarge by up to 30 per cent, expanding instantly from a dot to a full circle and thereby transmitting a powerful signal of attraction or affection. Women in Renaissance Italy and Victorian England, well aware that enlarged pupils make the eyes even more attractive, squeezed drops of belladonna into their eyes before going out with their paramours – significantly the Italian word *belladonna* means 'pretty woman'. In more recent times picture editors and advertisers have taken to artificially enlarging the pupils of the models in their pictures in order to enhance the sexual allure of their eyes.

Geisha in traditional make-up, Kyoto, Japan. She has painted her face a much-admired chalk white, thereby emphasising the attractant bright red of her lips, and the beauty of her eyes, however modestly lowered

Why it should work like this is not entirely clear. Since children have larger pupils than adults, it is possible that enlarged pupils may decode to signify youth. Or a man may interpret a woman's enlarged pupils as a sign that she is sexually interested in him and react accordingly in flight or flirt. Male homosexuals, on the other hand, prefer women with small pupils, as do women themselves.

'Cover girls are more than beautiful. They have come-hither faces. It comes from the eyes.'

POLLY MELLEN, CREATIVE DIRECTOR, ALLURE

The colour of the iris also plays a part in the sex appeal of the

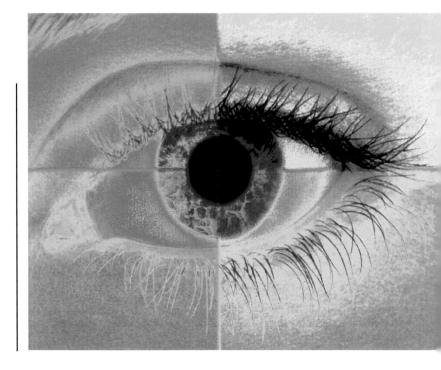

Computer graphic image of the eye – a prime receiver and transmitter of sex appeal signals

APHRODITE IN THE DESERT

Even if a woman is so heavily veiled that only her eyes are showing, she can still transmit powerful signals of sexual attraction. Douglas Botting reports from the Hadhramaut:

I was sitting in a small desert airport in Southern Yemen waiting for a plane from the Gulf to take me on to the port of Aden. The airport was a kind of clearing house for people from all over Southern Arabia – desert Bedouin, northern soldiers with long curved daggers tucked in their belts, British and American oilmen, bodyguards armed to the teeth with Kalashnikovs, Socotra tribesmen babbling in an unknown tongue – and me, and her. Before long I realized that every single male was staring at the person sharing the bench with me. I cast a sideways glance. She was an Arab woman dressed from head to toe in black in the strict Moslem way, so that it was impossible to form an impression of her body and even her hands were hidden by black gloves.

 Out of her entire anatomy only her eyes were visible – and it was on account of these eyes alone (and perhaps her calm, assured, superstar kind of poise) that she attracted the longing stares. They were sensational eyes – large, brown, liquid, gazelle-like, with clear bright whites, a wide iris and long black lashes. Her skin was pale and she was obviously young. She revealed next to nothing of herself, certainly next to none of the normal cues that signal female physical attractiveness in the West, she did not move or speak – and yet she was utterly unforgettable. I turned to look at her again and as I did so she cast a glance at me and I found myself staring at point blank range into those quintessentially erotic eyes. The corner of her eyes crinkled slightly then, and I realized that beneath that all-obscuring veil a smile had formed. Her eyes seemed to signal a conspiratorial look, as if she recognized that we shared a mutual perception of the comic side of the situation. Then she turned back to resume her cool, aloof, unblinking gaze into that sea of yearning male faces – truly an Aphrodite of the desert.

eye, both for men and women. The colour depends on the amount of melanin present in the iris, so subtle blue hues are the result of a reduced amount of melanin in the various layers of the iris, while a violet colour (the colour of Elizabeth Taylor's eyes) is due to blood showing through. Initial research suggests that women prefer men with dark-coloured eyes and men prefer women with light-coloured. But there are many exceptions. For some people a woman's amber eyes, a relatively rare hue, can have a startling impact, while many women report a penchant for steely grey eyes in a man. As film star Paul Newman recalled, it's a funny way to judge another human being. 'To work hard,' said Newman, 'as I've worked, to accomplish something and then have some yo-yo come up and say: "Take off those dark glasses and let's have a look at those blue eyes," is really discouraging.'

a hole in the head - the mouth

In some ways the mouth is even more versatile than the eyes. It can transmit outgoing signals through the sense of sight, sound, smell, taste and touch; it can also receive incoming signals through the sense of touch and taste, while the movements of the mouth and the sounds it utters, both speech and non-speech, along with the 'gestures' of the protruding tongue, are crucial elements in a person's repertoire of body language. The shape and size of the mouth as a whole, the colour of the lips and the colour and condition of the teeth they reveal, can all evoke significant sexual responses. The teeth are often the weak link. 'Americans don't like their women fat – and get your teeth fixed!' were the first words that greeted Greta Garbo when she reported to the MGM studios. When Josephine met Napoleon for the first time a rather catty Duchesse d'Abrantés reported: 'Her teeth were frightfully bad, but when her mouth was shut she gave the appearance, especially at a few paces distant, of a young and pretty woman.'

The kind of mouth preferred on a Western male is one that broadly corresponds to the accepted masculine virtues of strength and status – firm, straight, lean without being mean or thin, and unadorned. By contrast, the kind of

Lips that are fuller, more protuberant and highly coloured will transmit a powerful sexual message that can enormously enhance a woman's sex appeal

'We find no beauty of
countenance
complete without the
amorous curve of the
lips...'

ANNIE WOLF

mouth most favoured on a woman is set in a short lower face above a gracile chin, with a relatively short distance between the nose and the point of the chin, and with full, red, moist and even slightly parted lips.

It is easy to see why such a mouth has been described as a genital echo, (and for that matter the protruding tongue, a hypothetical penis echo). A round orifice contained within slit-like lips which swell and flush during sexual arousal has more than a passing resemblance to the female genitalia. Lipstick is used to emphasize the self-mimicry of the lips, both to colour the lips and make them look fuller than they might really be. No matter the colour changes dictated by fashion the preferred colour of lipstick always comes back to red – the colour of sexual excitement.

crowning glory – the hair

Oddly, while many male polls do not rate the hair amongst the top six most physically attractive features in a woman, female polls often place male hair among the top six features in a man.

The hair can be a significant factor in the sex appeal of the face. It can be sensually silky and pleasurable to the touch, it can give off sexually inviting odours, and visually it can enhance the sexual attractiveness of the face in two ways. The first way is by setting off the key attractant features of the face or modifying them for the better in some way – by defining the generally preferred oval or heart shape of a woman's face, for example, or lessening the proportions of the lower face by artifically increasing the proportions of the upper face, particularly the forehead. The second way is by signalling information about a woman's age and state of health, for luxuriant, shiny, bouncy hair signals youth and health in a woman – as does, to a more limited extent, the colour of the hair.

The reason why many men find blondes so attractive in most parts of the world is because natural blonde hair is a characteristic sign of youth. Few blonde girls remain blonde far into their twenties when the hair begins to darken. Blonde hair also indicates that a woman has not yet had a child, as blonde hair darkens after childbirth. Even Marilyn Monroe had to dye her hair. Many men in high places have followed her example: though age is less of a handicap to the male, white hair, can be perceived as unpalatable evidence of a man's fading powers. 'He doesn't dye his hair,' quipped ex-President Ford of the new incumbent in the White House, Ronald Reagan, 'he's just prematurely orange.' A bitchy Gore Vidal affirmed. 'He just bleaches his face.'

The hair provides a vital clue to a woman's health and age

the geometry of beauty

From earliest times to the present day the nature and mechanism of facial beauty, the magic formula, structure, geometry, alchemy, trick that underpinned the kind of face that men and nations would go to war for (or against) – Helen of Troy, Evita of Buenos Aires, Maggie of Grantham – has preoccupied some of the brightest and dimmest minds of civilizations ancient and modern.

First onto the track were the ancient Greeks. It was the Greeks who came up with the idea that a pretty girl's or boy's face was all a matter of maths. For them beauty was all about harmony, balance and above all proportion. The philosopher Plato, for example, contended that the essence of beauty lay in what he called the 'golden section', the belief that all things beautiful could be divided into thirds. The perfect face in his view was proportioned like this: the brow one-third of the way from the hairline, the mouth one-third of the way from the brow, the point of the chin one-third of the way from the mouth, and the width of the face two-thirds of the height. The sex and beauty experts of medieval Europe went along with this thesis but elaborated on it by dividing the face up into sevenths.

In fact, recent computer measurements have come up with their own version of the geometry and 'vital proportions' of the face. Faces judged as 'pretty' were found to share the following measurements: each eye was one-fourteenth as high as the face and three-tenths its width, and the distance from the middle of the eye to the eyebrow was one-tenth the height of the face (and the nose, incidentally, occupied no more than 5 per cent of the face).

what the composites say – is symmetry the answer?

Sir Francis Galton, a cousin of Charles Darwin, made a major contribution to the study of sex appeal, Victorian style, by his researches into the nature of the beauty of the human face.

This early contribution to the study of sexual attraction was actually an accident on Galton's part, a by-product of an inquiry in a rather different field of research. Galton had wanted to create a prototype criminal face, using the novel technique of creating composite photographs in which the faces of several people were superimposed to produce a single image that was the 'average' of the group. To Galton's surprise – and frustration – his composite portrait showed a face that was more likeable than criminal, and certainly a lot more attractive than the individual faces that went into it. Intrigued, Galton repeated the experiment using different photographs of both

The legendary Evita Peron, being congratulated by a foreign dignitary in Buenos Aires after receiving an award for her 'extraordinary merits'. One of Eva's merits was her universal sex appeal, which won over Argentina's masses as well as her husband, the country's dicatator

'If a girl has curviness, exciting lips, and a certain breathlessness, it helps. And it won't do a bit of harm if she has a kittenish, soft, cuddly quality.'

JAYNE MANSFIELD

TWO OR MORE FEMALE THINGS

In 1180 an anonymous physician in Tunisia wrote a book called *An Intelligent Man's Guide*, explaining how men were attracted to certain parts of a woman's face which could be grouped in lucky combinations of two and three. It made an ingenious but dotty list divided into winning combinations of 'Two Female Things' and 'Three Female Things':

■ *two round things:*   face, eyes
■ *two long things:*   hair, eyebrows
■ *two broad things:*   forehead, eyes
■ *two narrow things:*   mouth, nose
■ *two nice-smelling things:*   nose, mouth
■ *three white things:*   complexion, whites of eyes, teeth
■ *three red things:*   tongue, lips, cheeks

male and female faces. Each time the result was the same. Features common to the majority of the faces were reproduced in the final print, but peculiarities and extremes were eliminated. 'The result,' Galton reported, 'is a very striking face, thoroughly ideal and artistic, and singularly beautiful.'

More recent corroboration of Sir Francis Galton's findings has come from an influential American anthropologist, Donald Symons, who has a specialist interest in the evolution of human sexuality. Symons has proposed that according to the principles of evolutionary biology, beauty is indeed averageness. Evolutionary pressures tend to operate against people at the extremes of the population (the outer edges of the gene pool), while people with average physical properties (in the middle of the gene pool) generally have the best chance of survival, argues Symons. If this is the case, then the pressures of sexual selection will ensure that people with average features are more attractive than people with non-average features.

In 1990 this hypothesis was tested by psychologist Judith Langlois and a colleague using a computerized version of the photographic technique pioneered by Galton. Again, the composite, 'average' faces were found to be more attractive than the originals, and the greater the number of faces contributing to a composite (up to 32), the more attractive it became. However, there was one important discovery which Langlois did not pursue. It turned out that a few individual faces in her sample were rated as being more attractive than any composite, which suggested that while composite faces are attractive, the most attractive faces are not composites. Averageness and symmetry, it seemed, might not be the whole answer after all.

...or non-symmetry? what the computers say

In 1993, psychologists Johnston and Franklin developed a computer programme that allowed the user to 'evolve' on screen his or her ideal face. 20 male and 20 female subjects used the programme to create one ideal face apiece, and these 40 ideal faces were then combined to produce a computer-generated face which Johnston and Franklin termed the 'beautiful composite'. The faces of the female subjects, whose average age was 20, were then combined into what was called the 'subject composite'. In most aspects the make-believe dream-wish 'beautiful composite' and the real-life flesh-and-blood 'subject composite' did not differ greatly. In certain dimensions, however, there were significant differences. The 'beautiful composite' had a shorter lower face, with a nose to chin proportion that was typical of an 11- or 12-year-old girl, fuller lips from top to bottom typical of a girl of 14 (the age at which female lip fullness peaks), and a smaller mouth. And though the 'beautiful composite' contained features characteristic of early youth, as a whole it appeared to be of a sexually mature woman, not a barely pubescent girl.

The following year a group of psychologists from Scotland and Japan obtained very similar results using computer-generated composites of female faces. Photographs of 60 white British women aged between 20 and 30 and 342 Japanese high-school girls aged between 18 and 19 were processed to produce three different sets of composites – an 'average composite' formed from the faces of the whole group, an 'attractive composite' formed from the most attractive faces of the group, and an 'enhanced attractive composite' formed by exaggerating the differences between the 'average composite' and the 'attractive composite'.

Contrary to the 'average' hypothesis, the 'enhanced attractive' composites with built-in extremes were preferred to the average and attractive composites and were rated more highly than most of the individual real-life faces. These findings were the same across both cultures – the Japanese felt the same way about the British composites as they did about the Japanese ones, and vice versa. The scientists found similar preferences for a non-average shape with male faces. In short, in both races the faces that showed the greatest departure from the average were considered the most attractive. Writing up their results in *Nature*, the scientists listed the key features of the most attractive female face shape (see right).

Japanese face shapes showed similar differences in the eyes, mouth and chin. 'The similarity of attractive facial characteristics across two cultures,' wrote the scientists, 'is consistent with the claim

> **'There is no excellent beauty that hath not some strangeness in the proportion.'**
>
> *Francis Bacon*

FEMALE FACE

- *higher cheek bones thinner jaw*
- *larger eyes relative to the size of the face*
- *shorter distance between the mouth and chin*
- *shorter distance between nose and mouth*

that such characteristics are functionally significant.'

baby faces and the bambi effect

Dr David Perrett, the psychologist at St Andrews who helped run this computerized composites programme, not only doubts the view held for over a century that the average is beautiful, he contends that the more exaggerated certain features of a face are, the more beautiful the face will become. His model beauty is a woman with large eyes, full lips, high cheekbones and a small chin. The male ideal is much the same but more rugged. Film stars and supermodels tend to have even more exaggerated forms of the same type. Compared to movie stars of the Thirties and Forties, today's stars have even larger eyes and even higher cheekbones, all features identified as classic signs of facial beauty. They are also all classic characteristics of the baby face. Beautiful people, in short, are grown-ups with baby faces.

Cartoon characters are at their most appealing when they are depicted with simplified and often wildly exaggerated baby-like features – and are even more appealing when, like Bambi and Dumbo, they actually are babies. For such fantasy creatures large eyes are the most crucial requirement, for large eyes signal amazement, wonder, love. Betty Boop, the animated paint-and-trace sex bomb, is a classic example. Her eyes are so big that they take up virtually the whole of her face, leaving just enough room for a rosebud mouth to replace her chin.

Part of Twiggy's enormous success could be put down to her Bambi-like looks, as her manager, Justin de Villeneuve, was quick to perceive. 'There was this little Cockney girl in a little white gown,' he recalled, 'with her long neck and her huge, huge eyes – she looked like a fawn. She looked like Bambi; I knew then that she was really going to make it.'

Features typical of so-called cute children have been identified as: large forehead; large eyes; large pupils; features that are small and narrow. Even as far back as Chaucer's time a large forehead was a key requisite of good looks – large; broad; high; smooth and wrinkle-free. Psychologists have suggested that when adults observe other adults with features such as large foreheads they are automatically reminded of babies and very young children, with a consequent triggering of their protective instinct.

Irrespective of their actual age or sexual maturity, women are sometimes considered more attractive to men if they look more childish than grown-up, while men are more attractive to women if they look more grown-up than childish. Childish features in a woman

Walt Disney's classic cartoon deer fawn has given his name to an important element of sex appeal in the human face: the Bambi Effect

do two things at once – they convey youth and they arouse protectiveness (in evolutionary terms the ability to breed for some years to come and to persuade the necessary provider and protector to stick around while they're doing it). Mature features in a man, by contrast, convey sexual capability, status and strength (in evolutionary terms the ability to impregnate, to provide and to protect).

Cindy Jackson, who runs a plastic surgery advice bureau, is a firm believer in the baby face theory and has had repeated plastic surgery to give her a face modelled along the lines of a young child or animal. Large eyes, small nose, a look as vulnerable as possible – these are the things that will bring out the protective instinct in men, and in the process generate sex appeal. Says Cindy:

'There are a lot of different theories to do with facial attraction, but the one I go for, the one that has been true in my case, is the baby look. Large eyes, small turned-up nose, full lips, soft, smooth skin, and looking as young as you can – these have the same effect on people that a baby does, and it's this that attracts a man to a woman.'

'Beauty is in the adaptations of the beholder': the evolutionary view

But is a pretty face more than just a pretty face? Does beauty, after all, lie not in the eye of the beholder but, as Don Symons puts it, 'in the adaptations of the beholder'? Is it a consensus agreed by eyes and minds fashioned by millions of years of human evolution?

The external clues of the attractive human face indicate that a female is in the prime of youth and the best of health, fertile and ready and able to bear healthy offspring. These standards are invariable. Shown a series of photographs of the faces of women from a range of races, there was a consensus as to which ones were the most attractive amongst the Chinese, Indians, English, South Africans and Americans (both white and black). Though the psychophysics of male facial attraction has not yet been properly explored, Symons' educated guess is that some features (like external signs of disease-resistance) will be the same, others (like signs of youth) will be different. As Nancy L. Etcoff, a neuropsychologist at the Harvard Medical School explains, 'Although some aspects of judgements of human facial beauty may be influenced by culture or individual history, the general geometric features of a face that give rise to perceptions of beauty may be universal, and the perception of these features may be governed by circuits shaped by natural selection in the human brain.'

Symons' evolutionary viewpoint suggests that the physical signals

With her baby-domed forehead, large eyes, small features and cute chin, Twiggy's Sixties 'look' was the embodiment of the baby-faced Bambi Effect

I ALWAYS WANTED TO LOOK LIKE BARBIE:
'THE BETTER LOOKING A WOMAN IS, THE MORE POWER SHE'S GOT'

Cindy Jackson, a member of Mensa, has transformed her face and body by plastic surgery over the last seven years. This is her personal view on the power of feminine sex appeal.

Growing up I had a typical hillbilly sort of hick face – big nose, thin lips, funny teeth. My teeth turned out to be all right, so I built around them. The hair was all right too, but I had a kind of fat face. I looked like my father – I don't any more. I had always wanted a woman's face, but I had a man's face, very masculine, hard, strong. I didn't feel it was me. I was more sensitive, feminine, I wanted to reflect that in my looks and I wanted people to treat me like I was that way.

I started surgery back in 1988 when I was 33. The first things I had done were the upper eyes, then the first nose job, then the chemical peel, then some collagen injections which didn't last very long, then my lower face lift. Then I had my lower eyes re-done, because they were still baggy, then my upper lip operation – they turned my lip inside out. And recently, I've had my jaw remodelled.

Before surgery people always thought I was quite a capable sort of person, which I suppose I am, but they never thought I needed a helping hand or somebody to give me support. Men always let me open my own doors, split the tab and all that stuff. People treat you the way you look. I wanted to look like a Barbie doll.

You see, I grew up on this farm in Ohio and all around me were redneck people, thick farmers – it was like The Dukes of Hazzard. *I looked at my mother and the sort of life she had on the farm and I looked at the other women around me and there were no role models for me. I felt I had more in common with Barbie and the sort of life she would have with Ken, going out and doing all those wonderful things, being terminally engaged, never having to get married and have kids. I do have Barbie's hair pretty much, but I wanted her wide eyes, her small nose, her overly prominent upper lip as well.*

Men are controlled through feminine things. The better looking a woman is, the more power she's got within herself, whether it's economic power or sex appeal power. How many times do you see a man drop his jaw and lose coherence and be unable to talk when he sees a very intelligent career woman walk by in army boots? Never! But you take some nice woman dressed in a smart, quite tight outfit, with a nice wiggle and a wink in her eye, and the guy doesn't even remember his name.

The more a woman can get what she wants out of a man, the more men will come to heel. Men will treat weak unattractive women like dirt. I know. I used to be one. I don't put up with it now, I don't have to. I don't belong in this face, this body. I'm a complete impostor. But it works. I feel like this is where I belong.

'Come into the gene pool, it's lovely!'

With apologies to Spike Milligan

of female sex appeal are interpreted not according to any aesthetic code-book, but for what they reveal in terms of the woman's age, sexual maturation, hormonal condition, fecundity, health and other related conditions. What the woman is presenting by way of her skin colour and texture, profile, and other physical features is less a kind of sexy floorshow than a clinical diagnosis. In the context of sex appeal this sometimes makes for odd, though essential, reading.

Take skin. Humans are born with skin lighter than their parents. This darkens through childhood, then lightens at puberty, though a girl's skin will lighten considerably more than a boy's. Female skin is lightest at nubility and approaching ovulation, then darkens again during pregnancy, particularly in areas already darker than the rest (armpits, thighs, genital regions and the areola of the breasts). In 50-75 per cent of women a blotchy pigmentation of the face also occurs during the second half of the pregnancy. Light skin therefore appears to be an indication of endocrinal health and fecundity in a woman, and perception of this (unconscious for the most part, or at least uninformed as to the probable underlying reason) seems to be time-hallowed and global. In medieval England, for example, smooth white skin was so admired in a woman that the similes were endless – 'as white as a whale's bone', 'sea foam', 'milk, chalk or feather of swan', 'lily flower or the blossom on briar', 'starlight, ivory, silk or snow'. In contemporary Japan a white skin (along with blonde hair) is prized above all – so much so that in the raunchier Tokyo clubs even African striptease dancers will bleach their skin and peroxide their head and pubic hair so as to conform to the ideal.

Other skin characteristics are also vital clues in female sex appeal. A close, fine, shiny quality is at a premium. Absence of wrinkles, spots, flecks or other blemishes, including lesions, eruptions, warts, moles, cysts, tumours, acne and hirsutism is a good indicator of a corresponding absence of infections, ovulatory dysfunction and high testosterone level – in other words, a signifier of a robust healthy mate. Beautification is not about beauty alone, but has a hidden agenda. When women enhance their facial appearance with make-up and other cosmetic adornment, it is to enhance or diguise their health and fecundity cues, in Symons' view, rather than to advance their purely aesthetic advantages.

The jaw is another unusual sex appeal clue with a hidden agenda in women. As the computer face tests have shown, men find a shorter lower face and a gracile jaw to be attractive facial features in females. This may be related to the fact that during a woman's life the face undergoes many changes, including a general vertical elongation of the facial structure, probably due to higher levels of testosterone and a growth hormone secreted into the blood stream during pregnancy. The lengthening of the jaw broadly coincides with a decline in fertility and overall health and is probably one reason why women are considered to be less attractive the older they get. If the sexual attractiveness of the human face has anything to do with evolutionary fitness, then the preference for non-average face shapes suggests there will be a continuing evolutionary change away from the population mean. Towards what, one wonders?

FEMALE FACE

Dr Don Symons has identified the key features of the attractive female face as:

- *short lower face*
- *gracile jaw*
- *full lips*
- *high cheekbones*
- *lighter-than-average, unblemished skin*

To this list he might well have added:

- *smooth skin*
- *clear eyes*
- *lustrous hair*
- *good muscle tone*
- *animated facial expression*

HOW TO IMPROVE YOUR HAIR

There are two main elements to having sexy-looking hair. The first is the shape of the hair and the second is the condition.

The shape of cut you go for obviously depends on your face shape, body shape and lifestyle. Well-cut hair will automatically look healthier but whatever style you choose, it won't look attractive and touchable if it's not in the best condition. And that, after all, is what attractive hair is all about: for people to run their fingers through it.

Whatever texture your hair, it will look better when it's shiny – the reflection of light off the hair will go a long way to carrying off anything else you've done with yourself. The products that you use should be geared towards achieving maximum shine, so choose high protein water-based products that won't weigh the hair down.

You should also be able to move the hair – it shouldn't be so hairsprayed or lacquered into place that it ends up looking stiff or untouchable. Don't try to get your hair to do something it won't naturally do: if you have curly hair, for example, don't choose a style that suits straight hair, you'll just have to blow-dry the hair out whenever you style it, and consequently it will look dry, dull and lifeless, or you'll have to use lots of product on it, which will make it lack shine and movement.

Go with your own natural texture, even if at first you're not really into it. It's much easier to look after, requires lower maintenance, fewer products, less heat and styling, and will therefore end up looking much healthier. The less time you have to spend doing your hair and the less money you have to spend on products and the rest of it, the more time and money you have to spend on other things.

Always be open to change. Many people will stick with just one style because someone once told them that's the way they look best. But you can end up looking out of date or old-fashioned.

One of the sexiest looks, for both men and women, is when the hair falls over one eye – it's a hidden sort of look. Hair that is cut to the cheekbone, has a long fringe and is nipped in shorter at the neck is a classic sexy style. It shows off the bone structure and gives the face a nice shape, but still leaves you some hair to hide behind and play with.

If you look back at the icons of fashion and beauty you will find a high level of blond women and men, although whether the old adage that blond(e)s have more fun is true, I'm not so sure. If you want to become a white-bleach blond(e) you must consider your skin tone, otherwise it can look really odd. Of course some people dye their hair to look deliberately artificial, and it can look great. But if you're changing the colour of your hair that drastically you've really got to think about changing your make-up and the clothes that you wear too.

There's nothing worse than seeing someone with something on their head that bears no relation to anything else that's going on with them. It's the same with clothes – they should go with your hair, you should strive for a total look.

If you've got a really good haircut shape, and you've got your hair in really good condition, you'll feel more confident – and if you feel good about yourself you'll immediately portray a more glamorous, confident image.

MARK HAYES, UK CREATIVE DIRECTOR, VIDAL SASSOON, LONDON

MASTER CLASS

HOW TO IMPROVE YOUR MAKE-UP

The key to wearing make-up and looking sexy is to put it on so that no one can actually tell you're wearing it. Go for natural, earthy colours and don't worry too much about looking perfect. A lot of young people, especially, use too much make-up and too many bright colours – they end up with that artificial Barbie-doll look. If your make-up's too perfect, a man will be too terrified to touch you – you'll take on that Grace Kelly, ice-maiden appearance. And the older you get, the less you should wear.

A lot of women are frightened by their flaws, but I actually think men find women who aren't perfect more attractive. I often work in situations where there are lots of seemingly flawless models, and the guys aren't remotely interested in them, so don't worry or try too hard to disguise the flaws – most people don't even notice them, and if they do they'll probably find them endearing. Look at Cindy Crawford, for example. She was told to remove her mole, but she kept it, and it was the making of her – people now draw them on to copy her.

The biggest mistake that people make is to use make-up as a mask. It should be there to emphasise the good points, and not to camouflage the bad. If you've got small lips, you've got small lips – you can't make them look like Brigitte Bardot's just by painting a line around them. But you can stop them looking even smaller by avoiding dark matte lipstick, or drawing any hard lines around the edge of the lips. Instead, use two lipsticks, a darker one on the outside, and a lighter one on the inside.

To look really sexy, emphasise the eyes and the mouth. Bring out the whites of the eyes and draw attention to dilated pupils, by using darker eyeshadow

and kohl. Keep things simple, and work on the basis that light colours bring things forward, and dark colours set them back. I would use a light, but never white, peachy colour on the brow bone, and then a smoky colour all around the eye. Never use cold colours, like blues or greens, all over the eye – they are very unattractive. And for a really sexy look, put black kohl pencil inside the eyes and perhaps a few individual fake eyelashes on the outer corners – it gives the eyes a very penetrating look.

Always blend everything well, for the most natural effect.

When you get sexually excited all the blood rushes to your erogenous zones, including your lips, so work for this effect with your lipstick. Avoid red, red lips and go instead for a more blood red colour, the colour of children's lips, or the colour you get if you rub your lips very hard. And always add a dash of lip-gloss – that's very sexy. Avoid using too much base – too matte or porcelain a face will look rather fake and unapproachable: and let the skin glow. Put a little bit of colour on the cheeks, under the eyes, where you naturally blush. Today, people are much fitter and healthier, and this is the look that is admired rather than the fragile pretty, pretty look, or the sex-bomb look. Make-up can give you confidence, but it can't actually make you beautiful. Beauty comes from within, and nothing can compete with a good night's sleep and a good diet. But make-up used well can make you feel more confident about yourself, and if you feel confident, you look good.

A SESSION WITH VIRGINIA NICHOLS, MAKE-UP ARTIST, *VOGUE, MARIE CLAIRE, ELLE, THE FACE*

5 powers of persuasion – charisma, personality and power

'If women didn't exist, all the money in the world would have no meaning.'

ARISTOTLE ONASSIS

the mystery of charisma

Sex appeal is not just a matter of good looks and good grooming – it's also the way a person carries himself or herself, an aura of self-confidence and self-esteem, being at ease with your own body and inner self. It's the power of the personality, the inner psyche, the life force – mind, passion, drive, curiosity, creativity, what you will – to animate and fire the whole person – body and all. The great stars have this gift of total impact. John F. Kennedy had it, Jimmy Carter didn't. It's a potent brew that can serve more purposes than sexual relations alone – it can influence crowds, move masses, clinch big business deals. It can operate at a macro or micro level – Hitler addressing a Nuremberg rally, Julia Roberts giving us a close-up smile.

Paradoxical though it may seem, a man does not have to appear physically desirable for a woman to desire him. A woman can look with disfavour on a man's body, dislike his shape, his height, his size, his colouring, and yet still find him sexually attractive, if not immediately, then in the course of time. 'For many women, the body appears to grow beautiful and erotic as they grow to like the person in it,' writes Naomi Wolf. 'The actual body, the smell, the feel, the voice and movement, become charged with heat through the desirable person who animates it.' Gertrude Stein, the lesbian literary hostess of the Paris of the Lost Generation was not noted for her fondness for men, but she was to write of that short, squat, thick-necked Catalan genius, Pablo Picasso: 'There was nothing especially attractive about him at first sight, but his radiance, an inner fire one sensed in him, gave him a sort of magnetism I was unable to resist.' Clark Gable had the same quality. 'He had a magnetism,' recalled Joan Crawford. 'He had something no one else ever had. Everything about him was manliness.'

If there is any one word that encapsulates this hypnotic quality, it is 'charisma'. 'I understand your problem with your studio,' Michael Chekhov told Marilyn Monroe one day. 'You're a young woman who gives off sex vibrations no matter what you're thinking or doing.' Cybill Shepherd at an audition for *The Last Picture Show* displayed a similar charismatic presence. She was wearing jeans and a jacket and sat down next to a coffee table with a rose in a vase, 'She started

Laurence Olivier and Marilyn Monroe trading assets as The Prince and the Showgirl *(left). There is an intimate connection between sex appeal and politics appeal: Adolf Hitler's charisma could woo the masses – like the Hitler Youth and Maidens in Berlin's Olympic Stadium (above) – and win many an adoring woman's heart*

The phenomenon of Beatlemania: surging, yearning crowds, showing the factor of fame appeal in sex appeal

playing with the rose while she talked,' recalled the film's director, Peter Bogdanovich, 'and, like in a cartoon, I expected it to wither in the heat.'

Charisma involves an innuendo of erotic danger. 'It's a sort of bloom on a woman,' wrote Sir James Barrie. 'If you have it, you don't need to have anything else; and if you don't have it, it doesn't much matter what else you have.' A Swedish doctor by the name of Axel Munthe, aware of the crucial part charisma and its counterpart, confidence, play in the conduct of life, tried to grapple with the elusive nature of this vital quality:

'What is the secret of success? To inspire confidence. What is confidence? Where does it come from, from the head or the heart? Does it derive from the upper strata of our mentality or from the very depths of our being? Is it visible in the eye, is it audible in the spoken word? I do not know. I only know that it cannot be acquired by book-reading. It is a magic gift granted by birthright to one man and denied to another.'

Poise lies somewhere near the heart of the mystery – the appearance, illusion perhaps, of absolute self-certainty, the still, self-assured centre of a frenzied world. Not many of us are endowed with charisma – but many of us aspire to it.

the power of personality

Sexual attraction is not an exact science, nor even a steady state. The subjective attitudes of the people involved plays as big a part as objective factors such as body chemistry and differences of gender and sexual orientation. These subjective attitudes will vary according to the context in which people find themselves, where they are at in life and relationships, and what exactly they are looking for in a prospective sexual partner. It is the complexity and prolixity of all these factors which makes sexual attraction and its aftermath – sexual relations – such a richly mysterious and exciting lottery.

Except in the case of very short-term relationships it is rare that purely physical aspects of sexual attraction, important though they may be, are the only forces that come into play – not even with the male, who generally tends to be more closely focused on physical attraction than the female.

Sex appeal is about more than the simple gravitational pull of a body of flesh, bone and tissue enclosed in 6 pounds of skin. For inside that skin is the person who inhabits that body, and the nature of that person, the sum of the qualities which added together we call personality, exerts a highly persuasive influence on the perception of a person's attractiveness. In one UK survey, for example, it was found that personality was considerably more important to both men and women, topping good looks by some 30 per cent.

But what are the favoured qualities of personality? Judging by various surveys, polls, mailshots and Internet trawls around the world, the list of people's preferences includes: intelligence, sense of humour, kindness, understanding, honesty, respect, loyalty and one or more shared interests. In a recent survey of what single people of both sexes wanted from a partner, the top fifteen attributes shown on the right emerged, shown in descending order.

Most of these qualities are not intrinsically sexy in themselves but can, by their presence or absence, help to reinforce, diminish or otherwise transform the raw sex appeal of the body alone – qualities, in other words, which can shift the perspective of sex appeal from the overture to a mere collision of bodies to the prospect of a longer-term and even loving relationship.

A combination of physical attractiveness and an attractive personality features large in many people's sex appeal dream ideal – along with a whole host of highly idiosyncratic and less obvious requirements generally unique to each individual, such as the back of a knee or a left foot that turns inwards – the product of the long-simmering synthesis of that individual's life experience, memories and associations, fantasies and imagination.

The wish list of ideal qualities differs somewhat between the sexes. A survey of women's views of the ideal modern man (a serious prospective partner rather than a one-night stand or sun-and-sex romance) listed the most desirable qualities shown over, in descending order.

The physical attractiveness/attractive personality mix is well illustrated in this poll, as is the supreme virtue of a man's personality in a woman's eyes – head and shoulders clear of head (50 per cent) and shoulders (4 per cent), let alone hard brass.

Asked what they personally liked in a woman, men came up with a different list of qualities, with sex and looks very much higher up the scale of requirements (also shown over in descending order). 'Modesty' rated low in men's eyes, with 'cuddliness' a close second from bottom. The small ads in lonely hearts columns published in magazines and newspapers around the world reveal both the uniqueness and the sameness of what people are looking for in each other – cries of yearning in the fathomless void, an unquenchable thirst for love, sex, beauty, companionship, unification with a body-mate or soul-mate or both, fun and fusion.

what people really look for in each other

61% Friendship

58% Love

57% Honesty

56% Trust

55% Sense of humour

47% Faithfulness

45% Respect

39% Loyalty

37% Understanding

36% Kindness

30% Good conversation

29% Similar interests

29% Physical attraction

29% Good sex

12% Financial security

{SOURCE: SEX AND THE SINGLES. MORI}

QUALITIES IN WOMEN DESIRED BY MEN

- *Sense of humour*
- *Good looks*
- *Femininity*
- *Intelligence*
- *Sexiness*

(Source: Mori)

QUALITIES IN MEN DESIRED BY WOMEN

- *Personality*
- *Good build*
- *Facial good looks*
- *Intelligence*
- *Eyes*
- *Behind*
- *Height*
- *Money*

(Source: Mori)

Dating agencies and marriage bureaux are careful to warn their clients about the perilous gap between the delights of pure sexual attraction and the demands made by modern marriage or a committed relationship. In rare instances sexual attraction, if it burns strongly enough, can bind couples together in an unbreakable bond of erotic obsession, even though they have no other point in common. Equally, a partnership devoid of sexual attraction has its own built-in constraints. The ideal is an attractive personality in a sexually attractive body, the whole package all the more attractive for the fact that hopefully the person in question likes you too – for often there can be no one more attractive than a person who is attracted to you.

who likes whom?

There has been some debate as to whether personal attraction is based on the similarities between two people ('like attracts like') or the differences ('opposites attract'). The first thesis argues that the more two partners resemble each other in intelligence, humour, tastes, interests, attitudes, values, personality, background, sociability, compatibility, the more likely they are to be drawn to one another and stay with one another – always assuming that under the pressures of life they do not change and grow apart. However, many still favour the 'opposites attract' approach, arguing that in choosing a long-term partner we look for traits in the other that are missing in ourselves.

But the 'like attracts like' theory finds more favour these days, even though the matter is still a contentious one. In some cases, the congruence of similarities can even spill over into physical features – partners who have a similar ear-lobe type and middle-finger length, for example, have been found to be more compatibly attracted to each other. An extreme case of 'like attracts like' is that of siblings who are parted in infancy and meet and fall in love with each other after sexual maturity, not knowing that they are brother and sister. People in such instances can resemble each other to a remarkable degree, even down to chemistry and smell, and their attraction to each other can be instantaneous, total – and potentially tragic.

By contrast, the sex appeal of the exotic is also a powerful factor for some. 'A rational awareness that temperaments are miles apart, conversation topics hard to come by, shared experience non-existent,' writes one Slavophile English actor, 'is no match for the allure of a Russian accent and Tartar eyes.' But exotic relations (cross-national, cross-ethnic, cross-cultural, cross-class) are not necessarily examples of the 'opposites attract' theory so much as cases of 'something rich and strange' in which the exotic represents the fulfilment of a

THE AGE GAP

In every society in the world the majority of men prefer women who are younger than they are themselves. Among the Nambikwara Indians of Brazil there is just one word which serves to mean both 'young' and 'pretty' and one word to mean 'old' and 'ugly'. In more evolved societies the age gap between men and their preferred age in women is narrower than in more deprived societies. In Scandinavia the difference is one to two years. In the USA the age difference is between one-and-a-half and two-and-a-half years. In Greece it is about five years, in Nigeria and Zambia it is between six-and-a-half and seven-and-a-half years, while on Socotra Island, Yemen, the gap can rise to between eight and ten years, and in polygamous societies like the Tiwi of Northern Australia to 20 or even 30 years. In the USA the average age of a bride has risen to the early twenties in recent years. Among the Yanamamö Indians of Colombia it is 15 to 18, and in India the early teens. On Socotra it can be as low as 11 or 12.

The older the man gets the younger the relative age of the woman becomes. By the time a man is in his fifties his preference is for a woman ten to 20 years younger, though generally only high status males with abundant resources can easily actualize their preference. But even among lesser males the rule holds true, and computer dating services have found that as the male's income goes up the age of the woman he wants goes down – often by as much as 15 years or more.

These invariables hold true around the world and as far as can be judged through most of history. Such invariables do not always hold true in the rest of the animal kingdom – some male primates prefer older female primates, for example, provided they have already proved they can bear young. But in the case of man, that's how it is, like it or loathe it as many do.

person's inner fantasy or triggers a cross-referring associative memory.

Attraction can also be a matter of luck, opportunity, convenience – or even destiny. At its basic level sexual attraction between two people may be no more than a case of the most convenient person at the most opportune time. At its most evolved level it may take the form of an electrifying, eerily transcendental, all-exclusive, totally inevitable-seeming sex appeal encounter – a phenomenon often described as 'love at first sight'. One of the characteristic features of such encounters is the feeling on the part of one or other (or even both) of the persons involved that they have met or known each other at some mysterious, indefinable time in the past, have been lovers on occasion beyond memory. According to London psychologist Dr Glenn Wilson, this is not love at first sight but at second sight.

This thesis has been explained as a stage in sexual programming which begins even before birth. The blueprint for sexual attraction towards the sex of our preference is mapped out in the early years of life, using the physical characteristics of the parent of the opposite sex as a model. When our hormones go into overdrive at puberty this plan is then put into effect, but modified in the light of experience. Love at first sight is therefore a misnomer – rather it is recognition, love at second sight, for the love object has already been 'seen' in the course of the lover's genetic programming .

If this is true, love and attraction can both be a form of destiny, or perhaps pre-destiny. Equally, the search for the programmed model of the subsconsciously imprinted ideal love can lead to a kind of Flying Dutchman Effect, a restless wandering in search of the significant other, the very stuff of legend and high romance. Or it can result in a dissatisfied passing from one lover to another in the hope that one day 'the one' will be found at last.

However, love and attraction are underpinned by very strong evolutionary imperatives.

David Bowie enjoying 'Life on Mars' with two sex-kitten space companions – a futuristic interpretation of the Flying Dutchman Effect

faint hearts
never won
fair ladies

In circumstances or societies where there are no moral, legal or social curbs or restraints, the basic instinct of every male of reproductive age is to have sex repeatedly with as many partners as he can gain access to throughout the length of his sexually active life.

Given free rein, the total number of female partners a man in that position might have in an active lifetime might run into tens of thousands and the total number of sexual couplings into a significant multiple of that. Kings and despots all over the world and throughout history have behaved in this way, sending talent scouts as secret sex agents to scour the land for the prettiest women to satisfy the ruler's sexual pleasures, which would appear to confirm the relationship between a high power-drive, and a high sex-drive and a high testosterone hormone-level in men.

Men are biologically and sexually geared to repeated sex. The sexual physiology they have inherited from their evolutionary past is proof of this. A man's testes are small compared with the hyper-promiscuous pygmy chimpanzee but large compared with the maritally faithful gorilla. This suggests an intermediate degree of promiscuity on the part of our human ancestors, neither as monogamous as the gorilla nor as compulsively promiscuous as the chimpanzee. The relatively high libido level, fuelled by a relatively high testosterone count, drives his impulse to engage in casual sex and propels him to seek access to as many partners as our pair-bonding allows. The nature of a man's sexual fantasies (twice as many as a woman's and involving anonymous partners, multiple partners and strangers in acts and variations devoid of emotional engagement) facilitate his inclination to match his fantasy sex with the real thing in real life. To achieve all this a man is even prepared to lower his standards of acceptable desirability in a partner, thus permitting a higher head count than might otherwise be possible.

the coolidge effect

The ability of the human male to be sexually attracted to and sexually aroused by virtually any attractive new arrival on the scene is such a universal phenomenon throughout the male range of the human species that sexologists have coined a name to describe it – the Coolidge Effect, after a former US President. The story goes that President Coolidge and his wife were on a tour of government farms when the First Lady noticed a cockerel mating with a hen and asked the farm guide how often this sort of thing occurred. She was told

> 'A hen is only an egg's way of making another egg.'
>
> *SAMUEL BUTLER*

THE SEX APPEAL OLYMPICS – THE CHAMPIONS

At the height of the ancient civilizations, absolute power was synonymous with fantastic sexual activity and the vast harems of the potentates were tantamount to breeding machines for the spreading of the despots' genes. Record holders for the number of wives and consorts include:

- *Emperor Udayama of India:* 16,000 concubines

- *Emperor Fei-ti of China:* 10,000 women

- *Montezuma of the Aztecs:* 4,000 concubines

- *King Hammurabi of Babylon:* thousands of slave wives

- *Pharaoh Akhanaten of Egypt:* a wife (Nefertiti), 317 concubines and an army of consorts

The numbers have dropped in more recent times, mirroring the decline in political absolutism, but are nonetheless still impressive:

- *King Lapetamaka II of Tonga had the job of deflowering every maiden on the island, and at the age of 80, when Captain Cook visited him, was still carrying out his royal duties eight to ten times a day*

- *Moulay Ismail the Bloodthirsty, Emperor of Morocco, kept 500 women in his harem and sired 888 children*

- *King Ibn Saud of Saudi Arabia had sex with three different women every night for 63 years, making a grand total of some 65,000 different female partners in his lifetime*

- *The Belgian crime writer, Georges Simenon, claimed to have had sex with a different woman every 50 hours throughout his adult life*

- *The wife of the Boston Strangler went on record as saying that her husband had sex on average 19 times a day, his extra-marital activities not included*

Fewer women outside of the oldest profession have notched up such huge tallies, but there have been some impressive contenders:

- *Catherine the Great of Russia recommended sex six times a day and achieved a final tally of over 80 lovers, while the French actress Sarah Bernhardt was credited with more than 1,000 lovers, and another French actress, Mlle Dubois (c. 1770), named 16,527 individuals in her catalogue of lovers*

- *The record for the number of couplings with one partner in one session is 87, held by a couple in medieval France*

- *The world record for continuous sex without a break is 15 hours, held by Mae West and an American called Ted*

that the usual strike rate for the average cockerel was dozens of times a day. On hearing this the First Lady was heard to reply: 'Please tell that to the President.' The President, observing the same cockerel copulating again, asked whether the cockerel always had sex with the same hen. Oh no, came the reply, with a different one each time. Whereupon the President gave the farm guide a meaningful look and said: 'Please tell *that* to Mrs Coolidge.'

Evolutionary psychologists cite the Coolidge Effect as an example of evolutionary adaptation in human sex. 'The waning of lust for one's wife is adaptive,' noted Dr Don Symons, 'because it promotes a roving eye.' For those dominant males who are the living proof of the Coolidge Effect, repeated sex is just part of life's work. As pop singer Rod Stewart, a so-called 'serial blondogamist', once commented: 'The most memorable is always the current one, the rest just merge into a sea of blondes.'

What the male of the species is actually attempting to do is to impregnate as many of the females as possible in a splatter-gun effort to ensure the continuity of the species as a whole; while from a genetic point of view the male is involved in a systematic programme to pass on his genes to as many reproductive receptacles as he can persuade to take them.

What foils the male's tendency to random promiscuity is the woman. Here the differences in the reproductive mechanisms of the two sexes are all important. Male sperm are replenished at the rate of around 12 million per hour. By contrast, women are born with a finite number of eggs and will use just 400 in a lifetime. The act of sex demands a minimum biological investment from the male but can entail a maximum investment on the part of the female, involving a pregnancy lasting nine months and a child-caring period lasting several years. Given these basic and divergent start points, it is clear a woman must bring a radically different attitude and set of priorities to both the act of sex and the male with whom she chooses to have it.

The evolutionary process has favoured women who prefer partners who possess attributes over partners who incur costs, just as it has favoured men who prefer females who are fecund and young. Overall, women value economic resources about 100 per cent more than men do, though there are variations from one society to another – Japanese women, for example, value economic resources 150 per

A harem packed with voluptuous women, as in this Orientalist fantasy by Ingres, may look like the primordial male dream, but historically it was the preserve of only the absolute rulers of the ancient civilizations

'There are a number of mechanical devices which increase sexual arousal, particularly in women. Chief among them is the Mercedes-Benz 380SL convertible'
P. J. O'ROURKE

cent more than Japanese men, Dutch women only 36 per cent more. A 1993 survey found that 40 per cent of the women polled voted in favour of a 'solvent businessman' type, while only 8 per cent voted for a 'good-looking caveman on a hormone rush' type.

Even when the woman herself has economic resources – as in the affluent West or some matriarchal societies of Africa – such a woman will almost always require that a potential mate possesses even greater resources than her own. American screen star Grace Kelly put her finger on it when she remarked to a friend on the eve of her marriage to Prince Rainier of Monaco: 'I don't want to be married to someone who feels inferior to my success or because I make more money than he does.'

Given all this, it becomes obvious that good looks in a man, though desirable as an optional extra, may not add up to the kind of resources necessary in a long-term mating situation (unless, of course, his looks are his resources, as in the case of a movie star or pop idol). So what do necessary resources add up to and how do they reveal themselves to the world at large?

In assessing the answers to these questions, there are several stars to steer your ship by – clues, that is, to the resource potential of a potential mate. Some women have a rule of thumb in these matters. 'I can spot a millionaire in the street by the way he looks,' claims Ivana Trump, former wife of an American tycoon. 'First I look into his eyes, then I look at his shoes.'

Another key clue is a man's social status – his pecking order within the group, be it a gang or a tribe, a company or a corporation, a town or a nation. The higher a man's status, the greater the likelihood that he is a man endowed with greater-than-average resources. Men who are pushed around within a group are viewed with disfavour, while those who are off-limits through marriage or long-term relationship are usually (though by no means universally) treated with caution, no matter how favourably they are regarded, for their resources are committed elsewhere. The ideal is the 'eligible bachelor', a man of high status with resources that are still available for the partner of his choice.

Age is another clue. While a woman's socio-biological value decreases with age, that of a man increases, for generally he becomes wealthier, more powerful and more elevated in status the older he gets. And with increasing maturity comes sounder judgement and greater emotional stability, making it less likely that he will on a whim reallocate his resources elsewhere (though there are many sensational exceptions to the general rule). But there are certain disadvantages in becoming involved with a substantially older man. One is the likelihood of his dying in mid-commitment, so to speak. The other is the possibility of instability and strife due to incompatability brought about by an excessive age differential.

A cluster of male characteristics which numerous polls and surveys have indicated as being particularly important in choosing a husband or long-term mate include ambition and industriousness, intelligence, humour, dependability, compatibility, kindness, commitment, fidelity and – yes – love. All these qualities, according to evolutionary thinking, signal different aspects of the same thing – they all indicate the man's resource potential, his determination to acquire it, his ability to achieve it, his inclination to share it, his disinclination to divert it, his commitment to cherish, protect and provide for woman and offspring alike. Positive qualities of kindness and loyalty augur well for happiness and security, while intelligence indicates a man with an aptitude for learning skills, including parental skills, along with the ability to hold his own in a group or even influence its decisions. Add good looks, good health and an athletic build and you have a paragon of masculine virtues, a sex appeal god no less.

In most of the world women remain in a vulnerable position, reliant on the success and finances of the man for their own security. Even in those societies where a minority of women do have opportunities to acquire status and resources of their own, women will continue to follow their evolutionary instincts and indicate a preference for a man who has commensurate – or ideally greater – status and resources. In the USA today a woman who earns more money than her husband is likely to leave him, and one study found that the divorce rate

PERUVIAN LOVE SONG

The swapping of assets – beauty and fecundity for strength and resources – is an age-old and worldwide custom. Anthropologist J.G. Samanez describes a typical marriage bargaining ritual in rural Peru:

The boy goes with his entire family in the early hours of the morning to the girl's house. The mother, already prepared, sings out:
"Who looks over my fence at such an ungodly hour?"
The boy replies:
"The exhausted lover, no longer able to sleep, seeks the pigeon, la colombina, of his dreams."
"What merit does he have to ask for her?"
"He is young, hard-working, courageous."
"What does he own?"
"Land, cattle, and strong arms for work."
"What does he bring?"
"His family is here with the burro laden with food and amber chicha."
After a further song, towards daybreak the visitors are welcomed in. Food is laid out, drinking begins and negotiations start.'

was 50 per cent higher among couples where the wife earnt more than the husband.

As London business woman Jennifer d'Abo, former chairwoman of Ryman the stationery retailer, put it: 'A powerful man is attractive – a powerful woman is frightening.' This was a sentiment echoed by Idi Amin of Uganda – then a powerful man and a frightening one – in a letter of condolence to Lord Snowdon on his divorce from Princess Margaret: 'Your experience will be a lesson to all of us men to be careful not to marry ladies in very high positions.'

It has been suggested that the male drive to acquire riches and

Clark Gable, adored for his magnetic masculinity, nearly failed his first screen test when he was marked down with the comment 'Ears too big.' But for Joan Crawford – and millions of moviegoers – he had 'something no one else ever had'

display extraordinarily expensive status symbols and elaborate toys – the Blue Riband motor yachts, the giant inter-continental balloons, the Lamborghini and Harley-Davidson runabouts, the wildlife parks, castles, islands, race horses, flunkeys and dancing girls – is deep-down an evolutionary instinct intended simply to enhance his sex appeal. This is sex appeal as image – the clothes you wear, the car you drive, the house you live in, the friends you keep, the girlfriend you sleep with. As David Buss has put it: 'Men strive to control resources and to exclude other men from resources to fulfil women's mating preferences.' It has always been thus. 'Girls praise a poem, but go for expensive presents,' wrote Ovid, poet of love in the days of the Roman Empire. 'Today any illiterate oaf can catch their eye provided he's rich. Today is truly a Golden Age: gold buys honour, gold procures love.'

Not much has changed since Ovid was banished from Rome for an unspecified indiscretion involving one of the Emperor's grand-daughters. Wealth, power, fame and glamour – any one of them can do the trick. 'The best aphrodisiac,' pronounced the former US Secretary of State, Henry Kissinger, when asked about the attractive actress with whom his name was currently linked, 'is power.'

Power and wealth often go together (though not always). The richest man in the world is a Japanese hotel and railway magnate, Yoshiaki Tsutsumi, 60 years old, worth between $8.5 and $22 billion, and a notorious womanizer whose name has been linked with a succession of Japan's most famous actresses, all young, charming and beautiful. According to his closest friends he supports four or five households, each containing a 'wife' and children. According to his friends, he is like a butterfly, flitting from flower to flower. In modern Japan, where maintaining a number of households is a sign of a man's wealth and power, a symbol of his status, this is considered anything but shocking.

Fame and glamour are also great enhancers of sex appeal, and never far distant from wealth and power. Robert de Niro and Mickey Rourke may no longer be in the first flush of youth, but they are mature men of the world, famous and rich – and this puts them in a different league when it comes to sex appeal. By comparison, according to Karen Ford, the head booker at the Models One UK agency, some of the more gorgeous young hopefuls, male models among them, were no-hopers with next to nothing between

> **'Money cannot buy**
> **The fuel of love**
> **But is excellent**
> **kindling.'**
>
> *WH AUDEN*

> **'She was the original**
> **good time that was**
> **had by all.'**
>
> *BETTE DAVIS OF A READILY-AVAILABLE STARLET*

MALE SEX APPEAL – WHAT LAUREN BACALL LOOKS FOR IN A MAN

I find it hard enough to meet someone I want to have dinner with, never mind marry. I don't want to be bored – if they can smile it's a start. I like men very much, but I do mean men, not boys. I have no time for

egotistic, macho or humourless men. I don't like men who take life too seriously. I can't bear men that want women to tell them how wonderful they are the whole time – these sort of men can't deal with getting older, so they go out with younger girls and get their egos fed all the time. I actually don't think it's natural for men and women to live together for a long time, because they want different things.

the ears. Maturer men were sexier because they knew where they were going.

Fame alone can do the trick. Mick Jagger is besieged by the nubility from dawn to long beyond dusk. 'They are all trying to use him,' complained Jerry Hall once. 'They are all nobodies trying to be somebody. I'm up against this every day.'

As with men, how a woman judges the sex appeal of the opposite sex depends on what it is she is looking for at any given time in her life. The more she is seeking a permanent commitment, the longer her wish list ideally needs to be. But if she has something else in mind – a brief fling, a holiday romance, an adulterous affair – she may radically revise her standards or shorten her list.

A woman who engages in a short-term affair may do so for a variety of reasons. It may take the form of a nakedly erotic experience with someone she fancies in a purely physically sexual way, or a form of exploration and adventure. It nay be a personal statement of some kind, a protest, or even an act of hero worship. It can be seen as a ritual submission in a collective rite, or a cure for heartbreak. But for the majority of women in the world any form of affair entails a degree of risk – the risk of pregnancy without the security of a supportive male, the risk of the withdrawal of a pre-existing partner's resources, loss of security, or even of reputation.

Evolutionary psychologists argue that in the light of such potential costs there must be some strategy behind the risk-taking. Casual sex, a brief affair, they argue, must serve some short-term goal, which in no way need invalidate the woman's own steady-state aim of achieving a long-term or permanent union. A pre-marital affair may be a way of evaluating the compatibility and suitability of a potential marriage partner, a way of testing sexual make-up and desirability under field conditions; an extra-marital affair a way of securing a 'back-up' mate should something happen to her steady partner, or even as a means of bearing offspring with better genes, and therefore a better chance of survival, than they might hope to acquire through her current mate. For the male, casual sex serves his evolutionary purpose well, for the woman, with all the potential costs involved, it succeeds mainly as a short-term strategy for a short-term goal.

All this adds up to one thing. The female's definition of male sex appeal will vary according to her sexual stratagems at the particular time and context in which she finds herself. A woman looking for sexual adventure at one stage in her life may pass over the charms of the gentlemanly City type replete with Savile Row suit and tremendous pension potential in favour of one of the wild bunch –

with leathers and a Harley-Davidson – but she may diametrically reverse her choice at a later stage when the need for security for her children and herself has the edge over a zest for living and loving dangerously. But this isn't to say that every woman doesn't have an alternative inner fantasy ideal, her escape from such practical sex appeal criteria. As Erica Jong put it: 'In every woman's heart there is a god of the woods, and this god is not available for marriage or for home improvement or for parenthood.'

Although a woman who is into short-term love may seek men with different kinds of sex appeal according to the context, from the strictly evolutionary point of view her requirements for both short-term and long-term relationships share broad similarities. Whatever the nature of the relationship, she will expect something in return for the precious gift which she bestows, and this is almost always a gift in kindness or in kind.

At the end of the day, women dally in sex for love, while men dally in love for sex. Dorothy Parker put her finger on it, perhaps, when she wryly but shrewdly noted:

> 'Woman wants monogamy;
> Man delights in novelty.
> Love is woman's moon and sun;
> Man has other forms of fun.
> Woman lives but in her lord;
> Count to ten and he is bored.
> With this gist and sum of it,
> What earthly good can come of it?'

The evolutionary psychologist's view of sex appeal and relationships may strike many people as an unforgivingly bleak and cynical one. What room is there in such a primordial scenario of apparent red-eyed lust and naked greed for the civilizing virtues of love, respect, selflessness, the affairs of the spirit as well as the heart? But room there is. And though so much of the sex appeal of status, power and wealth may seem to reek more of the boardroom than the bedroom, there is moderation in all things, and the virtues of status and power can be interpreted in other ways than those of the jungle, and riches in ways that are not so blatantly material. Every modest man or woman will have a strength of some kind, every poor one a value that will be prized. Wealth, status and power should be regarded in relative terms therefore – for in the country of the blind the one-eyed man is king.

FEMALE SEX APPEAL – WHAT RUDOLPH VALENTINO LOOKED FOR IN A WOMAN

- Fidelity
- Recognition of the supreme importance of love
- Intelligence
- Beauty
- Sense of humour
- Sincerity
- Appreciation of good food
- Serious interest in some art, trade or hobby
- Old-fashioned and whole-hearted acceptance of monogamy
- Courage

HOW TO IMPROVE YOUR CONFIDENCE

One of the first things to realize when it comes to self-confidence is that everybody is probably feeling just as nervous and wobbly as you are. Even the most extrovert people, no matter how confident they seem, are often putting on a front.

A lot of people get hooked on the 'what might happen if...' question. 'What might happen if I get to the party and I can't talk to anybody,' or 'what if I dry up in the middle of a conversation?' There are two things you can do to overcome this problem. The first, creative visualization, is very like positive thinking. Visualize yourself talking to people and feeling comfortable with them. Try to picture yourself as you want to be. The second is to turn your thinking on its head. Put 'so' in front of the 'what ifs?'. 'So what if I dry up in the middle of the conversation, so what if I don't know what to do, so what if I do get nervous?' It isn't the end of the world if you don't know what to say – it might be a bit uncomfortable, but if the other person isn't saying anything either, then they are probably experiencing exactly the same fears as you.

Work out a contingency plan. Think about something that will give you a way out. Ask yourself what it would be like to ask the other person if they would like another drink. It can feel hard to do, but just because it's difficult, it doesn't mean that it's impossible. Once you realise that nine out of ten people also find it hard, it will become easier for you.

Self-confidence is all about self-esteem. If you don't value yourself or believe in yourself it will be harder to build your self-confidence. So do things that give you a sense of achievement, that actually make you feel more confident in yourself. If you are on your own again after a relationship, or are feeling a little shy or nervous, go to things where you can mix with other people. Not necessarily to something where everyone else is in couples, but maybe an organized supper party, or, if that seems too intimate, join a course – drumming, singing, whatever – something which is fun and has social interaction. As you start to mix and meet with other people, you will soon realize that a lot of people are just as nervous as you are.

There's always a part that goes beyond our comfort zone, but the more you try, the more comfortable with it you will become. And eventually, the things that were difficult for you will become much easier. Trying is half the battle – if you try and fail, accept it: 'I failed, but at least I tried and I'll try again.'

We all get nervous sometimes. We all trip on our tongues when we really like someone, we all make silly comments and think 'Oh God! I shouldn't have said that.' But learn to laugh at yourself, to not be too intense. If you trip on your tongue, you trip on your tongue – make a joke out of it. Laughter discharges tension, it helps to externalize the fear. Try smiling – you'll find that it is physically impossible to feel as tense.

Self-confidence is about acceptance –'I feel nervous, but I'm going to do it anyway.' People tend to programme themselves for failure, so it's a question of reprogramming and learning to feel more comfortable with anxiety.

If you feel embarrassed, be embarrassed – many people find it very endearing. If you put on a huge front and pretend to be something you're not, you'll be found out eventually, especially if you get involved with the person, so you might as well face it at the beginning. If you accept who you are, you are far more likely to get other people to accept who you are. If they like you, then they'll persevere. If they don't, there will be other people with whom it does work.

If you aren't someone who is terribly suave or sophisticated and knows all the fast-pat chat-up lines, just talk to the person, get to know them. Most people enjoy talking about themselves, it's a subject they know well. Ask them about themselves. If you're at a party it might be as simple as asking how long they have known the host or hostess. If you show interest in the other person, they are more likely to feel attracted to you.

Self-confidence starts with self-esteem and that starts with you. Instead of punishing yourself, or feeling bad about yourself because you're not the most confident person in the world, make a joke about it and be accepting of who you are. If you try to change yourself into some suave, sophisticated, ultra-confident person you'll end up a different human being to the one you really are, and if you were that other human being you'd end up meeting people you may not actually feel comfortable with anyway. People always look at everybody else and think everybody else has sussed it – but they haven't.

SYLVIA MILTON, PSYCHOLOGICAL COUNSELLOR IN PYSCHOSEXUAL AND MARITAL DIFFICULTIES AND TRAINER IN PERSONAL DEVELOPMENT.

HOW TO IMPROVE YOUR CHARISMA

Charisma is very rarely to do with beauty. It is more to do with a certain wholeness, a sense of being at one with yourself. It sets you apart from the merely mortal. Gérard Depardieu is a classic example of a charismatic person. He's not a handsome man, but he has presence. You want to watch him, you want to watch every roll of his eyeball, every flick of his eyebrow.

There are actors and actresses who have charisma on stage or on film, but who wouldn't necessarily have it if you walked into a room. It may be that in front of a camera or on a stage, given a certain character and the situation of the play, they are able to find that wholeness – they are given another conduit in which to put their aspirant charisma.

Many of us can look to moments in our life when we have probably felt charismatic, but it is hard to lock into it at will. But if you know you've got it, there are ways of sustaining it – using silence, knowing when to be quiet. There are also times when we can feel charismatic. Alcohol, for example, gives us release, it can reduce our inhibitions, make us feel less self-conscious and more

charismatic. But it usually does the opposite.

Talent of any kind is charismatic. You might pass someone in the street wearing glasses and tweeds with a boring haircut and not look twice at them, but if you see them at work, making a piece of furniture or turning a piece of pottery, they can attain a charisma. As they appear totally absorbed in their work, you become the outside admirer – it can be as magnetic as watching someone on film.

Charisma is a question of absolute self-conviction, of being totally unselfconscious, of not caring what others might think, of being able to live totally in the moment. And the paradox is that the charismatic person gets liked because he or she is not worried about being liked. It is something we aspire to. When we're in the aura of a charismatic person we hope some of it will be reflected onto us, we want it to be catching, through the charisma of another person we hope to gain some kudos.

STEPHEN BOXER, ACTOR
NATIONAL THEATRE AND ROYAL SHAKESPEARE COMPANY

6

The power of artifice – clothing and adornment

'Know, first, who you are – then adorn yourself accordingly.'

EPICTETUS

sex appeal and the clothes we wear

The human body does not normally surface stark naked in day-to-day life or average sex appeal situations. Generally it is garbed, adorned and modified in various ways according to the dictates of social custom or the whims or needs of the individual. Theories abound as to why we wear clothes and what impact they have on our sexual attractiveness. One obvious reason is that clothes protect our vulnerable, naked skins from weather, insects and all the knocks of daily life.

But clothes do much more than simply protect us. They denote our sex, our place in society, our function in society, our personality and attitudes, our current mood and what we are doing at a given moment. Clothes form part of our self-presentation and reveal much about ourselves to the world at large. In a study carried out in the North of England, teenage schoolgirls were asked to judge what type of person someone was from the clothes they wore. Answers ranged from adjectives like 'snobbish', 'rebellious', and 'shy' to more specific conclusions about people, such as 'this one drinks', 'this one has loose morals', 'that one has lots of boyfriends' and so on. But clothes are also the most easily manipulated part of our persona and it is relatively easy to transform the appearance of a man from a beggar to a businessman simply by giving him a sharp suit and a cashmere coat.

It is when we come to the sexual role of clothes that the real argument begins. There are basically two theories. One is that, from the sexual point of view, we wear clothes to hide our sexuality – the modesty theory. The other is that we wear clothes to advertise our sexuality – the immodesty theory.

The modesty theory, propounded by zoologist and behaviourist Desmond Morris and others, holds that we wear clothes to hide our genitals and other sexually significant parts of the body. The genitalia are such instant 'turn-on' organs and provide such incredibly powerful visual sexual stimuli, the argument goes, that they have to be covered up to prevent endless embarrassing bouts of sexual arousal. In the light of this theory, the first fashion garment would appear to be the fig leaf. In Christianity, when Adam and Eve take a bite out of the apple in the Garden of Eden, the hitherto innocent naked body

> **'One must either be a work of art or wear a work of art.'**
> OSCAR WILDE

Madame de Pompadour, celebrated mistress of Louis XIV and arbiter of eighteenth-century taste, in a portrait by Boucher c. 1750 (opposite). For seasoned naturists (above), our bodies themselves are adornment –
'And not in utter nakedness
But trailing clouds of glory do we come'
WILLIAM WORDSWORTH

Aphrodite in the desert: even when the body and face are hidden, the eyes can still transmit their silent signal

'There are no ugly women, only lazy ones.'

HELENA RUBENSTEIN

becomes a sexual body and nakedness is linked with sin and shame. 'The loin cloth,' says Morris, 'is culturally the most widespread of all garments. In any social situation demanding costume-shedding, it is the last clothing barrier to fall.'

Other parts of the body also transmit sexual signals, and different societies at different times have seen fit to try to switch all these signals off. Hence the heavily garbed and veiled women of the fundamentalist Muslim states, where even the basic outline of the female body is hidden by the formless folds of their prescribed costume. Hence also the rules of Victorian puritanism in the West, which persisted well into the twentieth century. Even the sight of a woman's bare navel was banned in pre-war Hollywood movies, and photos that included naked nipples were not allowed to be printed in newspapers until the Sixties.

This modesty theory has its opponents. There are a number of tribal societies dotted around the globe – particularly in the hot, humid Amazon Basin – where virtual nakedness is still the norm. There is no evidence that such people go about their daily business in a state of incessant sexual arousal because of the unobstructed view of each other's near nudity all day long. In fact, the opposite is true. Unlike many more heavily garbed people in the West, half-naked tribal people in the main are not prurient about the half-naked human body, they have few hang-ups about the sexual side of life, and they keep more or less strictly to their agreed code of morality. The impact of Christian puritan morality on such people has been devastating, bringing about the very condition the Christian missionaries purported to prevent, as a Colonial Office report on the Gilbert and Ellis Islands in the 1920s makes clear:

'Sexual morality in the past was high. Girls went naked until married, and were protected by usages of extreme ferocity. To molest a maiden was to court death by slow strangulation, or by being tied to a log and floated out to sea. Now, morality is not so fierce. British justice has abolished the death penalty, and the native is deprived of moral landmarks. Clothes, covering bodies which once went naked and unconscious, have contributed to this moral decadence by stimulating nasty curiosities, which never before existed.'

In a polemic tract against what he called the 'missionary menace' Newton A. Rowe fulminated at the damage inflicted by Western interlopers imbued with a fanatical anti-sexual ethic. 'The native was taught to regard his beautiful, semi-naked body as being somehow foul and indecent, while sex, of course, the supreme sin, was only to be mentioned with uplifted hands, a grimace and a mock shudder.'

How much more natural and more lovely had the scant garb of the Pacific islanders once been. Robert Louis Stevenson, visiting the Gilbert Islands in the 1890s, praised the sexy dressing of the Gilbertine girls before the missionary crackdown:

'The *ridi* is its name: a cutty petticoat or fringe of the smoked fibre of the coconut leaf, not unlike tarry string; the lower edge not reaching the mid-thigh, and the upper adjusted so low upon the haunches that it seems to cling by accident. A sneeze, you think, and the lady must surely be left destitute. Yet if a pretty Gilbertine would look her best, that must be her costume. In this, and naked otherwise, she moves with an incomparable liberty and grace and life that marks the poetry of Micronesia. Bundle her in a gown, the charm is fled, and she wriggles like an English woman.'

Sociologists favouring the immodesty theory argue that we don't instinctively know that our genitals are significant, and therefore we don't instinctively cover up out of a sense of sexual modesty. Far from wearing clothes to conceal the sexual aspect of the human being we actually wear them to positively enhance the sexual aspect of the human being. So naked tribes arouse sexual interest and excitement by putting clothes on rather than leaving them off. Clothes serve the same purpose as a gaudy bird's plumage – to further the process of sexual selection and attract a mate. The drive to embellish one's physical attractiveness is one of the most ancient cultural expressions of man. As American anthropologist Harry Shapiro put it: 'This urge to improve on nature is so strong that one is almost tempted to regard it as an instinct.'

Fashion, according to this theory, is no more than courtship by other means. In the age-old battle of the sexes, dress and the art of adornment are the offensive weapons, and to entrap and keep a mate men and women must generate constant sexual interest by changing shape, colours and appearance by every means, fair and foul.

> **SOUTH SEAS LOVE CHANT: THE RITUAL OF ADORNMENT**
>
> In the Trobriand Islands of the Western Pacific it is customary for the woman to massage the well-oiled body of the man with a mother-of-pearl shell, softly intoning a traditional chant as she does so. This is called 'making the beauty magic' – an act of beautification and love.
>
> *Who makes the beauty magic? –*
> *To heighten the beauty, to make it come out.*
> *Who makes it on the slopes of Obukula? –*
> *I, Tabalu, and my mate Kwaywaya.*
> *We make the beauty magic...*
>
> *I smooth out, I improve, I whiten!*
> *Thy head I smooth out, I improve, I whiten!*
> *Thy cheeks I smooth out, I improve, I whiten!*
> *Thy nose I smooth out, I improve, I whiten!*
> *Thy throat I smooth out, I improve, I whiten!*
> *Thy neck I smooth out, I improve, I whiten!*
> *Thy shoulders I smooth out, I improve, I whiten!*
> *Thy breast I smooth out, I improve, I whiten!*
> *Bright skin, bright; glowing skin, glowing...*

Claudia Schiffer on the catwalk, strapped into a creation that exemplifies the agony and the ecstasy of fashion

selective exposure

Not surprisingly, Freud and his followers had tremendous fun with the psychology of clothes, explaining them in terms of hidden sexual meanings: fur was pubic hair; lingerie was the moment of undressing; silk was the softness of the skin; the coat, the hat and the necktie were the phallus. Clothing, in short, was a socially acceptable form of passive exhibitionism.

J.C. Flügel, a disciple of Freud, went further. While it was Freud who established the importance of the erogenous zones in the psychology of sex, it was Flügel who developed the idea of the 'shifting erogenous zone'. Since the physically attractive features of a woman are distributed all over her body, his argument goes, it is difficult to take them all in at a glance, so the focus shifts.

It is a theory that has been embraced by the fashion industry. Fashion distributes a woman's erotic capital by means of selective exposure, emphasizing one erogenous part at a time – bust this year, bottom next, legs the year after, shoulders, arms, tummy each in their turn. If this is so, then many of the designs that appear on the catwalk would seem to subscribe to the immodesty principle. Hence the periodic bouts of the blatantly shocking, sexual dressing *outré* – a transparent black blouse one year, a literally bottomless dress another. Such fashion styles sometimes stray across an invisible frontier from the alluringly seductive to the blatantly exhibitionistic. Sexy dressing is all about decorum – just enough to excite, not too much to satiate or shock. Cecil Beaton once said of the Sixties mini-skirt: 'Never in the history of fashion has so little material been raised so high to reveal so much that needs to be concealed so badly.' Not everyone would agree with him.

Albert Ellis analysed the psychology of dress among American women. Fashion, he noted, seemed to decree that American women had to be dressed 'romantically, fashionably, distinctively, expensively, sex-enticingly and properly.' In order to meet these requirements a woman carefully chose her clothes so that they made her look shorter, taller, thinner, fatter, bigger-breasted, smaller-breasted or something other than what she actually happened to be. 'Fictionalization,' Ellis concluded, 'thus becomes the main purpose of clothes selection.' You become what you put on, and the greater the choice, the greater the number of different versions of you there can be.

looking good, feeling bad

Fashion designs accentuate those anatomical features of the female which act as visual triggers for the male – brassières to maintain an adolescent shape to the breast, high-heeled shoes to accentuate the hips by making them rise and fall when walking, bodices to narrow the waist and accentuate the breasts and hips. Cosmetics serve much the same purpose of emphasising the physical forms or – in the case of eyes and lips, for example – exaggerating it. Female adornment – lipstick, jewellery, eye-shadow, perfume, hair dyes and the rest – is resorted to by the female primarily because that is what the male wants, not necessarily what the female wants. Men seek female beauty significantly more than women seek male beauty. For both men and women clothing also serves to emphasise and enhance the parts of the body which are kept concealed, for concealment is generally more sexually appealing than revelation.

Women's breasts have not always been in fashion. In Bavaria wooden platters would be fastened to a woman's breasts to flatten them. The Circassians of Asia Minor would sew young girls into constricting leather garments for up to seven years at a stretch, and when they married it was the bridegroom's privilege to cut the stitches and let them out. An enterprising New York company called the Boyish Form Brassière Company marketed a bosom-confining device in the 'flapper' era which they promised would 'give you that boy-like flat appearance' that was then all the rage. Reverse processes became the vogue when big breasts were back in favour. The bodice was dubbed the 'bosom's friend'; when 'lemon bosoms' became all the range in the nineteenth century, one manufacturer took out a patent for 'an improved, inflated, undulating artificial breast', and a French firm advertised pink rubber '*poitrines adhérentes*' which could follow the movements of breathing with 'mathematical and perfect precision'.

But perhaps the most tyrannical and long-lasting of female garments was the corset. Designed to accentuate a woman's hips and give her a wasp waist, it appears to be a typical example of the absurdity of fashion, yet is intuitively tuned to the evolutionary imperatives of the waist-hip ratio.

Many complaints were made about the damaging effects of too tightly-laced corsets, especially by the menfolk. Playwright John

Creating a sensation. Fashion today is designed to exploit and shock – no longer just to protect, conceal or enhance

'Fashion fades but style remains.'

CoCo Chanel

THE SECRET LIFE OF THE SHOE

According to Freud the heel and toe of the shoe were phallic symbols while the inside of the shoe symbolized the vagina. But long before the concept of penis envy and the Oedipus complex hit the West the erotic potential of the shoe was being realized to the full. In the Middle Ages, men wore very long pointed shoes called poulaines *which tapered to an arrow-like toe point. The poulaines proved to be one of the most enduring forms of European male fashion and lasted for some 300 years. The success was due in no small part to their sexual symbolism and versatility. Bit by bit the poulaines grew in length till they measured fourteen inches from heel to toe. Conscious of their symbolism, the wearers often stuffed the long toes to keep them erect, and coloured the tips in a rather unsubtly suggestive manner. With such a shoe it was possible for a gentleman to lift the skirt of a lady sitting on the opposite side of the table without appearing to do so, and no doubt there were other applications to which it could be put if required. Perhaps with this in mind rules were passed in France governing the length of the poulaines. Commoners were limited to a six-inch long shoe, aristocrats to a 24-inch version, while princes and kings could wear them as long as they liked, though there were obviously practical limits (it was very difficult to bow and pray in church wearing such things).*

Bulwer protested in 1650 that all that these whalebone prisons achieved was to 'open a door to consumption and a withering rottenness.' The English philosopher John Locke was unstinting in his condemnation. 'Narrow breasts, short and stinking breath, ill lungs and crookedness,' he fumed, 'are the natural and most constant effects of hard bodices and clothes that pinch.' In Napoleon's time a 13 inch waist was considered perfect. But such fragile dimensions were a constant cause for alarm, as a London tradesman wrote in 1828:

'My daughters are living instances of the baleful consequences of the dreadful fashion of squeezing the waist until the body resembles that of an ant. They are unable to stand, sit or walk as women used to do. My daughter Margaret made the experiment the other day: her stays gave way with a tremendous explosion and down she fell upon the ground. I thought she had snapped in two.'

More than a 100 years later and still the fashion persisted. Gina Lollobrigida was famous for her 19 inch waist, and fashion designer Christian Dior demanded a 17 inch waist from his models – 'even if the wearer faints'. From the clinical point of view the damage could be considerable, misplacing the most important organs of the body and compressing them so as to interfere with their proper biological function. The corset showed off a woman's child-bearing hips to advantage but damaged her innards to the point where she couldn't actually bear children.

Plus ça change. Today it's Guards officers wishing to conceal their pot bellies while Trooping the Colour on the Queen's official birthday who tend to wear corsets. But women are still compelled to trade pain for glamour. 'Glamour is a nightmare,' recorded one fashion journalist of the latest trend. 'All I know is that after an evening of exuding glamour, I was carried to the car, incapable of the smallest, most delicate of shimmies, and I haven't been able to feel the end of my toes since.'

By contrast, male fashion has traditionally functioned on rather different lines. If female fashion works on the 'seduction principle', male fashion works on a 'hierarchical principle', emphasising socio-economic status rather than sexual beauty. The Seventies was a golden decade for machismo run riot, with the trendy male boldy displaying every symbol and totem of manliness – gold chains signalling wealth, unbuttoned shirt displaying hairy chest signalling virility, flared trousers tightly contouring the crotch signalling potency. Eighties man was the same only more so, institutionalized now, a member of one urban tribe or another, with power braces *à la* Wall Street, loud status ties, double-breasted suits, Thirties haircuts – the whole designer bit with mind-sets to match, all signalling loads of money and a seat at the power poker game. But was it, is it, sexy? 'I hate men who flaunt power through their wardrobe,' commented American actress Ann Magnuson. 'These guys are so manicured, pedicured and deodorized that they look as if they all have talcum powder in the cracks of their asses.'

The Western male did not always dress so restrainedly, only relatively recently becoming trapped in the regimentalized uniform of the business suit, collar and tie (or its theoretically liberated but strictly regulated variants – blue denim trousers and leather jacket, the sports jacket or blazer with sober-hued slacks to match).

In the fourteenth century, for example, the fluctuating height of the male hemline caused as much controversy as the fluctuating female hemline today. In the 1340s the hemline for men reached to the knee, but by the 1360s it had sneaked even higher, and had become part of the male sexual arsenal. 'Alas!' complained the prissy Parson in Chaucer's *Canterbury Tales*. 'Some of them show the very boss of the penis and the horrible pushed-out testicles that look like the malady of the hernia in the wrapping of their hose.'

The situation grew worse as male clothing became even more indiscreet, until eventually something had to be done to house the male parts. The codpiece, originally an item of wartime armour, proved to be the answer. Adapted for use by the civilian, the peacetime codpiece came in a leather version that was eventually transformed into a gaudy object made of brightly-coloured silks that was sometimes enlarged by padding and garlanded with ribbons and enriched with precious stones. The codpiece died out in Europe as

Self-adornment is not just the preserve of the female. Amongst the men of the Huli tribe of Papua New Guinea many hours are spent creating elaborate lifelike penis sheaths that enhance the hidden virtues of the real thing

fashion and public morality changed, but something similar was preserved in tribal societies around the world. In the New Hebrides, for example, tribal men would wrap the penis up in a huge bundle of calico up to two-feet long, the tip decorated with flowering grasses.

the subtle art of deception

As every actor and every would-be lover knows, make-up is all about the subtle art of deception – emphasising the sex appeal cues of the face (large eyes, full lips, high cheekbones) and eliminating the non-sex appeal signs of ageing (wrinkles, blemishes etc.) by whatever means. The principles of make-up haven't changed since it was invented, but the techniques have advanced in line with the growing sophistication of modern technology. Backed by the latest advances in biochemistry and biotechnology, cosmetic companies increasingly proffer better and faster miracle cures for the ageing skin, and where chemistry doesn't work one can always resort to the cosmetic surgeon's ever more adept knife. But as Sam Sagiyama, co-director of Shiseido, Japan's biggest skin care company, admitted, the ultimate cure for ageing is still not yet available. 'If you want to avoid ageing,' he has said, 'you must live in space. There is no other way to avoid getting wrinkles once you are out of the womb.'

Today what you see is generally what you get. Make-up enhances but does not actually disguise. This was not always the case. In days gone by, it was used to totally transform the quality of goods on display. One irate newly-married man complained in a letter to *The Spectator* back in April, 1711:

'Sir, I have a great mind to get rid of my wife. You are to know, Mr Spectator, that there are women who do not let their husbands see their faces till they are married – I mean that part of the sex who paint. There are some of them so exquisitely skilful in this way, that give them a tolerable pair of eyes to set up with, and they will make bosom, lips, cheeks and eyebrows by their own industry. As for my own dear, never man was so enamour'd as I was of her fair forehead, neck and arms, as well as the bright jet of her hair; but to my great astonishment I find they were all the effect of art. Her skin is so tarnished with this practice, that when she first wakes in the morning she scarce seems young enough to be the mother of her whom I carried to bed the

'I consider a woman as a beautiful romantic animal that may be adorned with furs and feathers, pearls and diamonds, ores and silks.'

Joseph Addison in The Tatler, 1711

The ritual of make-up is an essential part of the art of physical deception, to emphasise the best parts of the face and conceal the worst

night before...'

A Roman poet by the name of Martial wrote to a woman friend in similar terms many centuries earlier:

'Your hair is at the hairdresser's. You take out your teeth at night and sleep tucked away in a 100 cosmetic boxes – even your face does not sleep with you. Then you wink at men under an eyebrow you took out of a drawer the same morning.'

Archaeologists have found ancient Egyptian make-up materials dating back some 8,000 years and beauty parlours and perfumeries that were established around 5,000BC, along with handwritten instructions for the cosmetic and beauty treatments of the day. Make-up on the banks of the Nile in the age of the pharaohs was remarkably elaborate. Both sexes wore make-up and wigs coloured variously blue, green, red or black, and both sexes shaved their bodies. Green eye-shadow made of crushed beetles, kohl eye-liner and mascara, blue-black lipstick and red rouge were all used to startling effect. Women coated their nipples in gold, painted their nails red, and made up their faces using lead white or yellow ochre foundation, so that their skin shone like a white lily or glowed with a golden shimmer. From that day to this every society, whether ancient or modern, civilized or so-called primitive, has resorted to an infinite permutation of make-up practices.

For centuries a fair skin was obligatory for any woman with claims to beauty. The means of achieving this often unnatural-looking blanched appearance were many, and mad. One of the most desperate of cosmetics was invented by a Signora Toffana, who introduced women in seventeenth century Italy to a face preparation made from arsenic designed to bleach the face of the user. This produced a double set of white faces – the chemicalized faces of the women, and the bloodless white faces of their husbands, some 600 of whom were poisoned to death after close contact with the faces of their womenfolk. A favourite cosmetic bleach in Victorian times was a product called bloom which masked the face like a fine china clay – laugh and the face broke into a thousand wrinkles.

Although white was *de rigueur* as an overall background colour, rouged cheeks (for men as well as women) were widely considered desirable to signal a sexually attractive flush. The means of achieving this rouge effect were desparate. In 1754 Antoine Le Camus, a French beauty consultant, warned of a preparation of brimstone and mercury

The Suya Indians of the Mato Grosso, Brazil, not only have a highly developed sense of smell (see page 149), but a sophisticated form of male body decoration as well

Coastal dancer, Papua.
'It is a perfectly natural desire to admire and often to exaggerate whatever nature may have given us'
CHARLES DARWIN

'Sex appeal is 50 per cent what you've got, and 50 per cent what people think you've got.'

SOPHIA LOREN

which was used to produce a very bright rouge called vermilion. The side-effects were unpleasant. 'Some ladies mix it with paint wherewith they rub their cheeks,' wrote Le Camus, 'which is very dangerous, for by using it frequently they may lose their teeth, acquire a stinking breath and excite a copious salivation.' In Greece around this time cheeks were painted with a preparation called sulama, which gave the skin a splendid white porcelain gloss, and rouge. But sulama had one defect. If a lover happened to have dined on a dish containing garlic and later breathed over the woman's face it had the effect of turning her bright yellow.

So it went on – a diet of ashes, coal and tallow candles for pallor, an anointment of powdered pigeon dung, barley and vinegar for spots, a decoction of brandy, musk, frankincense, cloves, nuts and nutmeg for wrinkles... The list is endless, and its poignant ingenuity true for every epoch and every part of the world.

an infinitely permutable kaleidoscope

No other species seeks to change the shape, size, colour, texture, features and appearance of its body or parts on a totally voluntary basis or with such a range of techniques and such a variety of effects: painting; dyeing; scarring; cicatrising; piercing; shaving; binding; contouring; sculpting; carving; stunting; fattening; elongating; aetiolating; depilating; substituting; implanting; tanning and, just occasionally, leaving well alone.

Viewed through the wrong end of a telescope, so to speak, the human urge to self-adornment presents itself like the ever-changing patterns of a kaleidoscope – dazzling, strange, random, infinitely permutable – the only thing in common being the urge itself.

ADORNMENT AROUND THE WORLD

■ Japanese men tattooed their penises to resemble an aubergine or an apricot.

■ Bedouin men and women used to stain the whites of their eyes blue.

■ The Tiv women of Nigeria have their faces incized with intricate patterns.

■ The women of the Ubangi tribes of Africa wear lip-discs big enough to take a 400-foot reel of film.

■ The Bagobo girls of the Philippines sharpened their teeth to a point and then blackened them.

■ Malayan girls filed their teeth in the interests of beauty,

■ Boloki tribesmen chiselled their teeth to enhance their masculinity,

■ Western people undergo extensive dental surgery to have their teeth capped an unnatural white.

■ Chinese girls traditionally had their feet bound to keep their feet tiny.

■ Mangbettu babies had their heads bound to make their skulls long.

■ Girls of the Nigerian island town of Ogoloma are confined in fattening rooms and force-fed till they look like barrels.

■ Among the barbarous Mossynoici of ancient Asia Minor, the youths were fattened with chestnuts till they were as broad as they were long.

■ In Europe and America models and young girls strive to achieve a skeletal shape through starvation or other means, sometimes to the point of death.

■ The so-called 'giraffe-necked' women of the Karen tribe of upland Burma lengthen their necks with neck rings.

■ The Masai of East Africa stretch their penises by tying a rock to one end.

■ The tribal women of Senegal elongate their breasts by pulling on them with a rope.

■ Americans and Europeans change the size and shape of their breasts, bottoms, penises, noses, lips and other body parts by means of cosmetic surgery, and before long it may be possible, by means of whole face transplants, to change their faces for other, better faces, fresh from the morgue.

HOW TO IMPROVE YOUR DRESS

Your choice of clothing has a lot to do with what makes the opposite sex approach you. It influences how a person reacts to you and whether they feel comfortable with you.

Often we don't stand a snowball's chance in hell of establishing a rapport with the opposite sex because our clothes are sending out completely different signals to the ones we actually want to send out. For instance, certain colours can bring people towards you, and others

make them feel they can take advantage of you.

It's important to appreciate that women often like colours that men aren't particularly attracted to. Take the colour black for example. Through history and fashion we have come to see black as sophisticated and chic, and while a man will be quite proud to have an elegant-looking woman in a little black dress on his arm, it's not a colour that will get a nibble on the ear. Men and women also prefer different shades of colour. Men tend to like the redder reds; women prefer the fuschia reds, but unfortunately men are terrified by them.

You should also think about the way a colour actually brings the attention to where you want it, and whether it enhances or bears some relationship to your own natural colouring or not. A pink or red dress if your colouring is actually quite fair or light, or a neutral coloured Armani suit if you're dark, will not look the least bit sexy.

Texture as well as cut is very important. A smart but stiff fabric that shows off none of the contours of your body is unlikely to ever get a hug, whereas a soft microfibre, silk or a soft-knit wool, which shows off the contours of your body without being skintight or provocative, is good at breaking down the barriers – it makes us feel that we can put a hand on the arm, an arm around the waist, and that either would be a welcome thing to do. Something with a sheen or a bit of fuzz to it, like a cashmere or an angora, is a pretty huggable fabric – and the more touchable the fabric the more likely you are to get pawed (so make sure you wear it in the company of someone you're happy to be pawed by!).

Clothing is also a layer of protection. A man without a jacket or a jacket that is unbuttoned is more likely to get a woman touching him – it is as if a layer of armour has been removed. And for a woman on a

—————————— M A S T E R   C L A S S ——————————

blind date or a first date, where she doesn't know the man, a jacket can be a useful tool. She can shed it if she's enjoying him more, or keep it on for added protection or to assist a hasty retreat.

As a rule, women seem far more confident in the whole process of courtship, so they should underplay the signals; be subtle, and use texture and colour rather than reveal too much. A woman who wears an outfit that states only one thing scares the socks off most men; a guy who can handle it is also probably going to want a piece of it. If you have everything exposed it's going to be very difficult to establish any communication. Sure, you'll get to bed fairly soon if that's your objective, but if you need to build a rapport or get to know the person a little before anything happens, then you don't want to be too obvious.

Focus on your best assets. If you have legs you want to show off, wear the right length skirt rather than trousers, with a lovely pair of shoes that makes the most of them. If your legs aren't your best feature, minimize their impact by toning in darker tights and a softer, longer skirt, but perhaps be more revealing on the top half; if you have a lovely neck show it off.

For men, what to wear can depend on where you are or what the event is. What jives in London really doesn't cut it in the Highlands. Pay attention to small details. Worry less about the jacket and more about good shoes, good fingernails – it's the small things that make or break the man far more than the woman. Men are pretty dead behind the ears when it comes to recognizing a Prada bag from a Marks and Spencer number, but women know a quality signet ring from a tacky nine-carat diamond cluster. A Mickey Mouse watch can be as off-putting as a gold Rolex, something understated and in-between is preferable.

Grooming is also very important. Make sure your hair is healthy, washed and cut in an attractive style for you. If you have, say, one long eyebrow, learn how to get it trimmed or tweezed in the middle at a beauticians.

Confidence and comfort are the keys to successful dressing. Avoid anything that inhibits your ability to move. Just being fitter will also make you far more

attractive. Whether you're a size 16 or a size 6, or a tall or a small man, a fitter person will carry themselves 100 per cent better than someone who isn't. Your clothes will hang better, you'll look more confident and immediately more attractive. At the end of the day, we are all attracted to people who are confident about their bodies and make the most of them.

MARY SPILLANE, AUTHOR OF *THE COMPLETE STYLE GUIDE* AND *PRESENTING YOURSELF*, AND CHAIRMAN OF IMAGE CONSULTANTS *COLOUR ME BEAUTIFUL*

7

sex appeal semaphore – body language and sexual signals

'Tina was great-looking, plus she could move and she had that voice. Usually you can have a voice but you can't move, or you're good-looking but you can't sing. How can anybody have that much? With Tina there it all is – it's all there.'

KEITH RICHARDS ON TINA TURNER, AS SAID TO MAUREEN ORTH, VANITY FAIR

from red to amber and green

The body is rarely at rest, not even in sleep, and the movement it makes – running, walking, dancing, talking, communicating by gesture as well as by speech, by looking as well as by looks – all intensify and multiply the totality of the sex appeal that body generates. Every time a man or woman walks into a room or strolls down a street, he or she transmits a plethora of sexual signals – the more powerful the sex appeal the greater the strength and the number of signals.

In the early stages of sexual chemistry – mutual sexual attraction – much of the process is communicated in silence by means of body language and sexual signals. In fact over 90 per cent of all face-to-face communication is non-verbal, and since most people rarely make outright sexual propositions – whether physically or verbally – their success in attracting or being attracted by someone depends to a much greater extent than they are usually aware on their ability to send courtship signals and recognise similar signals being sent in return. The silent signals of body language reveal more about our true feelings and attitudes and intentions than the spoken word, for it is difficult (though not impossible) to fake such signals or misrepresent them.

But body language is not simply a set of signs or visual codes like the tick-tack system a bookie uses to indicate a horse's starting price at a race-meet. Everything you do – how you stand, how you walk, how you dance, how you move your body, get off a train, climb up the stairs, kick a ball, do nothing, or do everything – employs a form of body language that may or may not transmit sexual signals.

BLACK APHRODITE

English writer and traveller Anthony Smith reports from Kenya:

The most beautiful woman I ever set eyes on was an African girl of 17 or 18 scooping up water in the bottom of a well near Marsabit in Northern Kenya. She was black, well-covered and perfectly proportioned. She was wearing bangles and bracelets of aluminum and her skin was glistening with water. I don't know why a skin glistening with water is so attractive, but it is. She was doing a tough job, passing up buckets of water from the bottom of the well. She wasn't just at the bottom of the well, though, she was at the bottom of the human heap, and that old romantic cliché came into my head, 'Can I take you away from all this?' Her posture and the perfect way her body moved as she performed her task was fascinating. I was just happy to look at her. She was number one as far as I'm concerned.

Tina Turner: the reigning Queen of Rock 'n' Roll in action (far left). Exotically-garbed samba dancers go through their paces during the explosive festivities of carnival in Rio (left)

the body in motion

A human body in motion is a human body moving into a new dimension of sex appeal. A body that can move well, with grace, suppleness, confidence and an awareness of the aesthetics of human kinetics, can be an object of beauty in its own right – as can the antithesis of movement – statis, pure presence, as integral to motion as a pause is to music or a silence to the dynamics of speech.

Even the common walk can be a thing of magic, sending out a myriad of signals – sex appeal among them. There are a host of extraordinarily expressive varieties of walk – the Pimp Roll, the Harlem Cool-Go, the High Heel Totter, the Mince, the Mooch, the Wiggle, the Waddle, the Swagger, the Slope, the Slink and many more. Each kind of walk signals the attitude, image, emotional state, bodily condition and sexual awareness of the walker at the time. Anyone who can put one leg after the other can improve their sex appeal by learning to walk more provocatively, holding themselves tall, buoyant, positive, vibrant, springy, ready and alert.

Women move more smoothly than men, who walk with a swinging, free-striding roll of the hips, mainly because their bodies are built differently. A sexually attractive walk in a woman is paramount. Florenz Ziegfeld, founder of a famous pre-war Hollywood dancing troupe called the Ziegfeld Follies, would select applicants for the Follies by having them walk, skimpily clad, behind a white screen placed across the stage, 'Before I see their faces I want to see how they walk,' he explained. 'There's more sex in a walk than in a face, or even in a figure. A woman can have the most beautiful face and the most glorious form. But if the walk isn't exactly right, it can spoil the whole damn thing. Any woman who doesn't take advantage of her feminine assets by learning to walk right, loses a lot of her sex attraction.' Marilyn Monroe, one of the great sexy walkers, was reputed to chop half an inch off the heel of one shoe to make her buttocks wiggle more enticingly.

The average woman walks with a stride of three to five inches heel to toe. Reducing the length of the stride will give her a more sexy walk. If she tries to walk along an imaginary chalk line she will look sexier still, for she will *force majeure* stride out with a model's swinging

TOTAL SEX APPEAL – AN UNKNOWN MALE

The New Zealand writer, Katherine Mansfield describes the total sex appeal of her ideal male:

The first time I saw him I was lying back in my chair, and he walked past. I watched the complete rhythmic movement, the absolute self-confidence, the beauty of his body, and that 'excitement' which is everlasting and eternal in youth and creation stirred in me. I heard him speaking. He has a low, full, strangely exciting voice, a habit of mimicking others, and a keen sense of humour. His face is clear cut, like the face of a statue, his mouth completely Grecian. Also he has seen much and lived much and his hand is perfectly strong and cool. He is certainly tall, and his clothes shape the lines of his figure. When I am with him a preposterous desire seizes me. I want to be badly hurt by him, I should like to be strangled by his firm hands.

THREE-INCH GOLDEN LILIES

Jung Chang's grandmother was a noted Chinese beauty in her youth, partly because of her bound feet, which made her teeter when she walked – a highly erotic body movement in the eyes of the Chinese men of her day:

My grandmother was a beauty. She had an oval face, with rosy cheeks and lustrous skin. Her long, shiny black hair was woven into a thick plait reaching down to her waist. She was petite, about 5 foot 3 inches, with a slender figure and sloping shoulders, which were considered the ideal.

But her greatest assets were her bound feet, called in Chinese "three-inch golden lilies" (san-tsun-gin-lian). This meant she walked "like a tender young willow shoot in a spring breeze", as Chinese connoisseurs of women traditionally put it. The sight of a woman teetering on bound feet was supposed to have an erotic effect on men, partly because her vulnerability induced a feeling of protectiveness...

In those days, when a woman was married, the first thing the bridegroom's family did was to examine her feet. Large feet, meaning normal feet, were considered to bring shame on the husband's household. The mother-in-law would lift the hem of the bride's long skirt, and if the feet were more than about 4 inches long, she would throw down the skirt in a demonstrative gesture of contempt and stalk off... My grandmother was considered the belle of the town. The locals said she stood out "like a crane among chickens".

FROM WILD SWANS BY JUNG CHANG

sexy catwalk strut. High heels have the effect of shortening the stride, though shoes with heels higher than three inches will make a woman lean forward, and there is nothing less sexy than a woman tottering along on her stilettos with her body tilted forward. Walking with feet placed laterally wide apart is also unsexy – this is associated with the infirm and elderly. According to William Rossi, author of *The Sex Life of the Foot and Shoe*, the main focus of sexual interest when a woman walks is in the calf – not only in the curves of the calf but the mobility of the calf muscles beneath. 'The rhythmic tensing and untensing of these cords,' he writes, 'slimming down to the Achilles tendon just above the heel, can hold the eye fascinated.'

Some men have found the sight of a woman restricted in her movements and thus helpless and dependent to be an erotic turn-on, though normally only subsconsciously. Fashion has reflected this perverse view. African tribal women wore knobbled, clog-like sandals and Chinese women traditionally bound their baby girls' feet, semi-disabling them permanently. In medieval Europe women wore platform shoes with such high heels that they employed midgets to walk beside them, so they could rest their elbows on the midgets' shoulders for

Although considered a measure of feminine beauty, such manipulation of the body for the sake of sex appeal caused extreme pain: the bound, shrunken feet of a Chinese girl photographed earlier this century

balance. Even today some Japanese women wear tight-fitting kimonos, and many Western women are garbed in tight skirts and and stilettoes, creating the same fettered impression.

love dancing

A New York drama coach once said that if movement was the key to stage performance, then dance was the key to movement. 'Every aspiring actor ought to learn dance first,' he said, 'and so should every aspiring politician.' A person who can dance well, whether it is group dance or couple dance or solo, is a person who has learnt to integrate the functions of the mind and body that in normal life in Western society may often be non-associated or non-articulated – thought and emotion, reason and creativity, order and free expression, self and other people, inhibition and sexual display, the body as a vehicle of the passions and so on. A person who can dance well is a person who has gone a long way towards mastering body language, and a person who has mastered body language has gone a

DANCING THE BEE

In 1850 the French writer Gustave Flaubert travelled to Egypt where he encountered the Almeh, the Egyptian dancing girls:

On the stairs, surrounded by light and standing against the background of blue sky, was a woman in pink trousers. Above, she wore only dark violet gauze. She had just come from the bath; her firm breasts had a fresh smell, something like that of sweetened turpentine; she began by perfuming her hands with rose water.

Kuchuk Hanem is a tall, splendid creature, lighter in colouring than an Arab; she comes from Damascus; her skin, particularly on her body, is slightly coffee-coloured. When she bends, her flesh ripples into bronze ridges, her eyes are dark and enormous. Her eyebrows black, her nostrils open and wide; heavy shoulders, full, apple-shaped breasts.

Kuchuk Hanem and Bambeh begin to dance. Kuchuk's dance is brutal. She squeezes her bare breasts together with her jacket. She puts on a girdle fashioned from a brown shawl with gold stripes, with three tassels hanging on ribbons. She rises first on one foot, then on another – marvellous movement: when one foot is on the ground, the other moves up and across in front of the shin-bone – the whole thing with a light bound. I have seen this dance on old Greek vases. Bambeh prefers a dance on a straight line; she moves with a lowering and raising of one hip only, a kind of rhythmic limping of great character.

Kuchuk dances the Bee. She shed her clothing as she danced. Finally she was naked except for a fichu *which she held in her hands and behind which she pretended to hide, and at the end she threw down the* fichu. *That was the Bee. She danced it very briefly and said she does not like to dance that dance. Joseph, very excited, kept clapping his hands: "La, eu, nia, oh! eu, nia, oh!" Finally, after repeating for us the wonderful steps she had danced in the afternoon, she sank down breathless on the divan, her body continuing to move in rhythm.*

long way towards projecting sex appeal.

Dance has been the means for releasing emotion since the beginning of human time – and not just sexual emotion. Human beings have danced war dances, fertility dances, harvest dances, community dances, religious dances, dances that tell stories, dances whose meanings are obscure – and they still do. But directly or indirectly, sex is the prime mover behind all social dancing where men and women can release their impulses in rhythmic bodily movement.

Dance and sex have been bedfellows since one or the other was first invented. The dance is still the favourite venue for encounters in many parts of the world. The dance is still one of the most effective ways in which a couple can get to know each other's true inner selves. The dance is the most powerful erotic symbolic act, and it still provides the opportunity for the most perfect erotic harmony between a couple outside the privacy of the bedroom.

But some dances don't stop at expressing sex appeal and sexual emotion – they entail sex itself. Tribes and societies have all had their repertoire of love dances, brought out on nights of full moons, spring equinoxes, midsummer binges and improvised occasions for collective derring-do. The hula-hula dance of the Polynesian islands in its pre-missionary heyday was one such erotic dance. So was a notorious variant called the *tinwrodi*, once witnessed by a bemused Captain Cook. The *tinwrodi* was basically sex to music, and the best dancer was the man who kept the best time to the music throughout the sexual act. A modern variation, according to a report received from Kuala Lumpur, is sex dancing to Beethoven's Fifth Symphony.

Wrote one early authority on dance and sex, sex psychologist Havelock Ellis: 'Singing and dancing are still regarded as a preliminary to the sexual act. It will be seen that the most usual method of attaining tumescence – a method found among various kinds of animals from insects and birds to man – is some form of the dance.'

Today the Brazilian lambada is probably the best approximation to tumescent dancing in the faintly Western world. The lambada is an indirect descendant of other raunchy popular dances from South America such as the samba (a copulatory dance brought to Brazil by Angolan slaves) and the tango and the mambo (both spawned in the red light areas of Buenos Aires, just as jazz was spawned in the brothels of New Orleans).

Modern Western 'art' dancing has often attempted to express something similar by symbolic means, as has a whole army of guitar-

'She knew all the sensuous dances. She could dance voluptuously and without apparent order. She could dance even while her prone body touched that beneath it. She could dance supinely. Every fibre of her flesh obeyed her rhythmic soul.'

Ralcy Husted Bell

John Tavolta in the seminal Seventies disco film, Saturday Night Fever. *A person who can dance well has gone a long way towards mastering body language, and a person who has mastered body language has gone a long way towards projecting sex appeal*

strumming, crotch-thrusting rock stars from Elvis 'the Pelvis' Presley to the present. As one authority observed: 'The exploitation of the pelvic area is not essentially a sexual posture; the body must supply surrounding overtones to make it become so. The finger, wrist – or for that matter any other part of the body – may be eloquent of sex when given gestural or qualitative background so directed.'

So where does the current hybrid of rock and pop – rave music in all its tribal permutations, garage, house and rap to acid jazz, reggae, techno, trance, funkateer, hardcore, swingbeat and plain straight stompin' – stand in the sex dance spectrum of today? It seems these dances at times involve the emotions of sexual attraction and sexual arousal in their rawest and most elemental form. In this respect the newest form of dancing resembles the very oldest form, harking back to moonlit nights in the cradle of man, when a primordial hunk and a primeval chick first put one foot one way and another foot the other in a steady rhythm, thereby discovering the sexuality that lay at the heart of their latest invention – old-time dancing.

the music of love

The erotic or romantic power of music is true of almost every genre of music except purely sacred music – be it classical or pop or jazz or rock or rave or country or folk or the ethnic mix known as world music. It is true for music produced by orchestra, band, group, choir, instrument, synthesiser or solo voice. It is true everywhere around the world and almost certainly throughout human time. Music, love and sex are inseparable. In Greek popular music, for example, there are only two themes – love and death.

Even the most sublime passages from classical music can do the trick. 'No one who is in any way susceptible to music,' wrote psychologist Thomas van der Velde, 'can listen to the stormy orchestration of the second act of *Tristan und Isolde* without being stirred sexually.' Beethoven's Kreutzer Sonata was notorious for its erotic impact on sensitive Victorian ladies. The German psychologist Wilhelm Stekel personally observed one instance. 'When I was a student,' he recalled, 'I used to play the Kreutzer Sonata with a very passionate woman; she always became very excited when we played, but this sonata had a particularly strong effect on her. After reading Tolstoy's novel [of the same name], we again played the Kreutzer

Sonata, and after the Third Movement she was a like a Bacchante.'

But if the connection between sex and music is obvious, its workings are elusive and difficult to define. Some music is overtly romantic or sexual because the lyrics tell us as much. The theme of love and the emotions of the human heart were banned by the Church in Europe for over a thousand years – a situation without parallel in the history of mankind. When the ban was lifted the proscribed emotion poured out of the mouths of every man, woman, flute and trumpet from the Shannon to the Volga. Guillaume duc d'Aquitaine was to the troubadours what Elvis Presley was to the rock 'n' rollers. Described as 'the sexiest man of the eleventh century', he spent his time whoring and song-writing, presenting to the world a completely new concept of woman, a feminine creature to love and be loved.

If music today is more blatantly erotic than ever before – to the point of incorporating the vocalizations of sexual love – the principle remains the same.

SATURDAY NIGHT FEVER IN BRAZIL

Documentary film producer Eric Massey reports on one of the world's sexiest dances, the lambada. The venue is a small settlement on the banks of the River Amazon, the occasion a local Saturday night party in the jungle:

The heaving mass of bodies gyrating to the loudly amplified, hypnotically-rhythmic music of the lambada were oblivious to everything. The temperature was in the nineties with a humidity to match—just the conditions for steamy passionate embraces, for as I was to discover, the lambada is not so much a dance, more a Brazilian's idea of foreplay. The basic rules require that two bodies become one at the groin and thigh, with one arm each around the other's waist, the other held out tango style as the couple mimic the sex act in a series of sensuous wave-like motions. Sex, as we all know, is difficult standing up and can play havoc with the knees. Full intercourse while spiraling around in ever-decreasing circles with a partner closer to you than your own perspiration would seem to be a physical impossibility. If you could have put a crowbar between any of the entwined couples I swear that you would only have succeeded in bending it. On some areas of the floor, however, judging by the position of an uplifted "cummerbund" and the apparent absence of adequate underwear something close to orgasmic satisfaction seemed to be in progress. Looks of ecstasy and a quickening rhythmic motion aroused my suspicions that these young aficionados were achieving the impossible.

I decided to have a go . . . I left the floor physically drained and shirtless. I believe the lambada is a sexual experience around which a dance form has evolved, in which case I am surprised that it is not more universal. It should grow in popularity providing dance hall owners around the world are not held responsible for a further leap in promiscuity and an explosion in world population.

An open-air 'hop' for dam workers in Siberia in the days of the Soviet Union, the dance providing – as ever – the best opportunity for a romantic encounter

Music that celebrates sex and love can also be inspired by sex and love, a specific person, a real-life experience. Of Chopin's 225 musical compositions, 54 are dedicated to women, while Liszt has been described as the first great erotic music star, swooned over by aristocratic groupies from the fashionable salons of the age. With programme music, by contrast, what you hear is what you imagine – so Ravel's Bolero, a *danse lascive*, with its driving rhythm and 'crescendo orchestral', provides a very accurate tonal representation of the act of love.

But how to explain the sexual power of music? How can a collection of mechanical or electronic instruments emitting various kinds of noises touch us to the very depths of our love, libido and soul? How can a medley of sounds – no more – lead one critic to label the Russian composer Shostakovitch as 'without doubt the foremost composer of pornographic music in the field of art'? One pre-war American music critic by the name of Charles O'Connell reviewed a popular medley version of the love themes from Wagner's opera *Tristan und Isolde*. Arranged and conducted by Leopold Stokowski, the thematic version was condemned by O'Connell as being nothing more than a '22-minute orgasm', and he called Stokowski to task for emphasising the erotic content of the work 'to the point of indecent emotional exposure'.

Perhaps music psychologists come somewhere near to comprehending the impact of music on the emotions and its power to arouse, out of infinitely complex arrangements of sounds, a variety of sexual responses. Music, they claim, works directly on the pleasure centre of the brain, deep inside the primordial mysterious interior of the cortex, where our deepest emotions and most powerful urges have their origins. It is the right-hand side of the brain, responsible for our emotional response and sense of meaning and belonging, that rhythmic, concordant, tuneful music – including the music of love and sex – impacts most, thereby releasing emotions of longing and desire, tenderness and love.

Such emotions, in certain contexts, can play a major element in sexual attraction, either between two persons, or one person and a remembered, hoped-for, imagined or idealized other, or between the person who is listening and the person who is singing the song. What are the psychodynamics of sexual attraction whereby we are attracted to singers with certain kinds of voices? Frank Sinatra, Marlene Dietrich, Edith Piaf and a host of other solo singers have had a huge following. Is it a case of the singer not the song? And if so does the attraction lie purely in the voice? And if so why?

the seductive power of the human voice

Some voices give off sex appeal vibrations, singing or speaking, even if you can't see who the speaker or singer is or what he or she is doing. Richard Burton in the radio play *Under Milk Wood* and Chrissie Hynde of The Pretenders are cases in point. Cary Grant, Eartha Kitt, Alan Rickman and Anthony Hopkins all have the same sexually charged voice quality. Conversely, an unappealing voice proved the downfall of many a silent movie star trying to convert to the talkies – and can make or break public figures even today. 'The last great silent movie star' was how Princess Diana was once unkindly described.

Even a person's name can buzz. How far would Frances Gumm have got if she hadn't changed her name to Judy Garland, or Archibald Leach if he hadn't changed his name to Cary Grant?

Non-verbal 'speech' – so-called 'metacommunication' – can have a greater impact in a face-to-face enounter than speech itself. Researchers have calculated that in such an encounter only 7 per cent of communication is actually verbal, while 38 per cent consists of paralinguistics (non-verbal) and 55 per cent of expressions (mainly facial). In other words in an initial sex appeal situation, it is the sound of the words and not the words themselves that is all important. Richard Burton himself spotted this while performing the lead part in the Lerner and Loewe musical *Camelot* in New York in 1980, writing in his diary:

'This almost child-like piece of Lerner and Loewe's has the most extraordinary effects on people sometimes. Weirdly eerie. Some people, intelligent ones, too, are seemingly struck dumb, apparently speechless or incoherent with emotion. One thing I've learned: the emotional impact of a supple voice speaking lovely sounding banalities can shatter even the most cynical and blasé of audiences...'

The non-verbal elements of speech encompass volume, tone, pitch, voice quality (e.g. nasal, breathy or resonant), rate of delivery, length and timing of pauses, rhythm, accent, stress, nature and number of speech errors. The successful manipulation of these voice qualities can convey a sense of conspiracy, secrecy, intimacy, emotional overlay – even when the actual language being purveyed is meaningless or banal, or for that matter unintelligible.

Different voice qualities convey different things to different people. From the voice we hear we make judgements about the other person's sex, age, class, education, trustworthiness, personality – and

'I heard of a man who says words so beautifully that if he only speaks their name women give themselves to him.'

Leonard Cohen: 'Poem'

'Lauren Bacall has cinema personality to burn. She has a javelin-like vitality, a born dancer's eloquence in movement, and a special sweet sourness...plus a stone crushing self-confidence and a trombone voice'
JAMES AGEE

'I like sex and all that. Sex is a connection and so is talk. So which do you think is my priority? Sex is fine. It can be more than fine. But I can do a lot better, faster, talking.'

CARRIE FISHER

sexual attractiveness. It is possible to judge these things in the abstract by the sound of the voice alone, as in a telephone conversation with a stranger, or listening to a recording or a broadcast of someone talking or singing. And it is possible to make such judgements even if the meaning of what is being said is gibberish. One American actor, for example, was able to make the women in his audiences swoon by simply repeating the names of vegetables in French, while in the film *A Fish Called Wanda* Jamie Lee Curtis writhed in sexual ecstasy whenever John Cleese addressed her in a dotty but persuasive brand of mock Russian. Accent can be a powerful aphrodisiacal ingredient in a voice. American GIs in Britain during the Second World War counted the English accent of the native girls as one of the key features in their sexual attractiveness, while the English themselves have long had a special fascination for English spoken in a French accent, as have the French for French spoken in an English accent.

Men and women aren't judged by their voices in the same way. A woman's voice is used to form an impression of how humorous, sensitive or enthusiastic she is, while a man's voice gives clues to his emotional and physical power. Deep voices (whether male or female) give an impression of sexiness, sophistication, security. Sad voices have a lower volume, more solemn tone and deeper voice quality than normal, with slow delivery and uniform stress on the words. By contrast, happy and elated voices have a higher volume, sharper tone, high delivery rate, a breathless quality and noticeable stress on key words and phrases.

Somewhere among all these permutations of vocal expression lies the combination of sound qualities that denotes the sexy voice – the kind of voice that all by itself oozes an irresistible sexual allure. There is no one master combination – every individual is different, every larynx is a prima donna. Every would-be sexy talker needs above all to keep sexiness paramount in the mind – and practise.

In part a sexy voice is an accident of nature: great professional exponents of the sexy voice – actors such as Richard Burton and Alan Rickman, screen star Lauren Bacall or TV presenter Mariella Frostrup – were born with the voices they have got, but they also exercised and developed them. Everyone can improve on nature to some extent. Frostrup, for instance, was once described as having a voice that sounded as though she cleaned her teeth with Glenfiddich whisky every morning and smoked cigars to give it a rasping tone. Everyone can become aware in some degree of the dynamics of delivery that are part and parcel of the actor's craft. In that sense, every sexy talker's best friend could be his or her tape-recorder – or for that matter his or her best friend.

language and sex

The relationship between language and sex is an odd one. For a start there is an age-old connection between the ear and the female sex organs. Yugoslav folk stories refer to 'the ear between the legs' (the vulva), while as early as 4,000 years ago adulteresses in ancient Egypt were punished by having their ears cut off as a symbolic act of de-sexing. Later a number of folk heroes or religious icons – Gargantua, Buddha and Christ among them – were popularly supposed at one time or another to have been born out of the ear.

The origin of the word 'sex' itself is totally obscure. It first appeared in English in Wyclif's 1382 translation of the Bible and was first used in its contemporary sense by John Donne in his 1631 poem 'The Primrose'. English, in fact, is generally reckoned to be one of the sexiest languages in the world, at least in terms of the extent of its erotic vocabulary. In the early part of this century a Chicago medic by the name of Henry N. Cary, whose hobby was collecting philological erotica, produced a lexicon of dirty words in English, the list of synonyms for 'to have sex' occupying 29 pages and including such unfairly neglected euphemisms as 'fadoodle', 'rootle' and 'rumbusticate'.

Students of *erotolalia* (Greek, meaning love talk) – of whom there are few – are quick to point out how often the licking-sounding letter 'l' appears in words with erotic associations – for example lewd, lustful, lascivious, lecherous, libidinous, lover, voluptuous and so on. However, few erotolaliologists have progressed to a study of the way love talk is actually used to attract and arouse a lover. For a discussion of this subject one has to go back to the seventeenth-century erotic classic by Pierre de Brantôme, *The Lives of Gallant Ladies*:

'I have heard it said by many great knights and gallant gentlemen who have lain with great ladies, that they have found them a hundred times more dissolute and lewd in speech than common women and such and no less free and wanton in their speech than any courtesan... these ladies were so well accustomed to entertain their husbands with wanton words and phrases, and dissolute talk, even to making freely their most secret parts without any glossing over.'

TOP SIX SOUNDS OF LOVE

- The cooing sound
- The weeping sound
- The sound 'Phut'
- The sound 'Phat'
- The sound 'Sut'
- The sound 'Plat'

FROM THE KAMA SUTRA

Phutting and phatting – two lovers from the Kama Sutra *practise the language of love*

Erotic sounds – as opposed to erotic words – have also had their aficionados. It was inevitable that the classic Hindu manual of love, the *Kama Sutra*, should address itself to the subject, listing the top six sounds of love (see left). Women differ in their taste in love talk, the author continues:

'Some like to be talked to in the most loving way, others in the most lustful way. Some women enjoy themselves with closed eyes, others make a great noise over it, and some almost faint away.'

One learned scholar of erotophony, a certain Dr Dutt of Lucknow, reckoned the basic sounds of love were 'hing' and 'hong', while another, after painstaking research, concluded that in English the true love-calls consisted of 'O' and 'Ah' – though he was tortured by doubts as to what they might be in the click languages of Africa or the consonantal languages of Siberia and central Australia.

Given the treasure house of erotic synonyms in English, the language's greatest master is disappointingly uptight when it comes to talking dirty. The female organ was supposed to represent to Shakespeare, or so it was said, 'a kind of ineffable, suprasexual, mystical adytum' – but the best imagery the bard could come up with for this fundamental aspect of womanhood was 'crack', 'hole', 'tail' and – an inspired leap of linguistic invention – 'secret parts', while the male organ fared even worse with an unprovocative catalogue of 'tool', 'yard', 'organ' and 'thing'. The renowned author of *Antony and Cleopatra* even failed to come up with 'sex appeal', and the world had to wait for a Hollywood columnist to coin the term in the 1920s.

It was left to gastronomy to make up for the pornophonic deficiencies of England's master wordsmith. Sex and food, eyeing and gobbling, screwing and swallowing, have long been inseparable pleasures. The very words of endearment – peach, sugar, honey, dishy, cookie, sweetie-pie and tart – are redolent of the erotic ambiguity of the gastronomic lexicon of sex.

brief encounter – body language from first sight to first sex

A crucial aspect of sex appeal is the transmitting and receiving of sexual attraction signals the use of body language in all its complex variety.

FIRST SIGHT

The first four to five minutes of visual contact are critical. During this period we make up our minds on all the data we have acquired regarding the physical appearance, sex, stature, body shape, age, status, ethnicity, personality, mood and, of course, physical attractiveness and overall sex appeal of the other person. Is the person too tall, too short, too fat, too thin? Posture, gesture and facial expressions complete the rapid portrait of a stranger. While facial expressions (along with voice and eye language) communicate our emotions, posture and gesture indicate our strength of feeling and underlying mood. These first impressions are stored away in the memory bank and may be difficult to change or erase. Specific reactions at this first encounter stage include:

■ **Face scan** When we first meet someone we spend about three seconds making a scan of their face.

Our eyes flick backwards and forwards between the other person's eyes – this takes up about 75 per cent of the scan – then move down to the mouth and finally make a few broader sweeps that take in the hair and the extremities of the face. In this way we build up a complete data picture of the person's face, centred on the eyes and mouth. If the duration of the scan is extended to about four-and-a-half seconds there will be an intensifying of emotional arousal by both persons.

SECOND SIGHT

To determine whether someone is attracted to you or not, watch their eyes, for they speak a subtle, sensitive, highly revealing language of their own. How we look at each other and for how long are important factors. Looking confident, looking confidently and wanting to be looked at are all major components of the charisma of the star. Important features of the follow-up stage of a close encounter include the following:

■ **The smile** There is a moral looking time – violate it and it conveys a message ('I am interested'). Add a smile and you have made a statement ('I am especially interested'). Both sexes are highly responsive to a smile. A smile will ensure your encounter is friendlier, smoother, longer and closer than if you had not smiled. Women smile and laugh more than men. The laugh – a more intensified form of smile – is an important clue to how a woman feels. If she fancies someone she will throw her head back when she laughs, laying herself open by revealing her neck. If she does not fancy the person, her head will keep its normal posture when she laughs.

■ **Eyebrow flash** When a person meets another person for the first time and smiles, the eyebrows will automatically flash up and down. The other person can respond in the same way (which demonstrates a friendly interest and intent) or not. Sometimes a barely perceptible shoulder flash is also given. If two people give each other a shoulder flash when they meet, it is a sign that they find each other attractive.

■ **Dilated pupils** We respond favourably to people with dilated pupils which send 'love me – I love you' signals. Unconscious pupil dilation may convey a message of sexual interest. On the other hand, it may be due to nothing more than low light intensity, which will also cause the pupils to dilate (hence perhaps the popularity of romantic candlelit dinners for two).

■ **Gazing** Further eye contact increases information intake and increases excitement. In ordinary relationships people conversing will glance at each other for two-thirds of the time, looking at each other simultaneously for only a second or less at a time. The listener will spend 75 per cent of the time looking, the speaker only 40 per cent. Everyone looks more while listening – especially if extrovert or female. Close friends will look at each other more and people who are attracted to each other will look at each other for the maximum possible time. The most rewarding gaze technique is to make regular brief glances every three to five seconds, increasing to every two to three seconds as and when a heightening of interest and response takes place. Short-sighted women have a peculiar attraction for many men, possibly because their unfocused gaze seems more attentive than that of a woman with normal sight. Women gaze more than men and are attracted by eyes gazing at them. Established lovers can gaze into each other's eyes for lengthy periods. Shy people have difficulty looking directly at others, especially in attraction situations. Instead of gazing into the other's eyes they steal covert glances from beneath their lashes (as Princess Diana used to do). Minimal eye contact is to be avoided – it suggests submission, bad manners and dishonesty.

■ **Eye movements** An extended gaze can indicate a dominating disposition. A gaze that breaks away can indicate reassurance and friendliness rather than hostility or dominance – but it is important that the person not only looks away but looks down as well. A gaze that breaks off to the left suggests a creative, imaginative, intuitive person; to the right a structured, logical and numerate person. A gaze away of longer duration suggests boredom or indifference.

■ **Heavy lidding** A very effective form of gazing is the heavy-lidded look (à la Lauren Bacall, Robert Mitchum, Sylvester Stallone and Clark Gable) – described by the Spanish philosopher José Ortega y Gasset as 'the most suggestive, the most delicious and enchanting look – the look of eyes that are, as it were, asleep but which behind the sweet cloud of drowsiness are utterly awake. Anyone who has such a look possesses a treasure.'

■ **Winking** The wink can be a powerful sexual signal if it is employed appropriately. It carries a

message of special recognition and awareness and even a hint of complicity, a secret shared. Used before mutual interest has been established, however, it can be a turn-off – like a wolf whistle from an unwelcome stranger.

FIRST BODY REACTION
SHAPING UP
When people meet in a social situation certain physiological changes take place in preparation for a possible sexual encounter. Muscle tone increases, bagging around eyes and face decreases, body sagging disappears, the chest protrudes, the stomach is automatically pulled in, pot-bellied slumping disappears, the body assumes an erect posture and the person appears to become more youthful.

FIRST BODY MANOEUVRE
ORIENTATION
Men and women have different preferences when it comes to orientation, i.e. the positions they occupy, vis-à-vis each other. A woman feels threatened if approached from the side or from behind, and a man feels threatened if approached head-on or full-face. So if attracted to a woman it would be best not to sit or stand to the side of her, and if attracted to a man it would be better to approach him from a side angle and from there work round to the front of him. By the time these manoeuvres are complete the couple should be in the best position – a position of so-called '0 degrees orientation', in other words face-to-face.

SECOND BODY MANOEUVRE

POINTING
A man and woman who are mutually attracted will point their feet, knees, hands, shoulders or whole bodies towards each other.

THIRD BODY MANOEUVRE
PROXIMITY
A mutually attracted couple will lean in towards each other, or arrange to be as close as possible to each other, e.g. by arranging chairs next to each other, often in a way that excludes other people joining in.

FOURTH BODY MANOEUVRE
MIRRORING OR ECHOING
Two people who are attracted to each other and share their thinking and feeling in common often copy each other's postures and gestures. This is called echoing or mirroring. The couple will do things in unison, lean forward in unison, pick up a glass in unison and cross their legs at the same time, as if they are literally of one mind. It is unconscious behaviour, but can be consciously manipulated, and it increases as they get to know each other better, so that eventually their tiniest, most fleeting physical expressions mirror each other and even their conversational rhythms synchronize – as do breathing and heartbeat rates.

FIRST WORDS
We are affected by the sound of the voice (i.e. tone, volume, pitch and quality) rather than the actual language, which at first encounter may be meaningless small talk anyway. The quality of the sound conveys impressions about character, warmth, vitality, sexiness, etc. It is best to try to be confident and positive. The tricks of the actor – varying pitch, volume

and flow, and using colourful figurative language – enliven speech and maintain interest.

FIRST TOUCH
FORMAL
Usually this is a formal part of social convention – a handshake or rather warmer social peck on the cheek. If two people are attracted to each other, even these formalities can be electrically charged (though touching has to be performed with due regard to cultural and individual considerations).

SECOND TOUCH
PERSONAL
Further physical contact is more personal and less formal. There is a very strong connection between touching and liking – in fact it is likely that touching can lead to liking. Initially it may be contrived as if accidentally. In a survey of 4,000 American men and women in their twenties across forty states, women reported that they felt a lot less comfortable about being touched by men than men did about being touched by women. Incorrigible touchers, it seems, tend to be more outgoing, talkative, cheerful kind of people, comfortable with their bodies and physical appearance – and thus more open to sending and receiving sexual signals. Non-touchers tend to be more apprehensive about communicating in general, and are less talkative and more socially withdrawn – and thus more wary about sending and receiving sexual signals.

THIRD TOUCH
INVASIVE
Close contact, usually involving hugging or mutual embracing and invasion of personal space, are key features of this third stage of tactile communication. The first significantly sexual tactile gesture is the placing of one person's arm around the other's waist. From this point much else will follow. The comfort zone or personal space zone takes two forms – the casual personal zone (from 18 inches to 4 feet away) which is the space for social gatherings such as parties (and therefore the usual space in which sex appeal encounters take place); and the intimate personal zone (from 18 inches to zero) which is the space reserved for close friends, parents and lovers (and therefore the zone for advanced stages of sexual attraction – hence the expression 'feeling close to someone'). If the intimate zone is invaded and the person does not back off then sexual interest is obvious. Country dwellers have a larger comfort zone than people in cities, and will stand further away from you when shaking hands. Likewise men have a greater need for personal space than women.

FOURTH TOUCH
INTIMATE
The kiss on the lips is the critical crossing from platonic to sexual affection. Different types of kissing reveal different kinds of sensuality, e.g. eyes open or closed (97 per cent of women close their eyes, only 30 per cent of men do, mainly because for most men much of sexual attraction is a visual experience); lips open or closed (if the eyes are the windows of the soul, the mouth is the gateway); short kisses followed by lingering ones; French (deep) kissing, nibbling and biting. Kissing is a form of bonding – a very important part of advanced body language and loving relationship. Prolonged or more erotic kissing can lead to further stages of ever-increasing sexual intimacy.

FIFTH TOUCH
SEXUAL
The couple proceed to caressing the head and face and thence to touching and stroking the whole body. Stimulation of the erogenous zones follows, leading to sexual arousal and finally sex itself. Only lovers or sexual partners have access to the whole body surface of the other person – even parents or same-sex friends are excluded from large areas. Oddly, the lower leg and feet of the male partner is the one area that is seldom touched by the female partner.

OTHER SENSES
Simultaneous with progressive touching is the continuing involvement of the other senses, not only sight, sound and touch but smell and taste as well.

'Men love with their eyes, women love with their ears.'

OSCAR WILDE

courtship gestures

Women have a much greater repertoire of courtship signals than men, and unlike many men most women make use of it, often unconsciously, sometimes not. Dr Monica Moore of the University of Mississippi at St Louis spent 100 hours observing 200 white women aged between 18 and 35 years in a singles bar. None of the women had a man with her and there were never fewer than 25 other people in the bar. Each woman was observed for at least half an hour and during that time each woman was seen to perform flirting acts at the rate of about 70 per hour. This compared with 19 in the snack bar, ten in the library and five at a women's centre meeting. 'Those women who signalled most often,' reported Dr Moore, 'were those who were most often approached.'

Not even a beautiful woman can do without the body language of flirtation. A woman with maximum looks and minimum body language makes herself unattractive by erecting a barrier against friendship. Flirting is direct action by means of body language and sexual signalling, conversational gambits and other courtship ploys. It is almost entirely a female preserve. As a woman who ran flirting classes in Seattle commented:

'The most surprising thing I found was that most men didn't know how to flirt. I expected that. The shocker is, most men don't know when a woman is flirting with them. 99 per cent of guys in their twenties, thirties, forties take one look at a woman who is putting out her most obvious signals, gulp, and look down into their drinks.'

Compared with the female the male has a small repertoire of sexual signals and many men don't even know these.

Perhaps this is why, contrary to popular perception, two-thirds of the initial approaches are made by women – even though the majority of Western women, even today, declare that they are reluctant to do so.

male courtship gestures

PEACOCK PREENING

The man smooths and straightens his clothes, pats or smooths his hair into place, straightens his tie or adjusts his collar, brushes imaginary dust from his shoulders, rearranges his cufflinks, shirt or other clothing, and thrusts out his chin.

GENDER POINTING
STAGE 1
Sexually-aggressive males will then stand in classic cowboy pose, thumb or thumbs in belt, fingers pointing towards genitals. This can easily be overdone – too overt and too aggressive a gender gesture can be a turn-off for many (but not, of course, all).

STAGE 2
An accentuated version of the cowboy stance is for the man to stand with legs further apart and pelvis thrust slightly forward – the Elvis Presley gambit – usually when leaning against a wall or seated with his back against the chair back.

VARIANT
Less sexually-overt men may stand with hands on hip or in pockets, but still gender pointing.

BODY POINTING
ORIENTATING
A man will point his body towards the object of his interest – or maybe he will just point a foot (look under the table) or the lower part of the body (while the upper part remains in a more sociable posture). Couples will point their bodies towards each other. If a person is pointing towards someone who is pointing elsewhere, he or she should abandon the quest.

EYE HOLD
The man may use the intimate gaze, holding the other's gaze a fraction longer than normal, and it may be that the pupils are dilated.

female courtship gestures

PEAHEN PREENING
Women use the same preening gestures as men, smoothing and straightening clothes, patting or smoothing hair, brushing away imaginary dust from shoulders, checking bracelets and other adornments.

GENITAL POINTING
Women also use the same genital pointing gesture as men and may even use the hand-in-belt method of genital pointing, though much more subtly. A version in which the right hand is placed on the right hip is a very typical gesture of sexual interest (it was once commonly employed by Roman sacred prostitutes and Indian dancing girls).

BODY POINTING
Like a man, a woman will point her body, or a part of it, in the direction of the person she fancies. Often she

will use a foot to do this, but sometimes it can be a knee – if she tucks one leg under the other, she can point the knee of the folded limb in the direction of the man.

HEAD TOSS

The head is flicked so as to toss the hair back over the shoulders or away from the face – even when the hair is short.

SEXY LOOKS

THE PROTRACTED GAZE

Like the man, the woman may gaze a fraction longer, and if she is particularly excited her pupils may dilate.

THE SIDEWAYS GLANCE

With partly dropped eyelids the woman holds the man's gaze just long enough to attract his attention, then quickly looks down or away. This flirty look can prove an effective come-on for the opposite sex, infuriating for the same sex.

THE SIDEWAYS GLANCE OVER RAISED SHOULDERS

Another variant, a cliché shot in the movie and TV ad business, with the shoulder supposedly echoing the rounded female breasts.

THE DEMURE LOOK

A bashfully erotic look away is another version of flirtatious glancing.

FACE FLUSH

If the woman is seriously sexually interested her face may become flushed, or even perspire a little.

PALM AND WRIST EXPOSURE

This entails a woman pushing back her sleeves to expose the delicate skin on the inside of her wrist and turning her palms outward towards the desired man (as seen in smokers or women who play with earrings while flirting).

SYMBOLIC STROKING

Fingering or stroking cylindrical objects such as a cigarette, glass stem, pen or finger is symbollic signalling with an obvious message.

SITTING AND LEG POSTURES AT INCREASING LEVELS OF AROUSAL

1: THE LEG TWINE

The woman presses her legs firmly against each other while they are crossed at the knees (and perhaps even at the ankles), thus emphasising the shape by tensing the muscles and producing the high muscle tone characteristic of a person ready for sexual performance (a pose much used in pin-up pictures during the Forties and Fifties).

2: THE THIGHS LOCKED

If the woman tightly crosses her legs high, thus locking her thighs together, this will convey a simple if not obvious message – she is not available.

3: ANKLES CROSSED

If the woman merely crosses her feet at the ankles this conveys yet another message – it's all right for people to approach her.

4: CROSSING AND RECROSSING THE LEG

If this is performed more slowly and deliberately than usual it has the effect of drawing attention to her legs in an erotic manner.

5: SLOW STROKING

The woman slowly strokes the inside of her thighs, calf or knees, indicating a wish to be touched. At the same time she may speak in a low voice, thus conveying a sense of intimacy as well as heightened erotic awareness.

6: THE HALF-OFF SHOE

A woman will sometimes allow her shoe to fall partly off her foot and will gently push her foot in and out of it for a period of time. This has been interpreted variously as an intimate action that is a sign of increased receptivity or a phallic copulatory echo indicating heightened sexual arousal.

7: THE TABOO POSITION

There is an age-old, world-wide taboo against a woman sitting with her thighs open and legs wide apart. Breaking the taboo, unless wearing trousers, sends a powerful sexual signal. The posture is frequently used in cabaret acts and fashion ads and pop videos where the woman is portrayed as aggressively voracious and sexy. It is a position which is not advised in strange company, though it can inject a heavily eroticized charge in familiar company.

BREAST SIGNALS

Protruding the breasts is an overt sexual signal – often achieved by pulling down the top to emphasise the breasts or leaning back in a chair and putting both hands to the nape of the neck or back of the head as if to preen the hair.

MOUTH SIGNALS

The smile, pout, pucker, tongue flick and kiss gesture are all part of the mouth's repertoire of sexual signalling, as is keeping it slightly open with lips moistened with saliva and reddened with lipstick.

overt sexual signals

Unlike most 'discreet signals', 'overt signals' can often take the form of close physical contact, symbolic sexual gestures and blatant propositioning. Anyone employing such signals has to accept that his or her intentions can be read by everyone else in the social group and that either acceptance or rejection will be a matter of common public knowledge. Overt signals are the soul of indiscretion.

In a survey of sexual signalling in singles bars in America by researchers N. Allan and D. Fishel, a number of men were asked to evaluate 103 sexual signals employed by women in order of their effectiveness. The following were rated as having the highest impact:

- offering to have sex with a man.
- rubbing the breasts or pelvis against a man.
- running the hands through a man's hair.
- looking at a man in a blatantly seductive way.
- talking to a man in a blatantly seductive way.
- puckering the lips and blowing kisses at a man.
- sucking on a straw or a finger.
- leaning forward to expose the breasts.
- bending over to accentuate the curves of the buttocks.

Importantly, where similar overt signals were used by men they had a very negative impact on women. On a seven-point scale, for example, men marked a woman rubbing her breasts or pelvis against a man at 6.07, whereas women marked a similar action by a man at only 1.82.

Another form of overt signalling involves dressing. Several studies have confirmed what every male with a roving eye has always known – sexy dressing by a woman is a high-impact way of saying something. The most effective modes of sexy dressing include the following:

- wearing tight, revealing clothes.
- wearing a blouse with a low-cut front or back.
- allowing the blouse to slip off the shoulders.
- wearing a short skirt.

Allan and Fishel reported that sexualizing appearance was quite overt in singles bars. 'Women often walked around the room,' they noted, 'standing tall, protruding their chests, holding in their stomachs, stroking their own arms or hair – they seemed to exhibit themselves on public display.' One slim, attractive, big-breasted woman particularly caught their attention (and everybody else's, it seems):

'She often tended to say things that were scatterbrained and she had a nervous giggle. Her talk and her erratic laughter seemed quite secondary in the singles bar, as most men who talked to her were preoccupied with her chest and the way she displayed her chest by twisting and turning. Some men commented to us that they hardly heard what this woman said – or for that matter, even cared what she said. Such men preferred to look at this woman's chest than listen to her.'

By contrast, men who wear blatantly sexy clothes can achieve the opposite of what they intend, since the clear message they are conveying is their availability for a one-night stand. For most women most of the time this is a distinct turn-off.

how to tell you've gone too far

When it comes to body language, many men are mere beginners compared with women, sending fewer signals themselves and decoding even fewer in return. Men often totally misread female body language, seeing a sexual message in every body signal, even an innocent signal in a neutral situation. Women resort to various strategems to head off the resulting unwelcome attention from eager men who have misread the meaning of the incoming transmission:

- **Displacement activities** Foot-tapping, crossing and recrossing of legs, restlessness.
- **Defensive gestures** Crossing arms, crossing legs, crossing body with one arm by fiddling with watch or bracelet, resting one arm upon opposite leg when sitting down, etc.
- **Privacy postures** Hunching up the shoulders or lowering chin to chest.
- **Restless wandering eyes** Except in the case of shy introverts.
- **Alienating orientation** Turning away, pointing elsewhere.
- **Sharp actions** Quick puffs at cigarette, sharp language, sharp look, distancing nod, frown, yawn, bored stare elsewhere (e.g. at ceiling).

HOW TO IMPROVE YOUR BODY LANGUAGE

The problem most people have when making an entrance into a social situation is nerves and when you get nervous you can end up looking aggressive and unapproachable. If you can control the nerves a little bit you will improve the way you actually look to other people, which in turn will improve your confidence.

The first thing to learn is how to stand and breathe properly. This will help you calm down and achieve a much more elegant look. Your weight should be slightly forward on the balls of the feet, your knees straight but slightly relaxed, your tummy pulled in and your head lifted up as if it were following a plumb line hanging down from the ceiling.

You should breathe from the diaphragm which will in turn open the shoulders out without throwing them back. If you are breathing deeply you will be inflating your lungs to such an extent that it will be virtually impossible to appear round-shouldered.

Women like to be in control of their bodies. They tend to have a naturally controlled look about them, which I think stems from the fact that they always seem to be in control of their own lives, their partners' lives and their children's lives. To maintain this sense of control the first thing a woman should do is ensure her shoes are right, that they fit, aren't too high and have a heel that can actually be balanced on. If your shoes aren't the right height for your body, your weight will be thrown forward, your back will arch and you will end up making very peculiar body shapes. There's nothing worse than being at a cocktail party in a new pair of badly fitting stilettos. You may look great but if your feet are killing you it will show in your face immediately and you'll end up looking slightly constipated.

When it comes to walking, the ideal step depends on the length of your legs, rather than specific inches. If you've got long legs, then you are going to have a longer step. Stand upright and put one foot in front of you, keeping all the weight on the back foot. If you can place the front foot flat on the ground without taking the weight onto it and without arching your back that's probably the right step for you – about two-thirds the length of your own foot.

For men, it's a case of appearing as comfortable as possible without looking like laid-back Lenny. A man who stands there with glass in one hand, the other in his pocket and looking just so damned cool is probably going too far. There's nothing worse than seeing a guy in a pinstripe suit, braces, white shirt and tie standing with his back to the wall looking like he really doesn't want to be there. Ideally he should be relaxed to a point, but not over the top.

Never be confrontational and always be respectful to people, so try to meet their eye level, and try not to look down on them. Keep your shoulders back and open, but not forced so you end up looking angry. Never cover your body with your hands and arms, or sit in a slightly hunched or restrained way, or crochet your legs around you – it all indicates that you're uncomfortable with the situation.

When you actually come to approach someone I would advise always interrupting a group rather than just going up and introducing yourself to a single person. When you join the group you don't actually have to say anything, just wander over and smile at someone, not necessarily even the man or woman that you really want to speak to. If you've been introduced to anybody in the group earlier just say 'Do you mind if I join you?' and as they carry on with their conversation you will quickly pick up on what they are talking about.

If you really want to flaunt your sexuality, it's the old Marilyn Monroe thing – the scarf comes off, the head flicks back, the shoulders go back, the back arches, the chest sticks out. It's a little more obvious than elegant, and if you need to be taught it, you shouldn't be doing it. Some people are naturally confident and can carry it off, but for the rest of us, we should stick with being elegant – which in the end is much more effective anyway.

KATE SMART, VICE PRINCIPAL OF THE LUCIE CLAYTON GROOMING AND MODELLING SCHOOL

HOW TO SOUND ATTRACTIVE

The key to sounding sexier is to reduce or remove tension in the voice. Tension repels, particularly the person close to you. So warm your voice up by lowering it, dropping the tone and the pitch to make it sound less strident.

As you get to know someone, and as you sense them responding to you, the tone of your voice will automatically change. It's like ping-pong – as you do or say something that appeals to the other person, they in turn will respond to you in a way which makes you feel good and so you will relax more. As you relax your voice becomes warmer and drops lower.

When you start to speak to someone, think to yourself, 'I'm going to stroke him or her with my voice' As they look you in the eye you will start to feel something stirring inside you and as you do your natural reaction will be to back off. You might feel you can't handle the power that you sense yourself exercising. But if you trust the power, if you relax, if you allow yourself

to vocally stroke the other person and accept the response that emanates from that person, you will elicit a similar response.

This mutual interaction involves the mutual exercise of power – power over each other on an emotional level. Most people find that very difficult to handle, so they tend to speak *at* each other rather than *to* each other. They throw information at the other person, simply transmitting ideas and thoughts, rather than trying to persuade someone to understand and accept what they are saying. The trick is to speak less and more softly.

With strangers and acquaintances we tend to transmit information and ideas on an arm's-length basis, but when we have an emotional interest in the other person, we put our arms around the other person's shoulders, so to speak. In our mind's eye we align ourselves with the other person, we place ourselves side by side with them. When you want to communicate with somebody you remove the barriers, you overlap each

―――――――――――――― M A S T E R   C L A S S ――――――――――――――

other's space-bubbles, and your voice automatically helps that process.

The rules of communication are similar for both men and women, with one fundamental difference – women hold the whip hand. Men are conditioned to go hunting while women do the choosing. The men woo and the women say yes or no.

Women can sound seductive, they can sound appealing, their voices can say come closer, come be with me, be my partner – and then when you get close you may not be the man for her after all. If you think of any woman that tries to vamp, either on the silver screen, or on the stage or even in the pub, she lowers her voice, she takes the sharp edges off, she is saying come hither, come hither.

The man for his part must make his voice sound more attractive to persuade the woman to allow him to come closer. Your voice should become rounder, and fuller; you should turn the tone button on your voice so it becomes richer, softer, less aggressive. You should make it more musical, using more than the normal five notes in your repertoire. By using this vocal variety you instinctively press buttons in the other person's receptors.

The other key element to vocal variety is to mean what you say. If you can learn to transmit genuine emotions through your ordinary voice you will be amazed at the huge change in the vocal variety that you can begin to exercise.

In an environment where the qualities of the voice or the influences that those qualities are supposed to carry cannot be heard, for example in a pub, you may have to resort to other means of communication such as body language. But improving the resonance of your

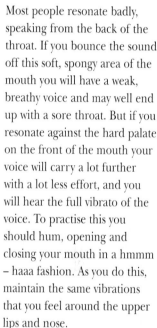

voice should also help it carry further.

We produce sound by pushing a column of air across the vocal chords. The column of air comes from our lungs and we expel it by use of muscles, principally the diaphragm. The diaphragm pushes upwards to force the column of air across the vocal chords which makes the sound, which in turn is then shaped by our lips, our tongues and our facial muscles.

Most people resonate badly, speaking from the back of the throat. If you bounce the sound off this soft, spongy area of the mouth you will have a weak, breathy voice and may well end up with a sore throat. But if you resonate against the hard palate on the front of the mouth your voice will carry a lot further with a lot less effort, and you will hear the full vibrato of the voice. To practise this you should hum, opening and closing your mouth in a hmmm – haaa fashion. As you do this, maintain the same vibrations that you feel around the upper lips and nose.

You should also use the energy of the diaphragm and your chest muscles to give you the thrust that will give you good vocal variety. Most people just wave the voice a little bit which begins to sound extremely boring after a while, because they are again using only four or five notes out of their entire vocabulary.

If you want to sound your most seductive you should be sitting down. You then sound at your most relaxed. You should also try not to lean back as this will change the quality of your voice. Speak softly and, most importantly, communicate.

PHILIPP PANNI, TRAINING CONSULTANT IN PERSUASIVE COMMUNICATION

MASTER CLASS

TEN WAYS TO ENHANCE YOUR VOICE

By the time we are three we have accomplished one of the most complex skills we will ever undertake – learning to speak. But even though language and the ability to communicate are the greatest tools at our disposal, we seldom give them another thought. The voice is a sensitive instrument, it mirrors health, thoughts and emotions, but, more people are in touch with the mechanics of their car than with the precious sexually powerful vehicle of the voice. Everyone can improve their vocal capabilities. It isn't a question of 'the beautiful voice', but of recognizing the importance of our unique instrument of communication and taking pleasure in its infinite variety. To achieve a sexually attractive dimension to your voice you must examine it, exercise it and experiment with it. Use every bit of yourself. The following warm-up exercises and relaxation techniques are easing and stretching ones and help the mind and body to feel connected to the voice. By doing them with your eyes shut you will be able to cut off external stimuli, and begin to work from the inside, letting go of self-consciousness and becoming more conscious of the self.

■ Sit silently for three minutes with your eyes shut and listen to the passing traffic, the sound of a door closing, the birds singing. Focus on the sound.

■ With your eyes still closed breathe in through your nose and out through the mouth, slowly making a funnel of air. Hear it. Almost feel it. Repeat this smoothly six times. This is the quickest and most effective calming exercise in the world.

■ Put your hands on your ribs and feel the breath filling your lungs. Breathe out, right out – and then a little more. As you breathe in, be conscious of your abdomen coming into play. Here is the powerhouse of your voice: abdomen; diaphragm; lower ribs; lungs. This is the place of your vocal rebirth, your sexual evolution.

■ Breathe in, speak out. Exercise your mouth and tongue. Get those under-used facial muscles working. They help to form the passionate words that you say.

■ Hum – do your lips tickle? This means you are bringing your voice forward, not holding it back.

■ Say the alphabet in one breath. In practice you will have more control than you think. Breathe in to a count of five. Hold your breath for a count of five. Breathe out to a count of five.

■ Try face and head massage. Start with the jaw and the chin. Don't forget the ears. Temples need easing. Hairline benefits. Massage all over your head. Rub the back of your neck and come round to your jawline again. Cover your eyes gently with your cupped hands. Count to 15. All these exercises free and deepen your voice.

■ Read out loud. Find a piece of prose which stimulates you visually, one where the pictures in your mind's eye are clear and vivid. Connect to these pictures. You are bound to feel something, emotionally. Your sensitive voice will go with the flow of your thoughts and feelings and inflect naturally. Visual imagination is an important element of the sexually seductive voice. If you can see the pictures of what you are talking about, so will the object of your desire.

■ Feel what you are talking about. A new thought or emotion brings a new note in the voice. Lift your voice and fill it with your own interest and commitment. Pause, give people time to digest what you've said allowing you to focus on the next fact. Always connect the thought to the word. Live in the present. Develop your imagination, visualize what you are speaking about.

■ Now that you are voice-conscious, listen to the people around you. Do warm-up, relaxation and breathing exercises from time to time. Read out loud. Sing in the bath, in the car, to the hills. Hum, yawn, grimace. Relax the face and free the voice. Your voice can stay youthful, flexible, powerful and attractive for the rest of your life.

YVONNE GILAN, CONSULTANT IN PERFORMANCE AND PRESENTATION SKILLS

x appeal is a
netrating stare, a
arkle in the eye, the
oadest shoulders you
uld imagine and a
rson not afraid to
press every aspect
his adventures and
securities and
lgarities.
MALE STUDENT, 21

me, the way my boyfriend
ks is secondary. I am
st interested in his mind.
e second sexiest man I
r met was tall, skinny,
d a mop of hair that went
rywhere, but he had the
ne dry wit and high
elligence. He's a rocket
entist these days.
ERICAN, FEMALE, TEACHER,
RLY 30s

he great class divide
an be an enormous
rn-on. What working
ass Northern lad
an resist that clipped
ueen's English of a
ell brought-up
oung lady?
ersonally, I have
arely been attracted
any girl who I
idn't consider as my
ocial superior' in
ome way.
ARKETING CONSULTANT,
ALE, 30

What attracted me to my fiancée was her face.
Sometimes, when she has her head tilted just
right, she looks like a little girl and it makes me
feel very protective of her. This is what I first
noticed about her.
MALE, 36, HETEROSEXUAL, NUCLEAR ENGINEER,
AMERICAN

OF COURSE
IT'S NOT JUST
PHYSICAL !

As far as I'm
concerned,
sex appeal
has more to
with what's
between the
ears than
between the
legs.
LIBRARIAN,
SUFFOLK

It's not an attractive body
which makes a person
sexually attractive; a sharp
intellect, a modest self-
confidence or even simply an
intuitive personality can be
far more seductive than
conventional good looks.
EMILY, STUDENT, 22

My first 'proper'
boyfriend was
tall, dark and
handsome and
very dull.
PLAYWRIGHT,
FEMALE, 30

He had an
incredible smile
and laugh lines
that spread
through his
whole face. It
was so sexy
that I wanted to
trace it with my
finger.
KOREAN WOMAN,
STUDENT, 22

The most sexually
attractive quality in a
person ? Confidence.
KOREAN WOMAN, STUDENT,
22

Accent is another temptress. A
rational awareness that
temperaments are miles apart,
conversation topics hard to come
by, shared experiences non-
existent, is no match for the allure
of a Russian accent and Tartar
eyes.
ANON, MALE, 44

To me, boyish qualities feature largely in
male attractiveness. The shirt hanging out,
the messy hair which signifies a certain
inattention to personal appearance.
THEATRE DIRECTOR, FEMALE, 30

The qualities I find attractive in a woman are the
ones that would make her a good partner for me:
intelligence, honesty, openness, wit , loyalty,
strength, gentleness, open-mindedness.
MALE, UNMARRIED, POLYAMOURY NEWSGROUP, INTERNET

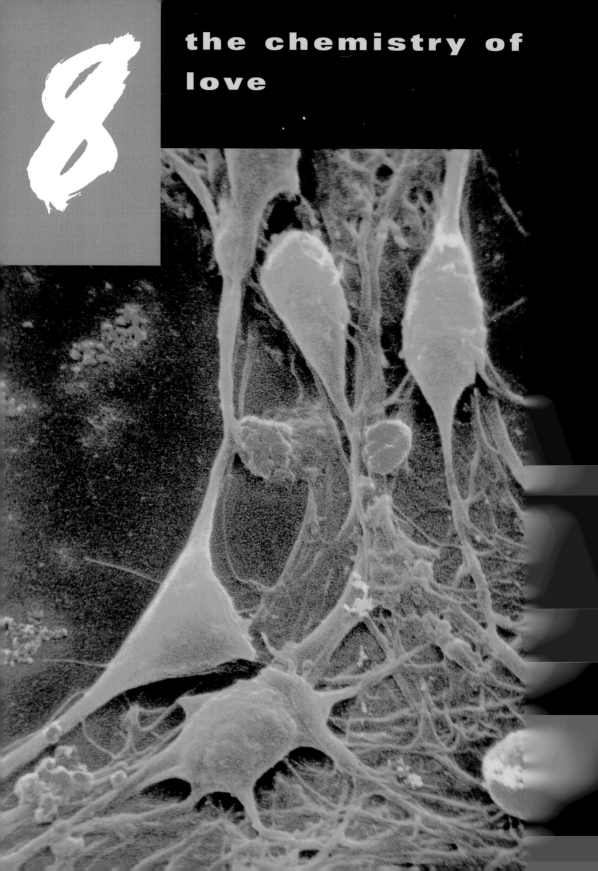

8

the chemistry of love

the most powerful sex organ in the world

The sexual chemistry of the body is one of the miracles of ancient science. Evolved over millions of years of biological evolution, the electrochemical system that processes the entire gamut of human sexual experience, from the twinkle in the eye to the passing of the genes, is a mechanism of sophisticated ingenuity, controlled by an organ which is itself one of the wonders of creation. Namely, the human brain. It is in the brain that sex really happens. And it is in the brain that sex appeal is noted, processed and acted upon. The sexual chemistry of the body in the final analysis is brain sex. For it is the brain that controls all the sensory, processor and motor activities of the body which make sexual happenings possible. And you don't have to be brainy to be sexy. Even an airhead can be a lothario or a scarlet woman – many are. In short the human brain is the most powerful sex organ in the history of the world.

It is the brain which controls the proper functioning of the body – including its sexual functioning – through a single, immense, highly complex and highly sophisticated electro-chemical control system. This control system and its central nervous system plays a crucial part in human sexual behaviour through its entire range, from sexual attractiveness and desire to coitus and reproduction. This is where it all ends up – the come-hither look, the sexy voice, the swooning scent, the warm caress, the urgency of lust, the anguish of love, even sex itself – here among the dripping glands, the pulsing blood vessels, the coursing molecules, the buzzing neurones, the impenetrable labyrinth of the brain.

sex appeal radar

A person's perception of, and reaction to, sex appeal begins in most cases with the impact of the external world on that person's sensory receptor system. By external world we mean some other person, the

'Sex-love - the cry of the race, the urge of being, the law of nature, the most fateful function of life, the dominant vital force'. The jungle that is the approach to a sexual encounter (above) is literally as complex as the tangle of neurones (left) that take sensations to the brain

sex appeal object. However, we say 'in most cases' because sometimes the significant other's sex appeal perception is internally generated, inside the elusive recesses of the brain's modes of memory and association; and it is perfectly possible to fall in love with the most beautiful woman or gorgeous man in the world, seemingly fully scanned by at least some of the body's sensory receptors, while alone with one's eyes shut in a darkened room in the depths of a dream.

'Real love possesses magic vision. A look, a touch, a word, a sigh, a smile – these tell all. Beyond them is desert – nothing.'

RALCY HULSTED BELL

Input of memory and association apart, the only way one person can perceive the sex appeal of another is through the senses. Traditionally these number five – sight, sound, smell, taste and touch. But many would argue that touch is not one sense but five (touch itself, plus pressure, pain, heat and cold), making a total of nine; while scientists claim to have discovered a totally new sense altogether, the pheromone sense, making ten senses all told. With this elaborate sex appeal radar it is possible for one person to scan in a wealth of data about another person's sex appeal, including not only physical attributes but a broad spectrum of other relevant information, including age, health, potency, fecundity, intelligence, personality, wealth, status, compatibility and all the rest – in a word, total sex appeal.

Man's best developed and most used sense is the visual, his most intimate his sense of touch, his most evocative but least understood his sense of smell, his most pathetic his sense of taste (only four tastes are discernable by the palate – sweet, salt, acid, sour – though some say these

'Sex is something I really don't understand too hot. You never know where the hell you are.'

HOLDEN CAULFIELD IN CATCHER IN THE RYE

only really amount to two, and all are dependent largely on the sense of smell). Man's sense of hearing is adequate but geared mainly to human speech, his ability to communicate by means of pheromones a matter of on-going research and controversy.

centre court nerves

Strictly speaking, many of our senses do not 'sense' at all, or at any rate do not make sense of anything in their own right. As the pioneer psychologist, William James, long ago declared: 'What we perceive comes as much from inside our heads as from the world outside.' It is how the brain processes and inteprets the signals it receives from the sensory receptors that counts.

It is not the eye that sees but the mind's eye in the brain. When a person spies another across a crowded room, it is the brain which actually sees him or her, the brain which unscrambles the scrambled electrical impulses it receives into a complex sequence of flashes of light that convey the data on hair colour, mouth shape, the fullness of her breasts, the width of his chest along the one million nerve fibres that lead off from each eye. It is the brain that reconstitutes the other's final image with the help of some 100 million neurons dedicated to the task. Similarly it is the brain that hears, not the ears, for it is the brain that makes sense of the bedlam of auditory signals which reach it to produce a kind of reality which is not the truth but the most useful and appropriate aural message for the listener at the time.

The vast complexity of this multiplicity of signals, inter-pretations, responses and actions – all triggered by a single, unaware, unassuming other in the corner of a crowded room – is enormous. The room itself is full of distracting alternative sexual and non-sexual stimuli, a smokescreen of fragrances, pheromones and aphrodisiacs, a cocktail army of signalling faces, semaphoring boobs, inviting eyes, licking lips, probing tongues, exploring hands, prying fingers, come-hither innuendos, swooning croons, and whispered sighs – all made doubly complicated by the fact that every signal may fire off thousands upon thousands of responses within a micro-fraction of a second – and every signal has to be processed twice.

For the brain to make sense of what it sees, hears, or for that matter smells, the processing of the sensory signals alone is not enough. The brain also needs to cross-refer what it perceives from these signals by comparing them with a memory bank of countless

---

PRINCESS DI IN LOVE – THE REALLY INSIDE STORY

Anna Pasternak describes the electro-chemistry of a royal encounter:

From the moment he caught her entrance Captain James Hewitt was aware of Diana. Fortunately, no one noticed their rapt attention as they faced each other with a measure of shock and disbelief. There was no mistaking it, they both knew.

Suddenly every nerve ending was raw and alive. Their stomachs churning in nervous apprehension, they could not take their eyes off each other, could not stop smiling. Their bodies were electric, aching to embrace...

She flicked him knowing, suggestive looks, peering up alluringly from under her eyelashes, and threw back her head as she reflected on a comment, slowly, sensuously stroking her elegant neck as she looked at him.

James watched, electrified. Never had he felt such a magnetic pull. The room was alive with her, with her soaring charisma... He could feel only the powerful connection between them, the current running wild and unearthed. As she handed him his cup he let her fingers mingle momentarily with his and he felt a voluptuous thrill shoot up his arms...

As she landed on him, cupping her hands behind his neck, James was both raging with desire and taken by surprise. Yet his antennae were on full alert... he was firing on all cylinders... they were ready to explode.

FROM *PRINCESS IN LOVE*

---

previous visual experiences stored in millions of cells in the visual association areas (or memory data banks) of the cortex. The same applies to most of the other senses. For example, some half a million coded sounds are stored in a sound bank and over 10,000 smells stored in a smell bank.

These data banks help complete the perceptory processing of the target object by relating him or her to other memories and associations stored in other parts of the cortex. In other words, the other can be straightforwardly processed to reveal, say, a woman who is not only pretty, desirable and bedworthy (no mean feat), but by means of some associative memory in the mind's eye of her admiring beholder – a former love affair, a past brief encounter, a fleeting but heart-stopping glimpse of a previous pair of eyes, a previous peal of laughter, a forgotten touch of the hand – she can gain a greater and much more disturbing presence, endowed with all the potential for a grand passion, an overwhelming love, a destructive obsession.

'Something magic started to happen. Oh yeah. It's an electrical charge, really, in the body. The body responds to something. Heart boom-bama-boom. Hands are wet...'

Tina Turner

As our much-quoted and highly prescient American doctor-in-love, Ralcy Husted Bell, wrote of the bodily enigma of sexual attraction in the Thirties: 'Unknown influences are at work in the depths. Various sympathies ebb and flow. Attractions rise like wisps of mist. Strange voluntary urges lift like wings. What are these forces? Can we ignore the tune of the nerves? Can moods be controlled? We know that these phenomena are physiological and psychological. But until we can solve them we must regard their victims with compassion, tolerance and imagination.'

unholy orders

So far the brain has been occupied with working things out; now it is time to act. It is into the hypothalamus, an organ the size of a cherry situated behind the eyes, with nerve connections to most other regions of the nervous system, that the other person must, in a sense, pass.

And it is inside this cherry that his or her fate is sealed. A drink, a dinner, a bed, a yacht, an offer of marriage; a brief encounter, something special, a mate for life; rejection, seduction, coition – out of the physically tiny but operationally mighty hypothalamus come the command and co-ordination decisions that will prepare the body for the appropriate course of action.

Though the hypothalamus weighs only one-sixth of an ounce (4.5 grams) and amounts to no more than 1/300 of the brain, it is immensely important and immensely complex, with far-ranging powers that are still not fully understood. Among its more routine everyday functions it controls body temperature, appetite and thirst. Among its more esoteric functions it is implicated in anorexia nervosa and runs a pleasure centre that delivers sensations so intense and satisfying that it banishes yearnings for food, sleep and even sex. The hypothalamus is involved in determining mood, the experiencing of emotions, and the motivating of sexual behaviour. Crucially relevant as far as sexual attraction and arousal are concerned, it exerts overall control of the sympathetic nervous system (which amongst other things handles the body's fight-or-flight response) and co-ordinates the function of the nervous and endocrine (hormonal) systems of the entire body via its connections with the pituitary gland. Though it may not sound like it, these are the functions that help determine the outcome of a person's sex appeal.

There are at this stage in the proceedings three parallel lines of communication for the onward transmission of sexual (and other) messages. Two of them consist of the two separate but mutually co-operative neural transmission lines of the autonomic nervous system – the sympathetic and the parasympathetic. The third consists of the hormonal communication line of the endocrine system, controlled by the pituitary gland. It is down these three lines that the orders for the body's sexual response – blast-off or shut-down, cast-off or melt-down – are despatched.

The sympathetic system enables the body to cope with sudden emergencies, such as fear and excitement (including sexual excitement), by revving up all the crucial organs of response. The parasympathetic system, counterbalancing each action of the sympathetic system with an opposing action, helps quieten things down again. To achieve these ends, the sympathetic system produces two almost identical chemical stimulants, adrenalin and noradrenalin; while the parasympathetic system produces an inhibitory chemical called acetylcholine.

The endocrines are small, relatively insignificant scraps of tissue located in rather obscure parts of the body. If you were to put them all together on a weighing machine – pituitary, thyroid, adrenals, ovaries, testes, pancreas and the rest, all in a rather sorry-looking cannibal heap – they would weigh a total of no more than about five ounces (140 grams). Lightweight in terms of avoirdupois the endocrines may be, but lightweight in terms of power they most

---

LATE-NIGHT EXTRAS

Other chemicals have back-up roles in the sexual chemistry of the human body.

Dopamine – *Produced in the brain it plays a key role in excitement and desire and is a necessary adjunct to sexual arousal. A large dose will send the libido soaring, while an overdose will lead to schizophrenia and an all-time high.*

Serotonin – *Synthesized in the brain, in the right quantity it helps trigger orgasm. A bit too little can lead to depression or violence. A bit too much – as in the antidepressant drug Prozac – can lead to anorgasmia in some cases. A lot too much – as in the drug Ecstasy – can lead to anorgasmia in all cases.*

Nitric acid – *As a side effect it has a highly positive impact on male erection.*

A neuropeptide *known as* VIP *for short, working in conjunction with the neurotransmitter* acetylcholine, *helps trigger and maintain male arousal, while* oxytocin, *secreted in the brain of both men and women during sexual climax, helps generate loving emotions such as mother-care and loving romance.*

certainly are not. For the endocrine system (along with the nervous system) is the great chemical regulator of the body's functioning, including continuing processes such as body growth, sexual maturation, the desire to have sex and the ability to reproduce.

The power the endocrines exerts derives entirely from the hormones they secrete. These chemical messengers secreted into the blood by one or other of the body's hormone-secreting tissues (the vast majority by the endocrine glands) are carried to target tissues elsewhere in the body to stimulate and regulate specific biochemical or physiological activities. By any standards, hormones are amongst the most remarkable substances in the body, not least for the part they play in the sexual life of the individual.

In the chemistry of love the hormonal system thus acts in a hierarchy of functions, with the pituitary gland, the most important of the endocrine glands, serving as the conductor of the orchestra. By controlling the pituitary the hypothalamus thus indirectly controls many other glands in the endocrine system, including those which are directly involved in sexual behaviour – the adrenals, ovaries and testes.

The chemistry of love in action: screen lovers Audrey Hepburn and George Peppard enact a passionate kiss at the climax of Breakfast at Tiffany's. *Done for real, the body's neural and hormonal chemistry will already be stoking up blood pressure, heart-beat and breathing rate to meet the challenge to come*

I had just arrived at a party with a friend, and suddenly someone plugged me into the National Grid. I actually believe there was a ribbon of energy running between me and this man on the other side of the room who I had never seen before. This was not love at first sight. This was the purest form of physical awareness of a man and of myself as a woman I have ever experienced.
PROJECT MANAGEMENT CONSULTANT, 27

Contradiction - in almost any form - is very sexually appealing. For example when her mouth is saying: 'My mortgage rate went down from 10.5% to 8.75% and we're using the saving to build a loft extension...' and her eyes are saying: 'The only reality left in my world is sexual passion, the only object of my lust is you...'
WRITER, MALE, 28, LONDON

My sex appeal ideal: same species, opposite sex.
SHEPHERD, 61, FRANCE

When there is a crackle of sexual electricity there is no mistaking it. It might be the purest form of communication - nearer telepathy than language - in that it doesn't matter what the situation is, who the person is, how old they are, how improper the sexual feelings might be, what they look like. Sometimes it is even annoying! 'My God! There's Claudia Schiffer standing over there rubbing baby oil on her breasts but I keep being drawn to that frumpy woman at the table with her cigarette holder and the made eyes'... Whatever.
WRITER, MALE, ANON

A long – very long – time ago, a person of the opposite sex said to me: "If you were as enterprising as you are seductive you would be devastating". I'm still trying to work that out.
BRIAN, TRANSLATOR, GENEVA

It is said that a person you truly love is someone you feel you have already met or known a long time ago, in some other context, as if from a past life. I am sure this was the case with an Arab girl I once knew at Cambridge. She lives on in my memory as a lush, laughing, life-loving reincarnation of one of those dark-eyed, raven-haired, bare-breasted palace dancing girls in the frescoes of the royal tombs at Thebes - one of Pharaoh's long-gone playmates from the Valley of the Kings.
COLLEGE LECTURER, SHEFFIELD

I have often wondered on the tiny odds of two people finding each other amongst a population of 4 billion and then falling in love. But somehow it happens - or so I've heard. If 'sex appeal' is a combination of everything that we find attractive, enjoyable, endearing and horny in another individual, then the odds against finding the ideal mate would be pretty remote.
Anon, male, English

My sex appeal ideal is a curvy dame with a beautiful face and shapely legs walking (dancing?!!) towards me with a sweet smile on her face (but not looking at me!!) and a nice easy-going attitude.
INDIAN, MALE, 28, SOFTWARE ENGINEER, AT YALE UNIVERSITY, USA

She should be visually stimulating. Embodying (consciously or unconsciously) the promise (real or imagined) of sexual satisfaction and - equally important - appearing to possess a satisfying answer to a most important question too: 'But what shall we do after we have made love?'
ANON, MALE, SIMIANE

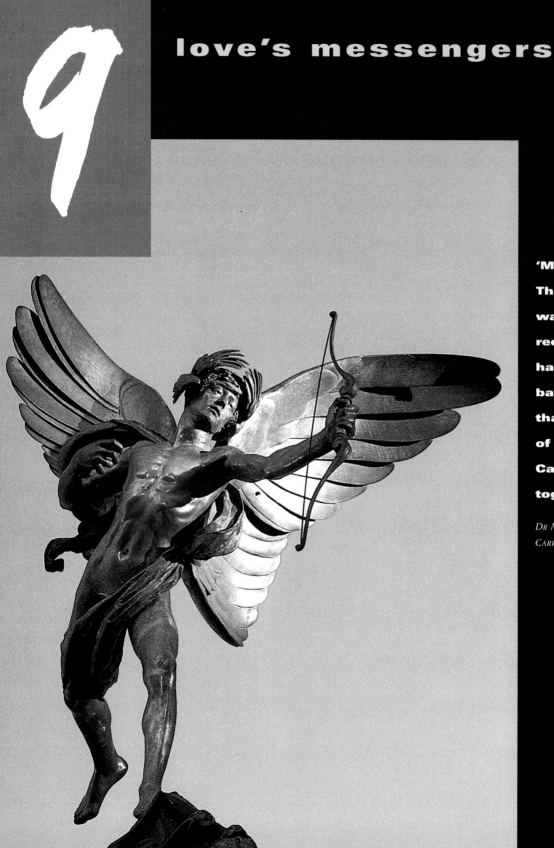

9

love's messengers

'Margaret Thatcher was always reckoned to have more balls than the rest of the Cabinet put together.'

Dr Malcolm Carruthers

back to
basics

The sex hormones are love's messengers. Secreted into the bloodstream by the gonads and other glands, they carry sexual messages to and from the brain, where in ways that are not yet fully understood they determine our sexual attractiveness to others, our sexual desire for others, and our biological ability to reproduce.

There are two main groups of sex hormones – the male sex hormones known as androgens (from the Greek meaning 'giving rise to maleness'), and the female sex hormones known as oestrogens (from the Greek meaning 'giving rise to oestrus', or female sexual heat). Androgens stimulate the growth, maturation, maintenance and functioning of the male reproductive system, oestrogens regulate the activities of the female reproductive system.

In the main, androgens are produced in the testes, oestrogens in the ovaries. But since the testes and the ovaries, along with the adrenal cortex gland, share a common embryological origin, lesser amounts of the male hormones are also produced by women in their ovaries, and lesser amounts of female hormones are produced by men in their testes, while the adrenal cortex produces small quantities of both.

As far as sex appeal and sexual desire are concerned, by far the most important of the male sex hormones is testosterone, while of the female sex hormones the two key ones are progesterone and oestrogen, which paradoxically happen to be made from the male hormone testosterone. It is these hormones that are responsible for all the major biological changes that happen to our bodies, from the deepening of the male voice to the bum fluff that adorns the face of the pimply youth, and from the growth of breasts to the ability to conceive.

the female cocktail

The sexual chemistry of women is more complex than that of men, which is not surprising in view of what their bodies are asked to accomplish. While men are basically activated by a single specific sex hormone (testosterone), women are activated by three (testosterone, oestrogen and progesterone). Testosterone powers the sex drive in women, just as it does in men, but as women generally have between 10-30 per cent less testosterone than men their sex drive is correspondingly that much less on average – as is their aggression, which is in large part curbed by the oestrogen sex hormone. Because testosterone is secreted continuously throughout the human female cycle, women remain continuously sexually receptive, unlike many other

Eros (opposite), the mercurial, mischievous, winged messenger of love. Below, the wonderful world of the sex hormone – polarized light micrographs of crystals of progesterone (upper) and the oestrogen, oestradiol (lower)

female animals. However, levels of testosterone in women vary during the cycle. They are at their highest around the time of ovulation (i.e. the period of maximum fertility), but after ovulation the hormone progesterone (which helps heighten the female inclination to protect and care for the young) inhibits the secretion of testosterone and the sex drive is diminished accordingly.

A woman's hormonal juggling act can be adversely affected by a number of things, most drastically by the onset of the menopause. Less well known is the impact of dieting. It is one of the great ironies of modern Western society that skinny, adolescent-looking women are perceived to be sexier than full-bodied, fully grown-up women. The fertility figures of the past, with their gently rounded bellies, broadly curving hips and full, motherly breasts, have been replaced by images of stick-thin supermodels. In fact these latter-day icons of femininity and beauty are, in reality, false icons, walking hormonal disasters. Everything that makes a woman sexy, from the testosterone that drives her libido to the oestrogens that enable her to conceive, are thrown into disarray by this wilful starvation.

All the hormones that drive a woman's sexuality are stored in the fat tissues that women today try so hard to eliminate. From birth girls have 10-15 per cent more fat than boys; as they reach adolescence their fat ratio increases, and by the time they reach 20 the female body will be made up of 18.7 per cent fat. A healthy, sexually attractive, sexually active woman needs this much fat to function on a sexual level. Drop much below that percentage and the system begins to malfunction. The body of the model is actually 22-23 per cent leaner than the average woman, and when a woman's fat-to-lean ratio falls below that percentage figure, infertility and hormonal imbalance often result.

'Big women are sexier,' claims comedienne Dawn French. 'We pump more oestrogen, have higher sex drives and fantasize more.' Women who go on diets of fewer than 1,700 calories a day experience a dramatic drop in libido (as do men). Researchers have found that plump women are twice as erotically excitable and ready for sex than thin women. Super slimness teetering into emaciation is not sexy.

testosterone power

It is to the tiny steroid substance testosterone that we owe, in the main, all the heavens and hells of sexual love, the agonized yearnings, the grand passions, bitter spurnings, the harassments, scandals, confusions and casual couplings that have characterized the love life of man since man was invented. The power of this steroid to inflame lust and love, to derail lives and change the course of history is constant and seemingly infinite. It is because of testosterone that the boy-next-door pants after the girl next door and she responds. It was because of testosterone that Helen caught Paris's fancy and President Kennedy dallied so resolutely with the White House secretarial pool. Many of the adventures, indiscretions and betrayals of everyday sexual life are down to testosterone – as well as those moments of ecstasy, of transcendence and fulfilment that make testosterone a hormone worth having.

Male sex hormones were first isolated by a German chemist called Adolf Butenandt in 1931 and have been blamed for a whole of host of things – from sexual excess of every kind to gang culture and genocidal war – ever since. There is some truth in the general perception that testosterone in the wrong hands – or, more exactly, the wrong balls – makes men potentially dangerous. And not just men but other male animals too.

For testosterone affects more than just sexual behaviour, which is dramatic enough. Ever since Roman times it has been known that testosterone – the Romans knew it as the 'male force' – is concerned with vitality as much as virility, particularly vitality directed towards male dominance in the human hierarchy. So testosterone is also the hormone of success, achievement, competitiveness, territoriality – all fought for and won (or lost) in the wake of testosterone-induced aggression.

At a primary level male aggression can be purely physical, as in the thuggery of the city street gang and the side-alley bully. At this level, sex and aggression are interchangeable at the drop of a hat, and the gang brawl is easily turned into the gang bang. Even at a higher level and amongst a nicer class of person – the emperor, tyrant, robber baron, mafia boss – the same principle applies only on a greater scale, and the dominance of the leader over the pack, be it an empire or a mafia family, has to be won by the exercise of aggression over his competitors.

But aggression doesn't have to be physical. In political cabinets and corporate boardrooms the leadership is usually achieved by the use of cunning, intelligence, know-how, force of personality, charisma – though it is usually testosterone that fuels the will to achieve, succeed and win by whatever means are deemed appropriate. From the evolutionary point of view, aggression was necessary in men (and other male primates) for hunting, for defending the family and the group, and for winning dominance in the hierarchy and gaining access to the females in order to leave more offspring than rival

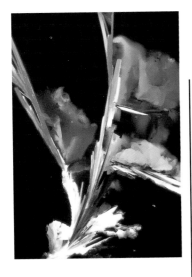

Polarized light micrograph of crystals of dihydrotestosterone (above), the most potent naturally-occurring male sex hormone. Responsible for aggression and the sex drive, it is the very stuff that fires both the lover and the hunter warrior (Guaica tribesmen in war canoe, Upper Orinoco, Venezuela)

males.

Not much has changed today. Testosterone still fuels the most explosive sports (like weightlifting and the sprints) and the most confrontational sports (like boxing and rugby) – hence the temptation to take anabolic steroids to build up testosterone levels in men and women alike. It is probably a powerful cocktail of testosterone and adrenalin (along with cultural conditioning and military training) that drives men again and again into the horrors of hand-to-hand combat, and a massive surge of both that helps wins most Victoria Crosses and other battlefield medals for courage. These days, though, a lot more men commute to the office than trot off to the jungle to hunt, and the hierarchy in the male pack is now expressed in terms of the motor car, for as a rule the pecking order is the parking order, and it's the man with the limousine that gets the chauffeur.

Research carried out by Professor James Dabbs, a psychologist at Georgia State University, confirmed the relationship between testosterone and those aphrodisiacal attributes of success and power. Using testosterone taken from salivary samples of men in a range of occupations from politicans and captains of industry to convicts and clergymen, Dabbs found that the high-flyers of society consistently had higher testosterone levels than the less successful members. Top football players, actors and entertainers, for example, all had high levels of testosterone. Clergymen tended to have rather lower levels than politicans and other gang leaders, implying that they led less dominant, and by definition, less sexually active lives. It is testosterone levels that determine, at least to a degree, the way men develop and whether they end up as political leaders and gang leaders, champs or wimps, studs or wets.

But Dabbs also found that, though women normally have less testosterone than men, female achievers, such as women lawyers, had higher testosterone levels than average women.

'It's all good biological stuff,' commented Dr Malcolm Carruthers, Medical Director of the Andrology Centre in London. 'Dominant people of either sex tend to have more testosterone than non-dominant people. Maybe that's why Eastern potentates had to go on proving themselves potent until they fell by the wayside, like poor old King Saud. When they were no longer potent they fell from power. When the leader of the pack loses his ability to dominate and in turn has less access to the choice females of the herd, then he ceases to be leader. A younger stag takes over, leaving him to limp off into the forest. You can see something like it at the Wimbledon tennis championships. When the winner of the Men's Singles Final leaps over the net to shake the loser by the hand, he is experiencing a sudden surge of testosterone, whereas the defeated champion is undergoing the opposite and limps off the court with his tail between his legs.' The effect of testosterone is a two-way business. Testosterone creates success and success in turn leads to a high that creates testosterone.

It is Malcolm Carruther's view that testosterone tests of the British Prime Minister and his Cabinet – and for that matter of the US President and his White House Cabinet in Washington DC – might provide an insight not only into the sexual and social drives of the individuals concerned, but their style of leadership and the nature of the government they controlled. 'All really great leaders are sexy leaders,' says Carruthers.

the big ball game

Since right across the animal kingdom testosterone levels are themselves determined to some extent by testicle size relative to body mass, it should follow that the bigger the testicles the greater the sex urge and power drive. Comparing one species with another, the premise seems to be broadly true – though not quite in the way, or for the reason, that one might expect.

For a start, there seems to be no obvious relationship between the size of the balls and the size of the body, nor is balls size determined for the pleasure or convenience of the male alone. By way of example, gorillas weigh four times more than chimpanzees, but chimpanzees' testicles weigh four times more than gorillas', which are relatively tiny. Or again, the testicles of the right whale weigh more than a ton and amount to 2 per cent of its body weight, while the testicles of the sperm whale, generally a substantially bigger creature, are comparatively small. Or moving to the world of birds, cock sparrows have huge testicles for such tiny bodies – bigger, relatively speaking, than those of a 50-ton sperm whale – while the comparatively gigantic male eagle is surprisingly poorly endowed.

Where does man stand in this apparently erratic scale of testicularity? As apes go, today's human males are pretty average – fairly well-hung compared with the bigger built gorilla, but punier than the smaller chimpanzee (though there is

Testicle size in human beings and other animals, like these blue-balled vervet monkeys, is a measure not only of the males' sex drive, but also the females' sexual behaviour

some evidence that our male ancestors once had bigger testicles). Why is this? The answer is surprising. Though the size of men's testicles determines the strength of their sex drive, it is the nature of women's sex habits that determine the size of men's testicles in the first place. And the same is true in the rest of the animal kingdom.

The basic rule takes us back to our evolutionary ancestors: the bigger the testicles, the more polyandrous the females. Or put it another way: the more promiscuous the group and the greater the competition from other males, the larger the testes; and the greater the sexual monopoly of the females enjoyed by the male, the smaller the testes. So since both gorillas and sperm whales live in harems, and since each male enjoys a monopoly over his harem and has virtually no competitors, biologically speaking he has no great need for extra large doses of testosterone and hyperactive sex, and hence no need for champion-sized balls. In fact, any mighty gorilla who heads a harem is lucky to have sex more than once a year with any one of his mates, and any male gorilla who does not have a harem is lucky to have sex at all. But the position is reversed in the case of the chimpanzee and the right whale, or for that matter sparrows, who do not live in harems but who have to compete with other males for the sexual favours of females who are basically polyandrous and mate with any number of males given the chance. Clearly the better hung the chimp or right whale or sparrow, the better chance it has of getting his girl before his rivals do.

Judged purely by the size of his balls, the human male is only an average ape sexually-speaking, with sperm production unusually low per gram of tissue, which suggests (as we all know from daily observation) that he neither lives in a harem (the numerous well-documented exceptions to this premise are probably statistically too insignificant to change the evolutionary norm) nor has to compete for wildly promiscuous women all the time (and ditto the well-publicized exceptions). The amount of testosterone produced by the human male is just sufficient to allow him to continue to compete successfully for women against a moderate level of competition from other males. The human female, on the other hand, has sufficiently less testosterone to remain faithful but turned-on by one man at one time.

But sexual drive is not solely governed by testosterone, and in virtually all human societies it is checked and modified by social and psychological factors. Most men do not go around raping women, and only a minority go around harassing them. 'It's a matter of control of one's urges and channelling of one's urges,' states Malcolm Carruthers. 'I think it's a personal, national and international tragedy that President Clinton hasn't been able to control or channel his high level of drives for whatever he does from eating a baked potato in one or two bites to whatever with women.'

President Clinton's romantic proclivities need putting in context, though, along with those of other great testosterone-enhanced leaders with an eye for the ladies, from President Kennedy and Chairman Mao to the long roll of honour of jolly rogering British premiers, among them Lloyd George, Disraeli, Palmerston, Melbourne and Wellington. For in no respect can even the great and the good of the human world compare with those sexual paragons of nature, the bonobos. The bonobos are pygmy chimpanzees and live in the forest of Africa. In bonobo country anything goes. The females are nymphomaniacs and have sex with virtually any other bonobo they encounter. A young female arriving at a tree where other bonobos are feeding will immediately proceed to mate with every male in every way. Copulation in bonobo society is incessant, indiscriminate and catholic. The big-balled males have little time for anything else, and devote relatively little of what is left of their surplus energy in trying to rise to the top of a heap.

Elephantine love in the wilds of Masai Mara, Kenya. The coitus of the largest land animal on earth is a spectacular event, but the testosterone power of the male is hardly commensurate with his body mass

the chemistry of desire

'Life invented sex as the most pleasant of all possible means to carry on.' Polarized light micrograph of cortisol, a key hormone in the complex chemistry of human love

It is testosterone that drives the sex drive. But the sex drive alone is just a lurching, untargeted urge. To generate desire, a personalized urge for someone in particular, an extra ingredient is required. That ingredient is noradrenalin (not to be confused with adrenalin, the fear and anxiety hormone). Noradrenalin is the turn-on hormone which produces the buzz, the high, the excitement and arousal generated by certain exceptional circumstances in life – like falling in love with the love of your life. It is the mixture of testosterone and noradrenalin which really puts the sparkle into the challenging areas of life, like politics, sport and sex. Successful men it seems secrete more noradrenalin and women more adrenalin. The former can be responsible for the hyperactive 'Jack the Zipper Syndrome'; the latter for nervousness and anxiety.

If sexual desire, generated biochemically in response to another person's sexual attraction, was to be turned into a neat and convenient formula, it would look like this:

TESTOSTERONE + NORADRENALIN

x CONDITIONING

= DESIRE

– conditioning being the modifying complex of psychoemotional attitudes a person brings to a situation as a result of his or her upbringing, development and life experience.

Malcolm Carruthers has identified six specific situations that turn on a person's noradrenalin, the turn-on hormone. He calls them the Six Cs (see box on upper right).

Cold conditioning may need some explanation. Apparently exposure to super cold conditions stimulates noradrenalin

THE SIX Cs

- Competitive behaviour (as in politics)
- Car driving at speed
- Coffee drinking
- Cigarette smoking
- Cold conditioning
- Coition and other sexual activity

production in the human body, which is why people roll themselves in the snow after a hot sauna, and feel on a huge high afterwards.

special situations

Situations in which people find themselves parting company with the down-to-earth norms of everyday life can also have a remarkable impact on their sexual responses.

One of the most startling effects of a special situation on libido and the processes of sexual attraction was in Hitler's bunker complex, deep beneath the streets of Berlin, as the city was on the point of falling to a vengeful Red Army. Berlin was on fire; the Führer dead. The Russians had set a ring of iron round the bunker complex; there was no way out for its inmates, and no hope for the future of the Third Reich. One of the men trapped in this underground rat-trap was Hitler's chief surgeon, Professor Schenk, who was later to give a remarkable description of what he saw during the countdown to Götterdämmerung:

'There was a kind of contagious mass-hysteria seeking a group outlet. Many of the same red-eyed women who had fled their Berlin apartments, in terror of rape by Red Army soldiers, now threw themselves into the arms, and bed rolls, of the nearest German soldiers they could find. And the soldiers were not unwilling. Still, it came as a bit of a shock to me to see a German general chasing some half-naked signal woman between and over the cots. The more discreet retired to Dr Kuntz's dentist chair upstairs in the Chancellery. That chair seems to have had a special erotic effect. The wilder women enjoyed being strapped up and made love to in a variety of novel positions.'

What was it that made these women cast aside their inhibitions and throw themselves at the doomed remnants of the dying Reich? Was it the alcohol that still flowed freely in this underground warren? Or some subconscious drive to go through the motion of sexual reproduction as a counter to the widespread destruction of life all around them? Whatever it was, the hormonal cocktail involved was complex and powerful, the whole sexual chemistry of the body – the adrenals, the testes, the ovaries, the sympathetic

Trying for a tan in mid-winter Russia, two sun freaks ignore the icy snow, one of the big-Cs (see above) that could give them a noradrenalin turn-on

system, the lot – churning away at full revs. This was a high to end all highs in the midst of a low to end all lows – sex appeal gone mad.

A classic experiment to test the effect of a special situation on sex appeal and libido was carried out in the early Seventies. The first part of the experiment was conducted on a high footbridge in the Rockies outside Vancouver. The bridge was 450 feet long, 5 feet wide, and 230 feet above a rocky canyon. Crossing the bridge was generally deemed to be a perilous experience, for the contraption wobbled wildly, apparently threatening to toss the pedestrian onto the rocks far below. To carry out the experiment, the researchers asked a group of volunteer male students to cross the bridge one at a time. Half-way across, at the point of maximum anxiety, each student was accosted by a beautiful girl. The beautiful girl, a heavenly apparition under such circumstances, would ask the student to help fill in a questionnaire. The student was then given the girl's home telephone number, with a request to give her a call that evening, if the student was so inclined. Meanwhile, another group of male volunteers were undergoing a similar test on another, lower bridge in another part of the canyon – a much less perilous and considerably safer bridge than the first. As each student crossed this second bridge he was confronted by another, no less attractive young woman, asked to help fill in the same questionnaire, and given another telephone number to ring in the evening.

The difference in the responses of the two groups of volunteers was very marked. Those who had crossed the perilous high bridge had filled in the questionnaire with far more sexually slanted answers than those who had crossed the safe low bridge. And that evening a substantially higher percentage of the high bridge students had telephoned to make a date than the low bridge students. Conditions of high anxiety, the psychologists concluded, did seem to induce heightened sexual attraction.

Australian surf lifesavers in action – the surging male hormonal cocktail is a complex and powerful chemical mix largely fuelled by testosterone and adrenalin

MASTER CLASS

HOW TO IMPROVE YOUR CHEMISTRY

Life can be compared to a trip in a glider. After being catapulted in our teens and early twenties to the peak of our innate physical and mental abilities by a powerful cocktail of hormones – particularly the sex hormones testosterone and oestrogen – we then go into a variable glide path for the rest of our lives, the rate of descent being largely controlled by the body's hormonal balance.

It is well known that women will undergo a menopause as a natural stage in their body's progression through life. It is generally less well known that many men may also experience a menopause, or in their case an andropause – not to be confused with the psychological mid-life crisis that happens around the age of 40 – featuring a number of similar symptoms. Among the mental symptoms common to both are fatigue, depression, irritability and reduced libido; the physical symptons include ageing, aches and pains, sweating and flushing, and decreased sexual performance and enjoyment.

In a typical andropause case the first and most obvious sign of crisis is loss of sexual interest and potency. There will also be loss of drive in professional or business life, together with lethargy and depression, and a sense of hopelessness and helplessness. Desperately casting about for a way out of this dilemma, such men may often resort to extreme measures – changing their jobs, for example, and their women – often with dire results.

Some of the unhappiest people I see in my clinic are men who have taken up with younger women and can't function adequately sexually to keep up with them. Their previous family has broken up, they've gone through all the social and financial traumas, and now they've got a dissatisfied young woman on their hands, a lot of problems, and no supportive family to help out.

There is one big difference between the male and female menopause, however. The female version is a natural, unavoidable process; the male one is to a large extent avoidable, at least until a relatively ripe age. Apart from the ageing process itself, there are several other precipitating causes for a premature reduction in the level of testosterone or a resistance to its actions. These include: stress; alcohol; obesity; smoking; glandular infections; surgical trauma (vasectomy or prostatecto-

my); medication (drugs toxic to the testis, such as oestrogens and corticosteroids) and environmental factors (xeno-oestrogenic substances in foodstuffs and water, causing undescended testes and lowered sperm count – a growing environmental hazard to all male species).

The negative impact of stress on the hormones of the body, particularly on those involved in sexual functioning, may lead eventually to sexual dysfunction, burnout, premature aging, heart attacks and other circulatory diseases. It is the long-term, unrelieved stress, when the adrenalin stress hormones have the upper hand over the sex hormones, that does the damage. Stress hormones have a catabolic effect, initiating an ageing process.

As for alcohol, often consumed as an antidote to stress, this can damage the testes permanently – so the lager louts of today may well be the lousy lovers of tomorrow. Alcohol can inflict lifelong damage which may not be apparent in a man's twenties or thirties but by his forties and fifties can already be causing all the problems of the andropause.

Vasectomy is one of the commoner reasons for a drop in male testosterone levels, but old age is, of course, the penultimate challenger to life, not to mention love. Among males in the West, however, there is a syndrome of reversible premature ageing, which can be attributed to a relative rather than an absolute deficiency of testosterone. The andropause can be safely reversed by a course of hormone replacement therapy.

Already an established treatment for women, HRT has more recently been introduced for men, using testosterone much as oestrogen is used for women. The results can be impressive, restoring virility as well as vitality, and banishing the more obvious stigmata of age.

By restoring a man's libido, you lift depression where anti-depressants have failed and generally put him back into the race. Testosterone can give back confidence, which in turn spills back into libido, which in turn helps enhance a person's sex appeal.

DR MALCOLM CARRUTHERS, PIONEER SPECIALIST IN HORMONE REPLACEMENT THERAPY FOR MEN AND MEDICAL DIRECTOR OF THE ANDROLOGY CENTRE, HARLEY STREET, LONDON

10 the sweet smell of sexcess

'Is it not every lover's ardent desire to inhale part of the beloved?'

CASANOVA

the
scented
ape

From time immemorial human beings have known that smell was a seductive aid and abetter of sexual activity. 'Do her armpits smell?' was the question Pablo Picasso and Georges Braque used to test whether a painting of a woman was carnal and real. When Napoleon came home from the wars he sent Josephine a note: '*Ne te laves pas, je reviens*' ('Don't wash, I'm coming home.') The French Emperor liked his Empress to bring a natural, unwashed body to the imperial bed.

Smell plays a greater role in human behaviour than is generally realised and there is a structural basis for a direct association between smell and sex. Smell has an emotional potency that other senses may not possess. Smell and touch are the senses which powerfully bond people. With colour and scent, it has been said, a person can control the emotional temperature of a room.

Smell can affect mood and behaviour, and there is increasing evidence that it is an important factor in choosing a mate. On a primitive level, it seems, we are looking for a person whose smell complements our own. Within seconds of meeting a person, we make intuitive sensory decisions about each other. If the person has the smell we are subconsciously looking for, we may undergo a process known as 'olfactory bonding', a phenomenon which may account in part for the most memorable romantic encounters and deepest friendships. As Rudyard Kipling once wrote: 'Scents are surer than sights and sounds to make your heartstrings crack.' But, warns Dr Susan Schiffman, professor of medical psychology at Duke University Medical Centre, 'two people can't maintain a relationship if they don't like each other's smell, on whatever level they perceive it.'

Smell is the oldest of the senses, operating within one of the innermost parts of the brain known as the 'primitive' or 'old mammalian' brain and at one time as the 'smell brain'. It is this ancient, near-animal brain which controls learning, memory, appetites, and the most basic emotional states – fear, rage, joy, love, hate and sexual arousal.

Everyody's sense of smell is as unique as their fingerprint. The individuality of our smellprints is determined by our genes, skin type, hair colour, diet and age. But we learn smell by association – it is based on our own life's experience. When we are born the cerebrum is empty. A baby, for example, is unable to differentiate between a good smell and a bad smell, and the first smell it will learn is that of its mother, a smell associated with safety and food.

Our ability to smell and differentiate between smells is inherited. All smells have molecular shapes which fit like a key in a lock into

'Smell is a potent wizard that transports us a thousand miles and all the years we have lived.'

Helen Keller

The head of Michelangelo's David *presents a fine-looking example of the human nose – the receptor for man's highly evocative but little understood sense of smell*

THE SCENT OF THE FEMALE

Few Westerners have a particularly sensitive nose. For those that do, the consequences can be extraordinary in terms of sex appeal, as American medic Ralcy Husted Bell discovered when he conducted an olfactory exploration of a current woman friend:

She irradiated what we now call sex appeal. It seemed to come from every part of her: lips, teeth, hair, ears, hands, feet, legs, breasts, arm-pits, eyes, odours, and the rest.

Every woman has her distinctive odours. What a variety she had! Many that were strange. About the wings of her nose the odour was clearly perceptible but faint, delicately rancid and four fingers deep – perhaps not more than three – fading into something almost if not quite aromatic, fascinating and provocative of desire.

From the roots of her hair came an odour of another kind – different, yet similarly provocative of desire for more, more, and always more. As it arose it seemed more like the perfume of some strange flower; and, oddly enough, it was less potent from the thick hair of her head than from the fragile curls of the nape. This may have been partly owing to associations – there is, as all lovers know, a subtle suggestiveness in the curls at the back of a woman's neck.

Then there were her glorious armpits! Yes, armpits that exhaled the glorified smell of honest sweat, the glorified smell of a clean negress, the glorified smell of goat, that so many married men get used to. Arm-pits that held the lure of privacy, of secrecy longing to be revealed. Glorious armpits! when not desecrated with perfumed powders.

The cleft between her large breasts was a nest of odours rising like mists from sacred blossoms. Corporeal odours below, growing more corporeal in depth of cleft and in descent of torso.

The skin of her ample belly smelled as it looked: smooth and like apple-blossoms in mid-April – even to the curious little odour spilled from the tiny, inverted thimble of her navel – an odd little odour, like a lone sentinel in a vast garden.

And like a breath from afar there arose indefinable, deft odours – odours like nuances – odours circling her large heart-shaped nates – odours starting from the tips of the toes, climbing on and on to blend in the climax of odours which first envelops life, beginning with the seed – that fountain of odours, so perfect in itself, so majestic, so impelling that it cannot be mistaken by the sons of men.

RALCY HUSTED BELL

receptor holes in the nose that correspond in shape to the smell. These holes are hereditary, so although you can develop your sense of smell by exercising your nose, it may be biologically incapable of recognising certain smells. As we grow up we build up an odour memory bank, a vast depository of smells and all the images and memories that go with them. Because we learn smell by association, the sense of smell is very subjective. One odour may unlock happy memories, another smell may unlock unhappy ones, yet another may trigger sexy ones.

Just as some individuals are better than others when it comes to smelling, so are some cultures. As a matter of course, for example, the Yanamamö of the Amazon and the Kanum-Irebe of New Guinea rub each other's bodies and then sniff their fingers to 'read' the olfactory message; while the people of the Suya tribe of the Amazon Basin classify people (along with plants and animals) by smell, placing them in four categories – bland, strong, pungent and rotten. However, in the Western world, where the visual sense predominates, smell has become the Cinderella of the senses. As smell expert Dr Michael Stoddart puts it: 'The idea that people should smell of people is deeply distasteful.' Hence the cosmetic industry's role in replacing such smells with perfumes, aftershaves and deodorants.

Though man's sense of smell is only a vestige of what it was, humans remain the most scented of all apes, for no other primate is so well-equipped with so many scent glands – some three million in all. The sebaceous glands occur all over the body, producing an oily, odourless sebum which bacteria break down into strongly-scented fatty acids. The apocrine glands (responsible for most of a normal person's smells) occur principally in the armpits (or axillae) and genital regions, as well as the anal region, belly button, nipples, scalp,

THE SCENT OF THE MALE

Until roughly a hundred years ago it was the male of the species who made the running when it came to wearing scent to attract a mate, if only by masking his own natural body odour. Even the cowboys of the old Wild West were not regarded as having demeaned their machismo when they tipped lilac water over themselves before going out for a night on the town.

The increased interest of the modern male in the beautifying impact of fashion and cosmetics is particularly focused on fragrance – specifically aftershave, cologne or eau de toilette (full-blown perfume, it seems, is still a male taboo). Though sales of male perfume come nowhere near the sale of female perfume, it is still big business, accounting for $1.7 billion in the USA at the last count (though some 60 percent of male fragrance purchases are made by women – buying for their men).

According to a survey carried out by the Fragrance Foundation of New York, 21 per cent of men have a favourite 'killer cologne' that they consider extra effective in attracting women. Men who admit to using men's fragrances to make themselves more attractive to the opposite sex also tend to be better groomed, more fashion conscious, more interested in exercise and more likely spend greater sums of money on clothes.

Whether such men are actually as sexy as they think they are is an open question, though if they actually think they are sexy they are already half-way to being sexy. The fragrance houses do their best to sell male scent as 'sex appeal in a bottle' – adding, in the yuppie years of the late Eighties, the no less powerful notion that designer fragrance was a signature of lifestyle and a prerequisite for success, along with the Armani suit, the red Ferrari and the portable phone.

According to Joachim Mensing, the director of communications at Lancaster, there are six types of fragrance-wearing modern man, and each type has his own appropriate fragrance – the unobtrusive, well-groomed, traditional conventional type will wear Aramis, Polo or Boss Spirit, while the sensitive, individualistic, introverted and unconventional type will wear Obsession for Men or Lagerfeld's Photo; the unconventional, avant-garde tear-away will go for Chanel's Antaeus, Moschino or Versace Homme. Fragrance use tapers off, however, once a man is married or settled in a steady long-term relationship.

mouth, nose, eyelids and ears, Our body hair acts as a scent trap to prolong and intensify the odours the apocrines emit. It is the odours produced in these glands that give human beings their characteristic smell. Saliva and urine are two other important sources of human smell, for odorous steroids are found in both, more in men than women. Musky steroids are also contained in armpit odour, including the scent attractant steroids androstenol, androstenone and androsterone, the first two also occurring as mating pheromones in pigs.

Human beings as a species smell differently from other species, and individual human beings also smell differently from each other. Every person possesses a unique chemical signature. So mothers can identify their children's T-shirts by smelling them, and many lovers can recognise their partner's body from its characteristic body odour.

The differences in smell between the two sexes are even greater than those between the races. For example, male odours in general are found to be strong and unpleasant, female odours weak but agreeable. German women tend to like their partner's odour, Italian and Japanese do not. In fact Japanese women do not like any male odour, whether it is their partner's or somebody else's. This is probably because armpit scent glands are so rare among the Japanese that anyone with smelly armpits is thought to be sick. Even fewer Koreans produce any body odour at all.

the fragrances of love

In the golden age of reeking innocence which preceded the hygiene age of Lifebuoy soap and deodorants, perfume was more an adjunct to the down-to-earth odour of unscrubbed bodies than a substitute for it. From almost the birth of modern man perfume of one kind or another – smoke, incense, unguent, lotion, pomade, nosegay, spray, cologne, pot-pourri, powder – has been a feature of private anointment and public ritual, religious, social, domestic or erotic.

The power of a smell to change a person's mood has long been recognised, and even (or perhaps especially) today's scents are used not just to aromatize the body but to raise the collective psychology of a human environment. In America workers work more efficiently when they are given occasional wafts of peppermint or lily of the valley, and European airlines resort to aromatherapy to help airline staff combat jet lag. Not surprisingly the power of perfumes to affect human moods has led to their close involvement in the erotic life of the human species.

Any seriously sensual appeal in a perfume has always lain in the

'Scent was a brother of breath. Together with breath it entered human beings, went direct to their hearts. He who ruled scent ruled the hearts of men.'

PATRICK SÜSKIND, PERFUME

animal base notes. Of these the most important is musk, a bitter-tasting, unctuous, reddish-brown substance which comes from a gland near the genitals of the musk deer of the Moroccan Atlas and Tibetan Himalayas (where it browses on aromatic shrubs for 11 months of the year and in the twelfth gives off such a stench that it can attract a mate from over a kilometre away). Musk imparts a warm, erotic note to perfumes.

Second in importance is civet, a soft, fatty substance with a foetid odour which is extracted from the anal gland of the wild civet cat of Ethiopia, usually after tempting the animal with bananas, eggs, fish and other delicacies, since the quality of the civet depends on the quality of the civet cat's food. Civet is used in many high-quality fragrances.

Castoreum, a secretion from the Canadian and Russian beaver, has a warm, leather-like note and is used in tincture form in a limited range of perfume bases. Ambergris, the so-called 'pearl of the whale', is even rarer, if only because it is so hard to find. A waxy calculus sometimes found floating in the sea or washed up on the shore after being expelled from the intestine of the sperm whale, ambergris has a golden, balsamic, slightly sweet scent with a violet, sometimes erotogenic note to it, and costs nearly ten times the price of gold and four times the price of French jasmine essence, one of the world's most expensive perfume ingredients (currently more than twice the price of gold).

Today it is mostly synthetic copies of these animal ingredients that are used in perfume manufacture. But the principle remains the same – many perfumes are promoted for their association with sexual attraction, as many brand names all too obviously show.

The role of animal sex attractants in perfume intended to enhance human sex appeal has been known for thousands of years. The Chinese used musk in perfume over 5,500 years ago. The earliest known book on perfumes, written in the 16th century, lists a formula for scent containing 20 per cent musk, 8 per cent civet and 12 per cent storax (a plant resin that smells like musk). Today 85 per cent of female fragrances and 94 per cent of male ones contain synthetic musk, while 39 per cent and 6 per cent respectively contain civet.

In high concentrations the odours of musk and civet resemble the human sex attractant steroids androstenol and androstenone, for

When natural body odour became associated with the reek of illness, Lifebuoy soap came to the rescue of both

though they are not steroids they have a very similar molecular shape which enables them to trigger the musky steroid odour. This is probably the reason why musk and civet are reputed to influence human sexual behaviour. Both were traditionally employed as aphrodisiacs with the power to attract the opposite sex. In the Middle Ages, the writer Petrus Castellus wrote: 'Civet will cause a woman so much desire for coitus that she will almost continuously wish to make love with her husband.'

Before the nineteenth century women wore musk as the strongest and most animal scent they could find to reinforce their own body odour. The discovery of antiseptics ended all that. Smell now signalled disease. Animal scents were out – after all, as one proponent of the new olfactory world order was quick to point out, what do you get if you ferment human excreta in a double boiler – the scent of musk! No wonder the French were scandalized when that redoubtable heavyweight of ladylike decorum, Queen Victoria, turned up in Paris reeking of a cologne with a musky hint – an aromatic deemed more appropriate to a salon *mondaine* than the empress of half the world.

Fragrances with animal base notes were replaced with floral base notes. This was more a difference of degree than of kind. For although a floral perfume is never generally recognised to be a blatantly sexy perfume, some plant scents have much the same impact as animal ones. Some of the major ingredients of incense, for example, closely resemble specific body odours. Thus frankincense resembles the sebum of dark-haired people, myrrh resembles the sebum of fair-haired people, styrax resembles the sweat and skin odour of dark-haired people, and ladanum resembles the head hair odour of all hair types. The base notes of many perfumes include a number of other plant ingredients, among them iris, cumerin, carnation (a clove note), some gum resins (which have a strong, musky steroidal smell), henna blossom (which gives off a powerful odour of semen) and above all perhaps vanilla (the diminutive form of the Spanish word for vagina), which resembles the smell of warm human skin.

'Generally men seem to love the smell of vanilla on warm skin,'

Guerlain's Shalimar, one of the most sensual perfumes ever created. With more than a touch of civet in it, it paved the way for the uninhibited restoration of animal notes in perfume, the key to sex appeal in a bottle

explains Roja Dove, *Professeur de Parfum* at Guerlain. 'It's something slightly sweet, very warm, a little secretive when it's in a perfume, and I don't think it needs much imagination to work out why a man might find it appealing. When you lie in bed with someone and you've made love and you have your nose in someone's armpit or nether region or whatever – these are generally warm, comforting, maybe slightly musky odours, and these odours make you think of vanilla.' According to Professor Michael Stoddart, there can be no odours more able to stimulate the deep, emotional levels of the brain than those associated – no matter how distantly and indistinctly – with sexual attraction. But only two plants are actually erogenic to man – costus and mace.

Though a growing number of men in the West wear scent of some kind, it is women who are the more frequent users, perhaps because they unconsciously associate the musky notes of scent with the musky body odours of men. 'Men's attitude to buying perfume is very different to women's,' notes Roja Dove. 'Men will come in and basically say, "If I wear this will I find a woman this weekend?" Whereas we have never heard a woman come in and buy a bottle of perfume from us and say, "Will this catch a man?" Maybe she buys it with that in mind, but she never says it.' Women wear scent to project whatever image they wish to create. Men seem to wear fragrance as a snare and a lure. In the opinion of Avery Gilbert, Vice-President of Sensory Psychology at Givaudan-Roure, some men wore fragrance as 'a kind of tactical, manipulative, social warfare.'

ah, pheromones...!

Ah, pheromones indeed! Scientists discovered them, the press hyped them, the public latched on to them as the blindingly simple, automatic QED the world had been waiting for, the universal explanation for such involuntary human phenomena as love at first sight, irresistible attraction and super sex appeal – an open sesame to a scorching erotic future. Pheromones were understood to do for sex what the moon did for tides and the atom did for bombs. All you had to do was somehow waft them in the direction of the person of your choice and presto! he or she was magically yours for eternity – or as long as you somehow kept wafting the pheromones. But was it as simple as that? What were pheromones exactly? Where did you get them from? And did they really work ?

For centuries it had been known that animals could communicate with each other silently and invisibly by means of secret messages which were understood only by members of their own

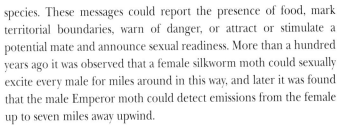

A keen angler, the Queen Mother once landed a monster 28-pound salmon after a three-hour battle. The phenomenal success of female anglers in landing record-breaking cock salmon has led to speculation that it is the human female pheromone that attracts these salmon in record sizes and record numbers

species. These messages could report the presence of food, mark territorial boundaries, warn of danger, or attract or stimulate a potential mate and announce sexual readiness. More than a hundred years ago it was observed that a female silkworm moth could sexually excite every male for miles around in this way, and later it was found that the male Emperor moth could detect emissions from the female up to seven miles away upwind.

But it wasn't until 1959 that Adolf Butenandt (who had by now won a Nobel Prize for his part in the discovery of sex hormones) discovered how it was done. Butenandt found that minuscule quantities of an airborne substance (in this case a chemical called bombykol), secreted by the female silkworm moth at a rate of 10 billionths of a gram per second, could be picked up by tiny hairs on the male moth's antennae and trigger an automatic sexual response. For this airborn chemical messenger Butenandt and his colleagues coined the generic name 'pheromone', from the Greek words *phero* (carry) and *hormon* (rouse to excite). Whether pheromones are a form of smell or something completely different is still a matter of debate. Whatever they are, they have in common the ability to alter the behaviour – including the sexual behaviour – of the body that picks up their chemical messages.

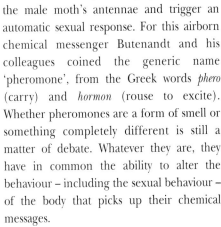

Further pheromone research has found that many other species are also responsive to the pheromone command mechanism. Ticks, for example, use them to gather the tick clans in cracks, crevices and caves. Ants need to use ten or more different kinds of pheromone to run an ant colony efficiently. Honey bees use some 30 pheromone communication systems to issue instructions and guidance to the honey gatherers, soldiers, nurses and undertakers in the hive. Just a few molecules of a sex pheromone drifting past a male hamster's nose will send the creature off on a frenzied hunt to locate and mount the female hamster emitting the pheromone.

Later it was dicovered that female monkeys produce a fatty acid pheromone substance called copulin which is tremendously sexually alluring to male monkeys. Since the maximum quantity of copulin is produced around the time of ovulation it was clear that the pheromone was under the control of the oestrogen hormone. If monkeys emit pheromones, why not humans?

The existence of human pheromones was first suspected back in 1952 when Dr Jacques Le Magnen, a French physiologist, noticed that female colleagues (but not male ones) were highly sensitive to the heavy musk-like odour of exaltolide, a chemical used in the manufacture of perfumes. Some of the women became highly aroused, a few became deeply upset, but all were most affected by the chemical during ovulation, which suggested that a sex-related pheromone was at work. During the Seventies scientists in Atlanta discovered a fatty acid substance in the human female which followed the same cyclic concentration as copulin – though perversely it was not male humans but male monkeys that were sexually aroused by female human copulin.

Subsequent experiments seemed to provide further evidence of the existence of human pheromones. Researchers found that whenever women spent any length of time together – in this case in a women undergraduates' dormitory – their menstrual cycles eventually coincided. Conversely if women spent much time in the company of men their menstrual cycles became shorter and more regular. Since female house mice exhibited exactly the same phenomena, and since it was pheromones that caused the phenomena, it seemed reasonable to assume that it was the transmission of human pheromones that was influencing the menstrual cycles of women, both in male or female company. But whether human pheromones also acted as a sexual attractant, and if so how, remained a mystery.

chemical sex appeal

If human beings can indeed emit pheromones to convey chemical messages, what kind of pheromones are they? Like many other mammals, human beings give off butyric acid from their skin and genitalia. As one scientist colourfully put it: 'A small cloud of the stuff follows them around like cheap perfume.' Butyric acid acts as a sex attractant for many mammals, so why not man? The big question today is not so much whether human beings transmit pheromones as whether they have the apparatus to receive them. If they do possess a pheromone receptor it seems possible that it is distinct from the smell receptor and operates at a subconscious level.

Two other candidates as human pheromones are androstenone

'Whoever would smell my scent, let him smell the rose.'

Prophet Mohamet

and androstenol. These two compounds are present in male axillary (armpit) secretions, urine and saliva. Androstenone is thought to have a predominantly urinous odour and androstenol a musky odour. Human beings are especially sensitive to androstenone, and women in particular can detect the minutest quantities of the compound.

As it happens, both steroids play an active part in the olfactory communication of the pig, and androstenone in particular plays a key role in pig sex, for as soon as the sow sniffs the scent of androstenone in the saliva of a boar she adopts a mating position, known as lordosis. Interestingly, the molecular structure of the boar pheromone androstenol is replicated in truffles, which is why French farmers use

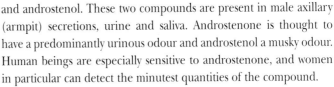

sows to snuffle them out. This is probably why little portions of this inordinately expensive fungus are eaten as an aphrodisiac by those who can afford them.

But what about human sex? There does in fact appear to be good evidence for believing that human armpit odours in general, and androstenol and androstenone in particular, have a function in human sexual communication. In fact, since the production of these steroid compounds is under the control of the gonadal hormones, the human axillary scent organ is to all intents and purposes a secondary sexual

A pig snuffles for truffles, homing in on the sex attractant pheromone, androstenol, found in these precious fungi. Science has not yet fathomed why the truffle emits the same substance that can trigger human sexual arousal

characteristic anyway, serving a presumably specific sexual function.

'It seems more than a coincidence,' reported Dr David Kirk-Smith, a leading researcher into human olfactory communication, 'that man produces these compounds from localized areas of the body which in animals would be considered sites of pheromone production and also has specific receptor sites for these same odorants in the nose.'

The fact that the sebaceous glands start functioning at puberty, peaking with sexual maturity and declining with old age, would seem to reinforce their possible importance in human sexual behaviour. However, in a fresh, pure form, human body smells are not easily detected by the human nose, and both appear to work at a subconscious level. Offensive body odour – the dreaded BO – is the stale, sour odour that is the by-product of wearing clothes, for clothing makes our skin a hothouse for the breeding of bacterial odour-agents.

As far back as 1840 research scientists were speculating that the sole function of the axillary gland was to produce a scent attractive to the opposite sex. In 1901 a German physiologist, Professor Hagen, commented: 'In human beings, in whom body scent is less useful, sexual attraction seems to be almost the sole effect which still has any significance. In this attractive power the axillary scent in man seems to be superior to the scent of the sexual organ or any other part of the body.'

It was well known, for example, that Greek male dancers would keep their hankies under their armpits and wave them under the noses of their female partners from time to time, and the German sexologist, Richard Kraft-Ebbing, noted: 'A voluptuous young peasant man told me he had seduced quite a considerable number of chaste girls without difficulty by wiping his armpits with his handkerchief while dancing, and then using this handkerchief to wipe the face of his dancing partner.' Perhaps it is not a coincidence that the nose of a woman of average height comes up to the armpit of a man of average height. And perhaps the presence of adrostenol and androstenone in human saliva accounts for some of the fun of kissing, especially the more deeply personal French variety.

Experiments have shown that at the very least androstenone exerts a degree of subliminal influence in human sexual choice. For example, in an experiment conducted in a dentist's waiting room, Dr Kirk-Smith found that women tended to prefer sitting on chairs that had been sprayed with androstenone, while men avoided them.

Androstenol, on the other hand, produced a more confusing picture. When Kirk-Smith asked a mixed group to pass judgement on photos of women, some of which had been sprayed with androstenol, both sexes rated the women in the sprayed pictures as more attractive. It has even been claimed that people are more likely to pay bills that are impregnated with a scent related to male sweat than bills that have no odour at all.

the industrial secrets of love

In the view of Dr George Dodd, one of the world's leading experts on the science and technology of smell, the sex pheromone is transmitted via the olfactory receptor and the olfactory nerve, registering in the brain as a smell bearing an unconscious but very potent 'smell language'. And he contends that other researchers have been wasting their time hunting for a single sex pheromone which has the same sexual knock-out effect on people as andosterone has on sows and copulin on monkeys – for there is no such single pheromone.

His own big discovery, Dodd claims, is to have isolated some 50 different human pheromones, produced by the glands of the armpits, the genitals and the face. This complex cocktail of pheromones falls into two categories – the attractants, which are secreted by the male in order to lure the female, and the primers, which produce biological changes in the female. The sexual scents can be further divided into seven families. According to Dodd, these families all correspond to known aphrodisiacs, such as truffles, oysters and champagne.

In Dr Dodd's tantalizing scenario these 50 pheromones, all present in human secretions, give each individual a distinctive bouquet – the hormonal equivalent of human body language – to which different people react in different ways. In 1993 he launched The Pheromone Factor, a bio-engineered human-identical pheromone perfume to increase a person's sexual attractiveness. Various combinations of odours could be mixed in different ways to produce different effects on people. The Pheromone Factor was one such combination. The hint of oysters and caviar washed down with champagne, in Dodd's view, could bring to mind the pheremonal allure of an attractive woman. One day he hopes to construct a pocket-sized artificial nose that will enable guests at singles parties (and perhaps not just singles) to sniff out others with compatible body odours.

That a human pheromone communication system exists may possibly be likely enough. But what it does exactly remains something of a mystery. The substance that sent moths and hamsters into a sexual frenzy seems to have a vaguer, more discreet impact on the infinitely more complex brains of humans. This did not deter the popular press from splashing the news. 'The sweet smell of sex!' proclaimed one headline. 'Not so sweet but oh so sexy!' trilled another. Here at last, it seemed, was the solution to one of life's most sought-after mysteries – the secret of sex appeal. Whoever acquired the potion, whoever was privy to the secret, was in possession of a power that was worth a king's ransom – or so it was believed.

This was the very stuff of male sexual fantasy come true. Awake the Sleeping Beauty with a pheromone-flavoured kiss and she would have you in the sack in a flash. Wave your pheromone-fragrant hanky in the direction of your favourite supermodel and she would have you pinned in a *Kama Sutra* clinch in a trice. With a brief squirt of a pheromone-flavoured in an eau de cologne they could all be yours. But what if the miracle molecule went up the wrong nose and activated the wrong person's olfactory bulb? What if it missed Michelle Pfeiffer and hit the old bat standing next to her? What if a bottle smashed and half the city downed tools and gave chase?

Does Dr Dodd's pheromone cocktail work? Journalists on a test run in London had some odd feedback but none reported becoming targets of unbridled lust, though one was jumped on by a dog. 'Sexual attraction is notoriously unpredictable,' commented TV journalist Francine Stock. 'Smell, though doubtless important, is only one ingredient in the alchemy. It just defies formula. Is there another little bottle with a sense of humour in it, since that must be responsible for more crumpled sheets than a thousand studied seductions.'

The traditional perfume houses have looked askance at The Pheromone Factor, arguing that there was enough sex in perfume already. Dodd's fellow scientists have been openly sceptical. 'It looks as though he has cooked up something from human sweat,' complained one, 'stuck in a few flavours from attractive foods and produced Dr Dodd's own version of human pheromone.'

the sixth sense

Hard on the heels of Dr Dodd came Dr Berliner, an anatomist-cum-entrepreneur who founded the Erox Corporation in New York to explore how human pheromones might enhance such products as perfumes and cosmetics.

Berliner was not convinced that pheromones were smells picked up by the smell receptors in the nose. In fact he was not convinced that pheromones had anything to do with the known five senses at all. He was particularly interested in an entirely different sense receptor inside the nose – a small pit-like receptacle first discovered inside the nostrils of various animals back in the eighteenth century and now known as the vomeronasal organ, or VNO for short. For a long time no one knew what function this tiny organ performed, if any, but by the mid-Eighties scientists were coming to the conclusion that the VNO was indeed a fully functioning sensory receptor for animal pheromones – a so-called 'accessory olfactory system'. Since no one was yet fully convinced that humans communicated by pheromones, however, the existence of a VNO inside the human nose was not properly investigated.

'Perfumes there are as sweet as the oboe's sound. Green as the prairies, fresh as a child's caress – and there are others, rich, corrupt, profound. And of an infinite pervasiveness, like myrrh, or musk, or amber, that excite the ecstasies of sense, the soul's delight.'

BAUDELAIRE

GLOBAL SCENTS APPEAL

Bint El Sudan was for a time the world's biggest-selling non-alcoholic-based perfume, legendary throughout Africa and the Middle East. The story of its creation is like something straight out of the Boy's Own Paper, a romantic by-product of the days of empire.

In 1920 an adventurous young Englishman by the name of Eric Burgess, of the London perfume company now known as Bush Boake Allen, was visited in his Khartoum office by a group of brigandish Sudanese tribesmen bearing phials of 48 mysterious essences they wanted combining into a single world-beating perfume. Burgess obliged, and a bestselling fragrance was born. Arab and African women wore it to enhance their personal sex appeal; their menfolk used it as an aphrodisiac.

In the course of time, Bint El Sudan became one of the unmistakeable smells of Africa, and though too powerful for the European nose, it remains a big seller in the Gulf. The bint, or girl, in the famous label, is based on a real girl photographed in the Sudan by Eric Burgess himself.

In the early Nineties, with the help of a team of specialists at the University of Utah Medical School, Berliner initiated a series of experiments which proved beyond all doubt that every human being possesses a VNO. The human pheromone receptor takes the shape of a tiny, cone-shaped, crimson-coloured cavity situated on the septum which separates the two halves of the nose about half an inch back from the tip (and in that position, incidentally, fearfully vulnerable to the cosmetic surgeon's knife in a nose job).

Tiny though it was, the human VNO turned out to be the largest in the animal kingdom, bigger even than that of a horse, and after a series of tests it was claimed that it was also fully functioning. Though the pheromone system worked rather like the sense of smell, it was quite distinct from that sense, for the VNO was stimulated by a different class of molecules and transmitted nerve impulses directly to a different part of the brain, the hypothalamus, the whole process remaining totally below the level of consciousness.

In 1993 a research group finally located the nerve cells that appeared to connect the human VNO with the brain. This seemed to prove conclusively that a neural network was in place to serve a 'sixth sense' in humans, additional to the senses of smell, taste, touch, sight and hearing. But the claim was greeted with scepticism in some quarters. 'It's fascinating stuff,' commented Dr Kirk-Smith. 'If this system exists it certainly deserves further exploration. One might expect any distinctive effects to be physiological rather than behavioural, given the importance of learning in human behaviour. Extraordinary claims require extraordinary evidence.'

Erox stored its human pheromones, synthesized from a sludge of human skin samples, in two large brown jars, one containing the female pheromone, the other the male, both jars together containing enough pheromone to stimulate four billion human beings, or more than all the post-pubescent people on earth. The conversion of the odourless raw pheromone into sophisticated perfume was masterminded by Pierre de Champfleury, formerly president of Yves Saint Laurent Parfums in Paris, and his consultant Ann Gottlieb, who had played a key part in the creation of Calvin Klein's world-selling Obsession, Eternity, and Escape. After submitting their specifications to three of the New York fragrance houses, they chose a scent from Firmenich to embody the female pheromone and a scent from Givaudan-Roure to embody the male one. Finally, in 1991 Erox launched the first perfumes ever to be developed round a synthesized human pheromone core – REALM Men (a cologne) and REALM Women (an eau de toilette).

A *Vogue* journalist who reported on the development stage of REALM pheromone fragrances expressed a lurking suspicion that many people probably share. 'I don't know about you,' he wrote, 'but I am beginning to find the idea of human pheromones extremely scary... I wondered how I would explain to my wife back in New York that I had been overcome by a group of beautiful women, dragged into one of those recreational vehicles so popular in Utah, and mated with repeatedly until I was no further use. What would this do to our marriage?' But nothing happened, and when he got back home his wife told him he smelled like a magazine.

'We have not identified a specifically aphrodisiac effect,' explained Dr David Dolberg, Erox's molecular biologist and patent attorney. 'Pheromones appeal to our sensuality, not our sexuality.' No question here, after all, of a human form of sow-like lordosis – no cocked ears, no cocked anything – and no little bottle of Love Potion Number Nine.

the theatre of seduction

If sex pheromones do work in human beings, they probably do so not in isolation but as part of a much bigger picture – within an interpersonal context of intricate signals from the other senses, and within a context of pre-programmed memories and their associated emotions.

In other words, it is unlikely a pheromone will lay someone out cold across a crowded room like some sex-golf hole-in-one. But as a back-up to the all the other paraphernalia of the theatre of seduction – the look in an eye, the gesture of a hand, the timbre of a voice, the shape of a shoulder, the mood of a place, a time, an encounter, music. candle and wine – all that – then perhaps a molecule in the nose and an electrical impulse in the hypothalamus or limbic system will provide the final shove that helps to win the day (or night).

Perhaps in man's distant evolutionary past sex pheromones were much more important, as instantaneous and involuntary in their effect as they are on many animals today. But evolutionary scientists point out that a sex-attractant pheromone system working in humans as it does in animals would have been counter-productive in terms of the kind of society in which human beings evolved. Man is one of the few mammals that is both gregarious and (for all the patent exceptions) largely monogamous. For a creature as sexy and social as man, living in a well-regulated society based on pair-bond, family and community, the existence of an irresistible fully-functioning sex pheromone that advertised a woman's fertility and drew panting men

THE SEX APPEAL OF FRAGRANCE

Humans have bodies that are among the most sophisticated smell-producing systems in the animal world, but paradoxically we have lost much of our sense of smell and turned our back on our own body smells in favour of perfumes containing animal and vegetable odours that are sometimes approximate mimics of our own.

These odours – some of them associated with the products of bodily excretion, be it faecal, urinous, seminal or oestrus-advertising – are closely linked with sexual attraction and in certain cases induce an unconscious erotic response, an enhanced level of sexual awareness brought about by mental associations with certain events in the perceiver's past.

The best and most expensive perfumes all contain strong erogenic ingredients, including urinous and even faecal notes (albeit not strong enough to intrude into the higher notes) which unconsciously stir vestigial memories of sex attractant pheromones. Most important are the so-called 'emmenagogues' – musk, civet, and castor, which are all odorant secretions from the follicles around the sexual organs of the three mammals in question. Ambergris, on the other hand, is said to have an 'indefinable odour of human hair'. Certain vegetable products also have an erogenic effect. Some plant resins, which help to give perfumes their body, contain resin alcohols with a similar structure to animal steroids, and may mimic the oestrus odour signals of the female, unconsciously stirring the deepest parts of the brain. Jasmine and other flowers have a faecal odour, while many orchids were believed to increase the production of semen.

The sexual attractant qualities of perfumes can be clearly seen from this simple breakdown of their main ingredients:

■ *The top notes are composed of the sexual secretions of flowers, produced in order to attract animals for cross-pollination purposes and often designed as mimics of the sex pheromones of the various animal species involved*

■ *The middle notes are created from resinous matter with odours resembling animal sex steroids*

■ *The base notes are made from the sex attractants of mammals and have distinctly urinous or faecal odours*

Reduced to such basics, perfume emerges as a cocktail of sex attractant odours at low levels of concentration. As zoologist and smell specialist Michael Stoddart puts it: 'Perfume accentuates the wearer's odorous qualities in the same way that well cut clothes accentuate the wearer's frame. The top notes consciously conceal what the base notes subconsciously strive to impart. The real message is in the small print.'

in droves from every corner of the prehistoric savannah every 28 days would have torn society apart and replaced the happy families scenario with perpetual tribal war.

However, these are early days. Scientists may or may not have stumbled on the industrial secrets of love, the blueprints and specifications relating to the muzzle-velocity and stopping-power of Cupid's arrow – but this doesn't mean that someone won't one day hit on a pheromone smell that tickles the inner recesses of the brain in just the right way. In the meantime a pretty face remains a pretty face.

MASTER CLASS

HOW TO IMPROVE YOUR SCENT

The ultimate sexually attractive smell of a person is clean, fresh skin and hair. It is the ultimate turn-on for another individual. If two people are attracted to each other, you can count on the fact that, subconsciously at the very least, they like each other's body odour.

Perfume, at its best, enhances your own smell. It marries with it, settles with it and promulgates it. If the perfume you wear is at odds with and in contradiction to your own body odour it won't work. Your character and your colouring can affect your smell. If you are very sultry in personality and very dark in colouring, you shouldn't wear a terribly fresh, green, uplifting fragrance. It won't match your odour type and will send out terribly confusing messages to everybody.

There are four key legs to the perfume table – the floral family, the *fougère* family, the chypre family and the oriental family. They make up the utter origins of perfumery, and one of the types will suit almost everyone without exception. If you experiment in the quadrant you feel most comfortable in, you will find a perfume that not only suits you down to the ground, but enhances your own personal odour.

Somebody who's generally dark in colouring, by and large tends to gravitate towards a heavier, sweeter, richer more oriental type of fragrance. Conversely, someone who is typically Scandinavian in colouring, with light skin and blond hair, will tend to gravitate towards a light, generally floral, slightly fresh, green kind of fragrance.

When you buy a perfume, get a small sample first, and see what sort of reaction you get. If it's indifferent or zero then you're on to a loser. But if the reactions are very

positive, especially from the same sex, you're on to an absolute dead winner.

If you dab a little perfume under the arms, in the pubic area and especially on your hair, you cannot fail to be missed. These localized areas disseminate the unavoidable sexual smell or signal of every individual, so by dabbing a little perfume there, you are effectively pushing forward and enhancing your own fragrance, saying: 'This is me. Like me or don't, but this is me'. Perfume depends on evaporation to function and the quicker it evaporates the more effective it is, so as well as these three key areas, always place it on the pulse points too – behind the knees, the ears, around the neck and between the breasts.

ARTHUR BURNHAM, INDEPENDENT CREATIVE PERFUMER, CREATOR FOR NINO CERRUTI AND CREATOR OF LE JARDIN AND LE JARDIN D'AMOUR FOR MAX FACTOR

the food of love

love

bomb

business

Aphrodisiacs must be almost as old as man himself. In historic times there are records from almost every civilized society of love potions that could work wonders. At one time or another almost every kind of comestible was judged to be the aphrodisiacal flavour of the month – even the humble potato. 'Will your ladyship have a potato-pie?' suggests a scheming hotpants in one of Beaumont and Fletcher's Jacobean dramas. "Tis a stirring dish for an old lay after a long lent.' Today the women's magazines run regular consumer reports ('Value for money. How was it for him?') on the latest (often meaning the oldest) aphrodisiacs to hit the leisure market, from Montezuma's Secret to Love Bomb and Red Rooster.

Basically an aphrodisiac purports to do one of three things. It can arouse your libido. Or it can increase your sex appeal by arousing the libido of the person of your choice, and thus his or her sexual desire for you. Or it can do both. An aphrodisiac can do these things in one of two ways – by internal consumption or external application. Of these the first – food, drink or drugs taken into the body – has more to do with the genuine article than the second.

Better to travel hopefully than to arrive. The aphrodisiac store 'Sultan Mesir Magunu' in the Grand Bazaar, Istanbul, peddles hopes and dreams of erotic bliss. Oysters and champage for two (opposite) – a traditional aphrodisiacal indulgence

venus in the kitchen

Of all the types of aphrodisiac to hit the brain via the stomach, food has been the most dominant in the history of human love. In part this has been due to an age-old phenomenon, expounded by a sixteenth century doctor called Paracelsus, which taught that the shape of a plant was a clue to the part of the body it could best help treat. It followed that plants shaped like the sexual organs of a man or woman would make the best aphrodisiacs. These included the avocado, the fig, the banana, the hermaphrodite-like mandrake root, which resembles the genitalia of both sexes, and the vanilla pod which resembles the vagina from which it derives its name. And it wasn't just plants. Animal organisms such as the oyster, which resembles the female pudenda in shape and texture, fell into the same category, as did man-made culinary artifacts. In ancient Greece, medieval France and modern Italy, for example, bread and pastries were often baked in the shapes of penises and vulvas and consumed at private feasts or carried around at religious festivals.

Smell was as much an associative turn-on as appearance, as one

'A well-fed stomach and a naked body breed lust in a man.'

Chinese Proverb

scholar of the subject explained: 'Vegetable juices, the smell of which was more or less reminiscent of seminal fluid or vaginal secretions, were credited with aphrodisiac properties and used as such by the people. It was the same with animals; particularly intense vitality, an abnormally long or violent period of heat, or a peculiar odour, caused certain animals to be appreciated for the stimulating qualities of their genital organs.'

From time to time the close association of food and sex has come under the scrutiny of medical sexologists. 'Sexual love is really a sort of higher eating,' declared Wilhelm Bölsche, a pioneer in the field. 'One of the most obvious links between the two,' added another expert, Alfred Crawley, 'is the kiss.' And rather more than the kiss, as William Fielding pointed out. 'It is a significant physiological fact,' he wrote, 'that one kind of nerve structures, called Krause's end-bulbs, which are unusually large and sensitive, are found principally in the clitoris, penis and lips.' In short, early researchers in this field tended to agree that the sexual urge, whose purpose was to perpetuate the race, was virtually the same as the nutritional urge, whose purpose was the self-preservation of the individual.

Until recently scientists were agreed that food could not produce an aphrodisiac effect biochemically. According to the French culinary bible, *Larousse Gastronomique*, the sexy truffle, a well-known alleged aphrodisiac, consists of nothing but 76.83 per cent water, 13.49 per cent carbohydates, 7.62 per cent albumen, 1.57 per cent salts and 0.49 per cent fats. Only recently has it been found that this lowly but pricey fungus also contains a look-alike adrostenol, the powerful sex-attractant pheromone. Similarly, a past chemical analysis of the oyster, another of the classic (but putative) food aphrodisiacs, revealed that this exalted bi-valve consisted of not much more than water, up to 90 per cent of the stuff, along with relatively small quantities of other

EXOTIC APHRODISIACAL RECIPES

From Brazil:

Take the dried genital of a turtle, monkey or otter. Crush to a powder. Mix with the root of the herb marapuana *and the fruit of the plants* puxuri *and* noz-moscada. *Shake well and take a little each morning for heightened desire. Or take the private parts of a male or female dolphin, depending on your sex. Mix in a glass of alcohol or sugar. Take as required. If you are a woman, substitute camphor for sugar and take a bath afterwards. For heightened pleasure.*

The proud rhino's horn. A mistaken belief in the aphrodisiac properties of the powdered horn has led to all species of rhinoceros being hunted close to extinction

elements which have little or no impact on sexual activity. Only recently has it been ascertained that the oyster is one of the best natural sources of zinc and mucopolysaccharides, important molecules of sugars and proteins – both essential for male sexuality and the production of testosterone and semen.

A number of other foods have enjoyed apparently inflated reputations as aphrodisiacs, including durian fruit (a creamy, stinky fruit from the rainforests of Malaysia and Indonesia), caviar, royal jelly and chocolate, although recent research indicates that these reputations may not be as inflated as was once thought. Take chocolate. There have been times when chocolate has been worth a king's ransom as a means of gaining sexual favours. In the Mayan brothels of Central America or the ruins of 1945 Berlin, a handful of cocoa beans or an army ration chocolate bar were the quickest way to a girl's heart. For historic sensualists like Casanova, the Marquis de Sade and Madame du Barry (mistress of Louis XV), chocolate was the favourite aphrodisiac.

It wasn't just the sensuous melting sweetness of chocolate that did the trick, the psychological feel-good comfort factor – it was also the chemistry. Chocolate contains caffeine-like substances which act as a stimulant, just as in coffee or tea. It also contains phenylethylamine, or PEA for short, a chemical closely related to the body's own dopamine and adrenalin. PEA revs up the brain to produce flushed skin, sweaty palms, heavy breathing and the feeling of being head-over-heels in love. PEA also prolongs a natural high by slowing the breakdown of pleasure chemicals called beta-endorphins. People with love withdrawal symptoms often develop a craving for chocolate, for as scientist Diane Warburton explains: 'PEA gives a feeling of post-coital bliss.'

Though there is growing evidence for a biochemical basis to aphrodisiacal foods, their efficacy remains mostly psycho-physiological, through associations aroused by taste, smell, texture, and appearance. Perfumed dishes generate amorous associations, and so do luxuriant ones. In a sex appeal food test a dish called fruit zabaglione – a rich, juicy, creamy concoction of strawberries and pear slices, Cointreau, rum, sugar, egg, cloves and cinnamon – was pronounced 'very sexy' by over half the test group who sampled it, mainly because of its sensually exotic and luxuriously sweet

'Sex appeal is best when you're drunk.'

INTERNET SURVEY RESPONSE

EXOTIC APHRODISIACAL RECIPES

From India:
If a man cuts into small pieces the sprouts of the vajnasunhi plant, and dips them into a mixture of red arsenic and sulphur and then dries them seven times, mixes them with honey and burns them at night, and if, looking at the smoke, he sees a golden moon behind, he will be successful with any woman, and if he throws some of the powder mixed with the excrement of a monkey upon a maiden, she will not be given in marriage to anyone else.

CLOSING TIME SYNDROME

In a research study of the behaviour of 137 men and 80 women in a bar between 9pm and midnight it was shown that while women's perception of the sexual attractiveness of the men in the bar had barely risen by midnight, men's perception of women had increased significantly. But the increase on the men's part did not in fact appear to be drink related, since it took place whether a man had six drinks or only one. It was not booze but the decreasing opportunity for fixing up a partner for casual sex as closing time drew near that appeared to be the real cause for the 'Closing Time Syndrome'.

'Don't all the girls get prettier at closing time?'

Dylan Thomas

ingredients, which were unconsciously equated with sexuality. These visual-sensory, olfactory-sensory, savour-sensory reactions do tend to predetermine an erotic response pattern, most marked in the period of relaxed post-prandial euphoria that follows a good meal in a relaxed, langorous ambiance in the intimate company of someone you fancy. As a German gastro-sexologist by the name of Dr Balzi put it: 'After a perfect meal we are more susceptible to the ecstasy of love than at any other time...'

Not surprising, then, that dinner for two is a classic move in the human mating game – dining out in the pre-coital phase, dining at home in the post-coital phase.

In all this foody sex fun alcohol plays a big role. Quite apart from any other qualities or associations it may bring to bear at a cosy dinner-for-two, whether in the form of a fine champagne or a Between the Sheets cocktail, alcohol is first and foremost a drug – the most widely used drug in our society with any real claim to aphrodisiacal properties. In fact alcohol does not increase libido, it simply takes away the inhibition that normally controls it. 'The super-ego,' it has been said, 'is that part of the psyche that dissolves in alcohol.' Excessive drinking over a long period however, can lower libido in men by permanently decreasing testosterone level, and in women it can cause infertility and endanger the proper development of the foetus. So, in gastro-sex there is no such thing as a free drink.

lords of the fly

In the popular mind the true, mainstream aphrodisiacs are drugs, both natural and synthetic. This is a grey, mostly under the counter area, where the modern pharmacopoeia mingles with mumbo jumbo straight out of folklore and the jungle. A full-blown aphrodisiac should ideally heighten the three main phases of a person's sexuality – desire, arousal and orgasm. Many drugs may affect one or other of these phases, but usually at the expense of the remaining phases.

Age-old folkloric aphrodisiacs are legion. There is not a street market in Africa, Asia or South America without a love potion stall or quack sex clinic dispensing dodgy recipes to arouse desire and resurrect a limping performance. In the West such products are usually marketed via the small ads in adult magazines. More colourful than efficacious, their inventory of ingredients makes odd reading.

Some of these folkloric aphrodisiacs derive their undeserved reputation because of their association with large, potent animals. The popularity of powdered rhino horn, tiger bones and stag antlers in China has had a scandalously catastrophic effect on the fate of the species involved, but often it is the unsavoury parts of more ordinary animals that are used. In Japan snake essence, powdered lizard and extract of white dog liver are much sought after, though most prescriptions consist mainly of plants, the more peniform the better.

The most notorious of the folkloric aphrodisiacs is cantharides, better known as Spanish Fly. In fact this toxic product is not derived from a fly but a rather beautiful iridescent green and gold beetle – the 'blister beetle' – which is found in Spain and other Mediterranean countries. Traditionally the beetles are anaesthetized, dried, then heated in an oven till they disintegrate into a powder of fine white crystals. Swallowed in a love potion, Spanish Fly causes genital burning, along with swooning and screaming which in more naive days was seen as evidence of sexual passion.

Tales abound of legendary feats of arousal under the influence of Spanish Fly. In sixteenth century Provence, for example, it is recorded that when some village women gave cantharides to their husbands to cure them of a fever, the sexual impact of the drug on the men was sensational. According to one of the widows, her husband copulated with her 87 times during the course of a 48-hour period before falling ill, but he remained so fired up that he coupled with her three more times during the course of his medical examination. Another of the priapic husbands had sex with his wife 40 times on the trot, only stopping when he developed gangrene of the penis and literally died on the job. Not surprisingly there was no repeat performance. The reality is that Spanish Fly is a deadly poison. Taken orally, a minuscule one ten-thousandth of an ounce (0.3mg) – just a few crystals in a cup of coffee – can bring about kidney failure. Even today, Spanish Fly fatalities still occur from time to time.

The secret of Spanish Fly – in fact a blister beetle, seen here emitting a blistering fluid. Long thought to have amazing aphrodisiacal powers, it is actually a lethal poison

jungle juice

Plants with aphrodisiacal properties attributed to them are almost as legion as foods. Some – like ginseng, damiana, vanilla, sarsaparilla – are relatively well known and easily obtainable. Others – like *iboga* from Zaire, *fo-ti-tieng* from China and *kavakava* from Tahiti – are exotic and harder to come by. Some are listed in the homeopathic pharmacopoeia, most notably yohimbine, a crystalline product

DAMIANA VODKA COCKTAIL

If one particular herb won't work why not try a cocktail with lots? The following time-hallowed recipe combines the sexually stimulating properties of damiana leaves and the de-inhibitory properties of vodka.

Infuse 1oz (30g) of dried damiana leaves in 1 pint (600ml) of vodka for five days. Strain through coffee filter.

Put the vodka in a cool place. Soak the damiana leaves in 1/4 pint (150ml) of spring water for five more days. Strain through a coffee filter. Keep the water but throw away the leaves.

Heat the water enough to dissolve 1/2–1 cup of honey according to taste.

Allow to cool then mix with the vodka. Bottle.

Drink one or two cordial glasses of the cocktail before bed.

'I have personally observed its amatory effect. Highly recommended.'

Dr Cynthia Watson, author of Love Potions

'Another one of these and I'll be under the host.'

Dorothy Parker

derived from the inner bark of the West African yohimbe tree, which has been used as a cure for impotence for centuries. If used homeopathically, it can improve male potency and increase genital sensation in both sexes. Not surprisingly, the world's greatest forest, the tropical rain forest of the Amazon and Orinoco basins, provides a number of plants with reputed aphrodisiacal properties, including guarana, muira puama, matico, quebracho, yage and ebena. Whether any of them are actually aphrodisiacs, rather than relaxants, stimulants or hallucinogens, is a matter of opinion.

Ginseng is the best known of the herbal aphrodisiacs, though whether it specifically affects desire, rather than simply increasing all-round well-being, is uncertain. There are four kinds – American, Siberian, Chinese and Korean, of which Korean seems to be the most powerful. Used in the East from time immemorial, ginseng (so ancient texts proclaimed) 'bestows the power of a bull on men both young and old'.

A women's magazine recently sent field researchers out to test ginseng's erotic qualities. The woman reporter gave it 4/10 and the man 8/10. She reported: 'High energy levels but not particularly horny'. He bounced out of bed saying, 'Let's go out for a run', which was not what she had been led to expect. In fact, scientific tests have shown that ginseng does have an arousing effect, but according to Dr Malcolm Carruthers 'it is not much stronger than coffee'.

the fountain of youth

To date the scientific view is that at least 99 per cent of aphrodisiac folklore is based on wishful thinking rather than scientific data. 'There are no traditional "aphrodisiacs" that can bring about erotic biochemical and/or physiological results,' was the categorical conclusion of sexologist Duncan MacDougald, an authority on the subject.

A few decades ago there were hopes that monkey glands might prove the miracle route to sexual rejuvenation. In fact they didn't, but in an age of sophisticated biochemistry and genetic micro-engineering it comes as no surprise that three synthetic drugs have been produced which show marked aphrodisiacal effects.

The first to appear was L-dopa, a drug used in the treatment of Parkinson's disease. Geriatric patients treated with the drug underwent amazing rejuvenation and were observed to jump out of bed and chase pretty nurses round the ward with amorous intent. However, L-dopa had no effect on young people of normal health.

The second synthetic was a cocktail of drugs – 'l-tryptophan, an anti-depressant and a tranquillizer with anti-serotonin and adrenalytic properties' – produced by the Clarke Institute of Psychiatry in Toronto to treat schizophrenic patients. The cocktail – referred to as Brand X – had a remarkable impact on the sexual behaviour of some female patients, who jumped into bed with each other, sexually assaulted the male cleaning staff and propositioned the nurses, exposed themselves in provocative poses and masturbated wildly in public. High on Brand X, the whole ward was a riot of what the medics in charge reported as 'compulsive pathological sexual activation'. Based on this experience, it would seem to have commercial possibilities as an authentic aphrodisiac.

The third drug was a synthetic derivative of the putative aphrodisiac yohimbine, which works by increasing blood pressure and brain levels of noradrenalin. Known only as RS15385, and still undergoing trials in pill form in Europe, Australia and America, the new drug has been hailed as the first true aphrodisiac. On the basis of results so far, RS15385 would seem to have a dramatic effect on male potency and promises to reinvigorate the sex lives of millions of men.

the columbus effect

Behaviourally speaking, the greatest enemy of desire in a long-term relationship is ennui, and the greatest cause of ennui is the diminishing of the sex appeal of the other partner due to over-familiarity. As G.B. Shaw put it, 'Beauty is all very well, but who ever looks at it when it has been in the house for three days.' Lamentable though it may be, the process is normal and natural. After a period of active love-making in the first year of marriage, there is a dramatic falling-off, and the marriage settles down to a low and ever-declining rate of sexual activity. Sexual boredom is perhaps the commonest underlying cause of marital breakdown, and unfortunately no matter how hard the afflicted couple may try, there is generally only one certain cure (though the cure may kill the marriage quicker than the condition) – to take a new sexual partner, or a series of partners. The sexual novelty generated by this drastic remedy will restore sexual activity to its former high rate, though there is a price to pay in personal and social side effects. The phenemenon is known as the Columbus Effect. At a casual level it amounts to promiscuity. In its more institutionalized form it is known as serial monogamy. It is probably the most effective, though damaging, aphrodisiac known. At the end of the day, it would seem that the best aphrodisiac is other people.

> **'Candy**
> **Is dandy**
> **But liquor**
> **Is quicker.'**
>
> *OGDEN NASH*

12

true love and total sex appeal

the agony
and the
ecstacy

Love can go by many other names, depending on whether Cupid fired an arrow, a cross-bow bolt or a .350 magnum parabellum. Flirtation, crush, romance, affair, infatuation, obsession, erotomania. The rising scale of erotic intensity can lead to rapture and ecstasy on the one hand, murder and suicide on the other. 'The supreme adventure is still falling in love,' wrote Germaine Greer. 'In love – as in pain, in shock, in trouble.'

Some see it as a sickness, with recognized aetiology, symptoms, treatment and prognosis. At its most extreme it has a lot in common with fever and other physical traumas. Psychologically it can cause pain, even breakdown. 'Oh darling,' Camilla Parker-Bowles agonized to Prince Charles in the Camillagate tapes. 'I'd suffer anything for you. That's love. It's the strength of love. Night night...'

Romantic love is essentially erotic, intense, unstable, fleeting, compounded of physical attraction, romantic idealization and sexual urgency. Often it takes the form of an illicit affair or holiday romance, and usually it is doomed. Often it is fuelled by the obstacles that are put in its way (the Romeo and Juliet effect), stoked by erotic imagination rather than erotic activity, love rather than love-making, longing rather than fulfilment.

In hopelessly stalled cases of romantic obsession the passion is sublimated into something else – if Dante could have have slept with Beatrice, would he have bothered to write *The Divine Comedy*? If the obstacles are not removed the lovers crack under the strain; if they are removed, the passion dies down in a kind of humdrum togetherness. 'Love by its nature must be transitory,' wrote pioneer feminist Mary Wollstonecraft 200 years ago. 'The most holy band of society is friendship.'

Art and literature contain countless case histories over thousands of years, from Homer to Tolstoy to Mills and Boon – among them some of the finest utterances ever made by the human race. Western-style romantic love – now a technical term in the lexicon of sexual psychology – flowered in the European Middle Ages and has survived the ups and downs of fashions and culture shocks ever since. In the sex revolution of the Sixties romance took a nosedive. 'We believe that people should screw all the time, anytime, whomever they wish,' declared a Yippi pamphlet in Sixties New York. 'This is not a program demand but a simple recognition of the reality around us.'

In today's rawly bawdy and clinically sexual climate some of the conventions associated with romantic love ('the agony and the ecstasy' and the rest) can seem simply quaint. In some extraordinary

'People are the only thing people have since God packed up. By people I mean sex'
JOHN UPDIKE, COUPLES

Any woman who thinks she's over the hill at 25 and one of the living dead at 30 can take comfort from this account of a young man's older love-of-his-life, total sex appeal heaven:

She had large, dark, languorous eyes, and she was silent, luxurious, tranquil as a cat. She was passively amorous. Her silence was a form of eloquence. It started the sap flowing through the endocrines. Every poise of her body and neck was a sexual challenge. The languid way she sat on a sofa drew males to her as sweet flowers draw the bees. And she was female. I don't think that she ever had a male thought, nor the faintest, most fugitive, masculine emotion. She was all female and the female was all woman.

Above all she was interesting. She had a manner. She had a mind, and that also had a manner. You couldn't separate her dignity from poise, her reserve from latent power, not her desire from your own. She made it a joy in a man to talk. She inspired spontaneity. Stranger than all else, she was too womanly for women to gossip about. She was a man's woman.

It would be impossible, however, to say just what it was that attracted me to this comely passionate blonde, nearing 40, and older than me by 20 years. In one way, it was as if I had known her since childhood. I can phrase it only as a feeling of intimacy.

RALCY HUSTED BELL

instances it is a case of leap before you look. When 30,000 couples got married simultaneously in Seoul's Olympic Stadium two years back, many of the couples had never met before and some of them couldn't even speak each other's language. Sex appeal? Love?

But is romantic love just a Western invention, dreamed up by the troubadours in the South of France in the thirteenth century? 'There is no word for love in the language,' wrote anthropologist Margaret Mead of the Manus islanders of New Guinea. 'There are no love songs, no romantic myths, no merely social dances.' A comparison of sexual relations in five countries – USA, Singapore, Nigeria, Burma and India – showed romantic love still surviving in America at one end of the scale and virtually non-existent in India at the other (at least as the basis for marriage).

Some forms of romantic encounter preclude all notion of love and even of sex appeal. Among the Maoris an ancient and favourite way of marrying a girl was to get up a war party and drag her off by force – this saved years of haggling for consent with a multitude of relatives. Among the old native American tribes of North America it was customary when a man married the eldest daughter of a family that he also took by right all her other sisters, whether they fancied him or not (or vice versa). Among the Todas of India the reverse was true – once a man married a girl all his brothers had the right to sleep with her as well.

the power of love

But love, it has been said, is the key-note of life. It makes no difference if a man loves one person once in his life, or hundreds of people through the whole of his life. Love is the cause for which passion bleeds. Love is the dynamics of life. 'It rivals God,' wrote Ralcy Husted Bell towards the end of a long and amorous innings. 'Probably it is one phase of God, since its spiritual consequences, so far beyond our utmost conception, seem infinite. It seems to me that great love is a religion – perhaps the only great religion, since its source is the continuance of life, and because it creates a heaven in the midst of life's hellish phantasmagoria.'

Love is inevitably a consequence of the perception of loveliness. It writhes under constraint. Its very essence is liberty. It is compatible neither with obedience, jealousy nor fear. In its most pure, perfect and unlimited form its votaries live in confidence and equality.

Love has long been celebrated by the arts. Now it has become a subject for science. The classical age recognised three forms of love, modern writers up to 18. 'We can tell how love affects us,' wrote a dubious Henry Ward Beecher, 'but we cannot tell what love is.' Undeterred, contemporary psychologists have had a go, attempting to dissect love – the state of sexual affection – into its component parts. Thus Rubin devised a nine-point Loving Scale, Shostrom invented a Caring Relation Meter, Lasswell worked out a 50-item True-False Register, while Lee came up with the Six Colours of Love (SAMPLE for short – see right).

WHAT KIND OF LOVER ARE YOU ?

SAMPLE stands for six Greek words denoting different forms of love – storge, agape, mania, pragma, ludus and eros. Storge type lovers tend to be affectionate and companionable but devoid of passion. Agape lovers are generally patient, dutiful and altruistic. Mania type lovers tend to be obessive, jealous, even manic (as the name suggests). Pragma type lovers are practical, realistic, strong on compatability. Ludus lovers are playful, hedonistic, easy-come easy-go. Eros type lovers, not surprisingly, are into the erotic side of love, physical attractiveness, sensuality, imtimacy, rapport. Men tend to be more ludic and erotic than women, women more manic and pragmatic than men.

Men and women have different needs and disparate dreams and bring a different psychological and physiological apparatus to bear on the question of love and loving relationships. The consummation of love, which is often the end of love with a man, is only the beginning of love with a woman, a test of truth, a gauge of future pleasure, a sort of engagement for an intimacy to come. 'Man's desire is for the woman,' wrote the poet Coleridge, 'but the woman's desire is rarely other than for the desire of the man.' It is a woman's love, more than her body, that needs a mate; she finds no attraction in being merely possessed. The differences in hopes and expectations can lead to an irreconcilable tension. As Harry told Sally in the film *When Harry Met Sally*: 'Men and women can't be friends. The sex part always gets in the way.'

the decline of the steady state

In many parts of the Western world we live in a state of sexual confusion in which not only love but marriage and any kind of sexual steady state is viewed with apprehension and suspicion. This attitude is not new. Back in 1931 Robert Brittault concluded: 'For a male and a female to live together is biologically speaking an extremely unnatural thing to do.' Mae West said something similar but put it in a different way: 'Bigamy is having one husband too many,' she quipped. 'Monogamy is the same.' And she went on to say: 'Marriage is a great institution, but I'm not sure if I'm ready for an institution yet.'

With the gradual dissolution of the old communities in many Western countries, the lonely hearts columns and dating and marriage agencies have to some degree taken over the traditional role of the matchmaker. Over one million women between the ages of 25 and 34 are registered with dating agencies in the UK – a figure that has doubled in the last ten years. The agencies play a paradoxical role in the affairs of the human heart today, for in one way they are the sex appeal brokers of our time, in another they have brought back the age-old ethos of the arranged marriage. An agency questionnaire is like a résumé of this book – fill it in and you have the sex appeal profile of yourself – and who and what it is you are looking for.

the rise of the serial monogamist

In some countries in the West today there appears to be a trend away from conventional one-on-one monogamy towards serial monogamy. In a research study of divorce in 62 cultures around the world, Dr Helen Fisher concludes that serial monogamy is not so much a sign of social collapse as a return to the true grassroots of human behaviour. In her view, such a system is completely comprehensible in evolutionary terms. 97 per cent of other mammals do not practise long-term pair-bonding, and human beings evolved it not as a marriage for life, but as a stratagem that brought parents together long enough for the man to provide protection for the woman while she reared their offspring. By Dr Fisher's calculation, that phase lasted four years. Her study of divorce world-wide indicates that if a couple is going to divorce, they will do so at the end of that four-year phase. Sexual restlessness could thus be interpreted as an adaptive mechanism which evolved in order to provide the essential genetic variety that every species needs. There are many scientists who do not go along with this thesis, but given the high failure rate of modern marriage, serial mogamy might be a practical short-term compromise, even though it has built-in problems and suits the male more than the female. For any relationship that provides two-parent stability during the critical early period of child-rearing must be better than nothing.

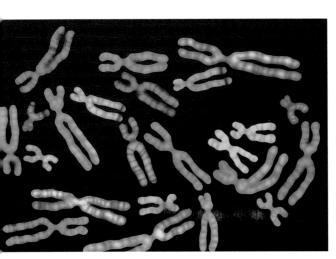

Sex appeal – from the twinkling of the eye to the passing of the genes. A coloured light micrograph of human female chromosomes made up mainly of DNA, carrying genes that determine the characteristics of the individual

the end of sexual civilization as we know it

Three decades and two generations since the sexual revolution of the permissive Sixties the old foundations have not just been shaken, they have been blown to smithereens. The breakdown of the old social structures – and with them marriage, family, community – the feminist revolution and the gay lobby, the radical shifts in people's priorities and preferences, the growing acceptance of androgyny and sexual ambiguity, the extraordinary advances in genetic engineering and medical technology, the apocalyptic catastrophe of AIDS, the singles option of auto-eroticism (half the flats of Paris are occupied by a single person), 'virtual sex' and sex in Cyberia – at the end of the twentieth century the world of sex is exploding in all directions like the very universe it has itself helped, on one tiny planet, to populate with human life.

And so where does all this leave sex appeal? Never has the importance of sex appeal been so widely appreciated, never has sex appeal been so avidly sought after, never have industry, media and the popular culture at large beavered so hard to satisfy the demand for sex appeal. And yet, never has sex appeal dazzled and delighted to such a confused and uncertain effect.

the egg and sperm race: 'take me to your breeder'

'Sex appeal,' we wrote at the beginning of this book, 'is the interface – the crucial, electric, mysterious interface – between the humdrum neuter everyday and the explosive sexual life of the individual and the species.' And we quoted Charles Darwin: 'The final aim of all love intrigues is nothing less than the composition of the next generation.' So it was once – so it was, indeed, when we started on this book. But, as we come to the end, so it is no longer. Consider, for example, just a few of the following recent developments in the science and technology of parenthood, which have made human fertility treatment one of the most high-profile and avant-garde branches of medicine:

■ The British Medical Association has approved a scheme for women to carry ovary donor cards, permitting their eggs to be used for research or implantation when they die. This scheme may be extended to children, so that in a few years' time it is possible that a child could be born by artificial techniques using an egg from a genetic mother who was a pre-pubescent 12-year-old killed in a car crash.

■ Near Washington DC a genetics institute buys human eggs for $6,000 for a cycle of three egg donations and then sells them to infertile women. There is no upper age-limit on the age of the women who buy them.

■ It is now possible to select the gender as well as the race of a child by artificial insemination. The London Gender Clinic offers to help couples produce 'designer babies' of the gender of their choice, most white customers wanting girls,

The future of sex appeal? Droplets of sperm being added to a petri dish containing ripe ova for in-vitro fertilization

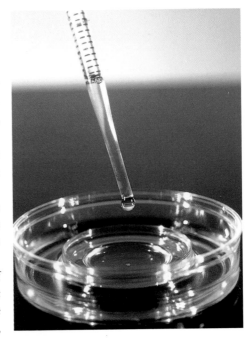

most Asians wanting boys – a practice condemned by the British Medical Association in all except strictly medical cases (e.g. when gender-linked diseases like haemophilia are involved). Before long it may be possible to manipulate the genes that make up human DNA and thus change the hair colour, intelligence and other characteristics of the unborn child.

■ Around the world tens of thousands of babies have been produced using frozen-thawed sperm. Now, as a form of male birth control, Professor Carl Djerassi of Stanford University in California, the 'father' of the Pill (and a very rich man), has proposed that young men in their prime should freeze their sperm samples in a liquid nitrogen sperm bank at a temperature of –196' Celsius, undergo a vasectomy to avoid the risk of an unplanned child, then retrieve their sperm sample 10, 20 or 30 years later to start a family by artifical insemination with the woman of their choice.

What was once the stuff of science fiction is now daily reality. 'The lid on Pandora's Box is open,' declared the chairman of the ethics committee of the British Medical Association. The brave new world of the designer baby is a long way from the glitzy frisson, the sensual spontaneity of the world of sex appeal – a long way, for that matter, from the urgent passion of sex itself.

THE ETERNAL QUARTET

Today a child can go out to play with not one but four different kinds of fathers – the genetic father (the sperm donor), the biological father (the sperm implanter), the legal father (who could be the donor in some countries) and the social father (the man the child regards as father).

sex in cyberia: 'strap in, tweak out, turn on.'

For the lonely, the jaded, the curious, the adventurous – all those in short for whom sex in the real world is either lacking or falling short – futuristic technology has now brought a brave new world of fake-believe called virtual sex, where almost anything can be made to seem to happen with almost anyone, though almost always nothing ever really does.

Virtual sex is one way in which state-of-the-art computer-generated technology facilitates the scientific fantasy of escaping our physical nature into a world of assumed identities and virtual selves. And in this new-found land of Cyberia a new lexicon of buzz words has been coined – cybersex, cyborgasm, erototronics, teledildonics and of course virtual sex itself.

Already the virtual reality (VR) user can take part in VR scenarios

A *CRI DE COEUR* FROM CYBERSPACE

From the depths of Cyberia a gay lonely hearts signal spells out a detailed decription of the kind of person the sender is looking for. Will the Internet come up with a happy end?

He is looking for a guy something like me: Canadian, 47, white, 6'4", 207 pounds, brown hair and deep-set blue eyes. Mom said I looked a bit like Marlon Brando when I was younger. I think I look a bit like Stephen Fry or Jeremy Brett.

He is black, 41 years old or younger. He has a firm body and tight-fitting skin. Boyish looking, small frame a plus. Overall handsome, with some flaw such as a burn or scar or small gap between the front teeth a plus. Tight short brillo-pad hair. No beard. Well-hung inordinately turns me on but is not necessary. He wears glasses. For me black skin is such a turn on, it overrides attributes I would otherwise find unappealing.

He is very tactile. He loves to kiss and cuddle for hours at a time. He is sexually very versatile. He likes to sleep tangled together. He loves to stare into my eyes for minutes at a time. Candlelight and fireplaces turn him on.

Ideally he would be Buddhist or New Age. Liberal views. Not a Republican. Altruistic. He does not consider it insane I gave away everything I owned, including my house, to help the Ethiopian famine victims.

He is a bit of a Peter Pan. He has not lost his childlike wonder. He enjoys charades, practical jokes, impersonations. Kids like him. He likes to talk to strangers. Likes to laugh himself silly. Likes big dogs and farm animals. Likes vegetarian food. He is interested in computers, the Third World, rain forests, the future. Plays the guitar and sings – folk, reggae, gospel, classical, sentimental, not country and western or rap. But no tobacco or hard drugs. This is not negotiable. Once a week marijuana, alcohol and poppers are OK.

He does not wear heavy colognes or deodorants. I want a guy with a pleasing natural body odour. I have an exceptionally keen sense of smell, and most colognes guys wear just make my nose tickle. But there are some natural and artificial scents that turn me on big time.

Though he might be boyish or androgynous, he does not exhibit effeminate or camp affectations in dress, body language or voice. It is the affectedness I find objectionable. Natural high-pitched voice for example is quite OK. Female clothing completely turns me off, so cross-dressing would not work. He loves to dress in bright solid colours or high contrast, sporty boyish looking. He avoids expensive stylish clothes.

He has a nice short masculine name like Jim, Steve, Chip, Trevor, Travis, Curtis, Tim, Don, Ken or Roy. A unique African name like Shakunya would also be nice.

His excusable 'flaws' are: low IQ, poverty, philandering, brattishness, temper. He is not a chronic whiner. He should be able to handle my faults: lack of concern about clothing (often wrinkled or torn), thinning hair, unusually liberal views, morning dog breath, manic depressive.

P.S. A guy who fits this description wandered into my life the day after I posted it on the Internet. It was love at first sight and he is moving in tomorrow.

BOBBY, VANCOUVER, CANADA

of combat, adventure, scenic flight and fantasy, even dance the night away in a virtual night-club. And already, it goes without saying, virtual sex is up and sighing in the form of Virtual Valerie and other virtual sex sirens who use computerized come-ons to tempt the VR lothario towards cybersex bliss in an interactive sexual encounter.

Before long there will be a Virtual Victor. As one 36-year-old mother of two explained: 'Virtual reality sex is very appealing to women of my age. I like to have options and this is another alternative – one night it's a date, the next a vibrator, the next virtual sex. It's also safe sex with someone I know well: myself.'

teledildonic sex appeal

True interactive sex must await the perfection of 'feely' sensor technology to deliver the '3D digital orgasms' which magazines like *Future Sex* predict will one day provide an alternative to the emotional snarls and physical perils of today's real thing. As yet the 'dick sleeve' and 'data bikini' which comprise the prototype 'feely' hardware

Erotic application of virtual reality. The man gropes his virtual conquest, whose image is provided by his headset, data glove and an unseen computer system

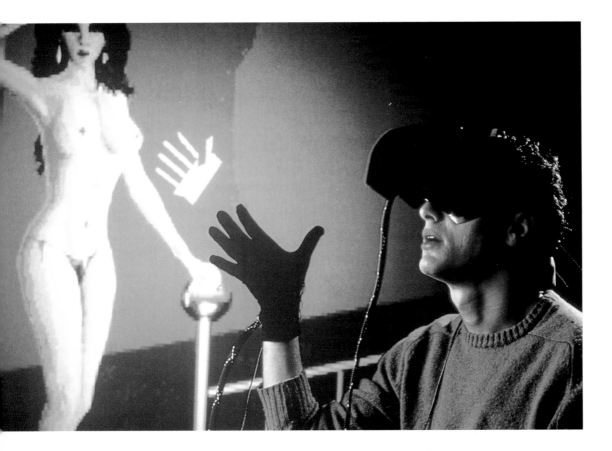

designed to be worn over the male and female genitalia are grotesque robotesque contraptions which seem more like ganglia out of *Blade Runner* than Woody Allen's celebrated 'orgasmotron' in the movie *Sleeper*. Undeterred, virtual sex nerds promise realistic desktop cyborgasms with the computer virtual date of your dreams by the end of the century. Wearing a diaphanous bodysuit embedded with a multitude of effector electrodes, they claim, you will be able to plug into the telephone network and connect with someone similarly garbed and in this way partake of the joy of erotic interfacing without having to meet. After all, the pleasure centres of the brain can be tickled by a flower, a sunset, an ice cream, a daiquiri, dope, sex – a host of things. So why not tickle the brain direct, by electronic or other means?

Related technology is taking virtual sex into other even more futuristic directions. Professor Kevin Warwick is a cyberneticist at Reading University working in the field of virtual sex and teledildonics, a technique for communicating physical sensations over a distance which promises a more interactive form of virtual sex. A film or video image of a virtual sex partner is projected on to a bed (after transmission across the world by satellite if need be) and can then be caressed erotically by a real partner who joins the virtual partner on the bed. A range of sensed feelings, including touch and smell as well as sight and sound, can be built into the teledildonic experience, and Professor Warwick can see a time, not too far in the future, when a virtual sexual experience can be obtained with the virtual person of your choice, using fully developed 'genitally-sensitive' aids of the sort demonstrated in the 1992 American movie *Lawnmower Man*.

Obviously teledildonic sex has the potential to reach a vast market, including for example couples who are geographically apart and want to make love long-distance. 'You'd put on your headsets, turn on your computers, modem each other and have sex that way,' claims Carla Sinclair, editor-in-chief of the American futurist magazine *bOING bOING*.

By harnessing new digital computer technology developed for the television and film industry – specifically, morphing and digital cloning of film and video images of people's faces, bodies and movements (known as 'motion capture') – the real-life lover may one day be able to enjoy a startlingly broader choice of virtual partners, from the beauties of times past and not-so past, like Queen Nefertiti and Marilyn Monroe, to the supermodels of today, or the girl or boy next door, or your absent partner or spouse.

robot love

Virtual sex remains exactly what it says – 'virtual', an illusory simulation. Critics contend that dreams can never be truly turned into reality in this way and that virtual realists are not recreating reality but simply losing their grasp of it. However, advances in robot technology offer the possibility of a virtual sex partner who is a lot closer to the real thing, and if robot technology is combined with advances in the fields of biochemistry, genetics and reconstructive plastic surgery it is possible to envisage a robot lover of an admittedly distant future with human-like intelligence and neuro-emotional responses, built-in sex appeal, synthetic flesh and all the necessary anatomical purtenances – a huge advance on the pump-up rubber dolls still imported from Taiwan.

According to Professor Warwick, robot intelligence resembling that of human beings will be around within the next 50 years, and it is possible to envisage such an advanced robot equipped with fully developed sexual responses.

One day, perhaps, a whole range of physically realistic, sexually responsive robots, each with an inventory of superlative sex appeal specifications to suit every taste, will be available for purchase or hire by a growing segment of the human populace jaded with the real thing and thirsting for novelty.

Perhaps one day the cybersex appeal ideal of your dreams will be yours for the asking at your nearest cybersex appeal emporium. 'A robot lover, sir? Of course, sir. Got lots. Straight, bi, gay, transsexual or hermaphrodite, sir? Erotomaniac or girl-next-door-type? Apple bottom or pear, hourglass or straight-cut? A touch of oriental for the evening, or something a little more robust for the poolside, a belly-dancer from the Congo, perhaps, our bargain of the month? And for madam, our new line in cyberhunks, maybe? Or a really smart new toy-boy from our Stuttgart factory? A superstud? A Schwarzenegger look-alike? Of course, madam. Well-hung or long-life or both? You can choose voice type and chat mode to suit your mood – husky, schmalzy, classy, or blue, double bass or falsetto, Eskimo, Zulu or Papuan Pidgin, monosyllabic, inarticulate or dumb. Dumb, sir? Blonde, sir? I'll see if we've got one in stock...'

Is all this pure cyberballs? Perhaps, but so were old movies about men on the moon. Is any of it desirable? Opinion is divided. Carla Sinclair finds some points in favour of non-human sex, arguing that at least you can't catch AIDS from cybersex and that traditional sex will always remain an option. Lisa Palac, editor of the Californian magazine *Future Sex*, sees artificial sex as a potential for good – a way round the fear of intimacy that many people have always had – 'But I don't think we are ever going to have an experience that simulates reality so closely that when you open your eyes in a virtual reality world you are not going to be able to tell whether the sex you are having is real or not.'

Sex in Cyberia may be read as a doomsday scenario by some. But most doomsday scenarios (*Brave New World* and *Nineteen Eighty-four* for example) have almost always proved excessively pessimistic. Sheer cussed human nature always wins through in the end. So it will surely be with human sex and sex appeal. Physical and romantic love at a human level will always prevail – perhaps in conjunction with cybersex technology as an optional aid rather than a complete alternative model, let alone the dominant form of sexual relations.

Sexual desire and its sibling sexual attraction have remained among the profoundest of human experiences, and given rise to some of man's most immortal utterances in art, literature and song. Could any of us seriously imagine any original, non-programmed lines in celebration of human sensual love being spoken or appreciated by a robot lover, even if it was an exact copy of a Bardot or Brando at 20? Only a complete flesh-and-blood human being in love could spontaneously utter something as simple and poignant – and as mischievous – as this naive-seeming little paean in praise of physical love and sex appeal:

> 'When I am sad and weary
> When I think all hope has gone
> When I walk along High Holborn
> I think of you with nothing on.'

MASTER CLASS

HOW TO FIND A MATE

Many people, when they meet a potential partner for the first time, expect there to be some instant spark of chemistry. It's a hangover from the romantic perception that surrounds the quest for finding a mate, and it can prove terribly misleading. Of course, it does happen. It might come down to something like pheromones, but it's almost certainly to do with a connection at some level. It could simply be that a couple's experiences have coincided at that moment. It is a sympathy that transcends the purely physical. Men, more than women, expect to experience some kind of instant rapport of this sort. But, more often than not, when people do experience it, the whole thing is liable to end in tears. Instant chemistry is not a very reliable indicator, and it certainly doesn't have to be there at the outset.

Try to not to dismiss someone on first meeting if the so-called chemistry isn't there. People frequently develop wonderful relationships after simply growing on each other, and simply liking each other provides a much better basis than instant sexual attraction.

Commonality of hopes, beliefs, feelings and values, agreement on such major things as religion, politics, divorce, children and money are all terribly important. Most people marry best or form good long-term relationships when there is a basis of common aspirations, experience (including educational and cultural experience) and attitudes.

Age, of course, is another factor. It is a sadly frequently repeated truism that men want to marry or remarry women younger than they are. It is all under-pinned by a woman's ability to have children, and inevitably creates problems. A lot of women, on the other hand, then don't want to marry a man much older than they are – they may have been widowed once already.

From around the age of 35, women begin to have less choice when it comes to finding a marriage partner, and men more and more. By the time you reach the fifties age-group, there are masses and masses of women and fewer and fewer men. But those who there are are starting to die off. Others, wounded emotionally or financially by divorce, decide not to risk remarriage,

while the growing social acceptance of homosexuality and bisexuality also means that men no longer have to marry against their instincts. The effect is simply to reduce the number of men on the marriage market.

Though it is also perfectly acceptable for a man of 55 to marry someone younger, it still doesn't work the other way round. Women in their thirties for instance seldom look for a younger man, partly because, relatively speaking, a man of 30 is less mature than a woman of 30, and by the time a woman has reached 50 she knows very well that a man wants to meet a woman who is younger than him. The toy-boy syndrome doesn't happen very often, and when it does the relationship tends to be an affair rather than long term.

People are still looking for love, but today purely romantic love is no longer enough. The pressures on partnerships and marriages are terrific and something as flimsy as 'being in love' isn't a sufficiently strong basis. The economic aspects of marriage have also changed. The old divisions of labour, where the woman wasn't working and needed a man to support the household has, in some quarters, gone almost by the board.

Today, amongst women in their 30s, the stipulation is that the man should not be earning less than themselves, whereas the man is less likely to be bothered about how much a woman earns – so long as she's solvent. Some men in principle are quite happy if a woman is earning more than they are, but it can make quite a lot of men feel a little nervous, principally because of what it implies about relative status and the kind of lifestyle the woman will have become accustomed to. For many women, the *amount* of money a man earns is less important than whether he is successful in his chosen field and in his own terms.

Having said that, the quest for a partner should be fun. First and foremost you should enjoy it. Keep an open mind, and not have a too cut-and-dried image about what is going to be important to you. Look forward to meeting new people and remember that there are a lot of bonuses to be had en route. It's worth finding someone that's right because life is a lot more fun when there is somebody to share it with.

MASTER CLASS

HOW TO KEEP A MATE

For every strength there is a concomitant weakness. Action profiling is a system of behavioural analysis which allows for the differences in a relationship and sees them as complementary strengths. It is a means of understanding our behaviour based on non-verbal information. It derives from the primitive movement patterns that we display unconsciously when we become involved in an action that requires us to think. It is the unusual situations, rather than the ones we have learnt how to react to, that display these sorts of patterns.

Basically, we move in three planes: the horizontal plane, when your mind is trying to get to grips with its environment and finding out what there is around it; the vertical plane, which tends to be a statement as to where you stand in relation to this environment, what you think is important, and what you plan to do; and the sagittal (fore-and-aft) plane, which is where you involve your mind in what you're actually going to do about the environment – are you going to go into it or withdraw from it?

Everybody has got his or her own unique choice – he, for example, might spend 40 per cent of his activity getting to grips with the environment, 45 per cent in making things happen and 15 per cent on stating where he stands. His partner, on the other hand, might spend 45 per cent of her time stating where she stands and less time in the other planes. So, in effect, they complement each other, with one spending energy where the other doesn't and vice versa.

As long as we can understand this process of complementariness, we can understand and make allowances for the fact that when we are at one stage in the process, our partner might be at another. If we don't understand it, the very things that attracted you could end up ultimately repelling. Someone who is indecisive, for example, may initially be attracted to someone who takes control and likes to be in command. As the first flush of excitement wears off, however, this very difference may become a source of irritation. But the important thing to remember is that it is exactly the same person, behaving in exactly the same way that once attracted you.

When you are interacting with people you have four potential means of interaction – sharing (literally sharing your ideas, views or actions with other people); being private (your preference is to keep yourself to yourself, to keep what you plan to do and what you are thinking close to your chest); remaining neutral (if you make a statement and someone picks you up on it, it's fine with you, if they don't and wish to remain private, that too is fine); and finally, versatility (sometimes you like sharing, sometimes you feel like being private).

The problem is that many people vary how they interact as they move through the three planes – someone who likes to share their ideas as they are getting to know their environment may become private when they are deciding what they are going to do about it, and become sharing again when they decide how they are going to act on it. This can be very disconcerting as people find it hard to understand why somone who seemed so open and above board to start with, suddenly turns their back to make the decisions by themselves.

Very often people feel like they are being shut out, when, in fact, they aren't. It is this interaction and failure to understand what's going on that is one of the most serious causes behind relationship breakdown because people find it so very puzzling.

PENROSE AND BILL HALSON, DIRECTORS OF THE KATHARINE ALLEN MARRIAGE & ADVICE BUREAU, LONDON

bibliography

Ackerman, Diane, *A Natural History of the Senses,* Chapmans, London, 1992

Allan, N. (ed.), *'Singles Bars',* Urban Life Styles, Dubuque, Indiana, William, C. Brown

Allman, William F., *The Mating Game,* U.S. News & World Report, July 19, 1993

An Intelligent Man's Guide, Tunisia, 1180 A.D.

And God Created Bardot, BBC1, September, 1994

Argyle, Michael, *The Psychology of Interpersonal Behaviour,* Penguin Books, London, 1990

Ash, Juliet and Wright, Lee (ed.), *Costume,* Cassell, London, 1963

Asimov, Isaac, *Asimov's New Guide to Science,* Penguin Books, London, 1987

Bain, Alexander, Professor of Logic in the University of Aberdeen, *Mental and Moral Science. A Compendium of Psychology and Ethics,* London, 1884

Baker, R.R. and Bellis M.A., *'Number of Sperm in Human Ejaculates Varies in Accordance with Sperm Competition',* Animal Behaviour, 37:867-9

Baker, R.R. and Bellis, M.A., *'Human Sperm Competition: Infidelity, the Female Orgasm and Kamikaze Sperm',* Paper delivered to the fourth annual meeting of the Human Behavior and Evolution Society, Albuquerque, New Mexico, July 22-6, 1992

Bancroft, Dr John, MRC, Edinburgh, *interview,* 1994

Beauvoir, Simone de, *The Second Sex,* Four Square Books, 1966

Bell, Ralcy Husted, *Memoirs and Mistresses, The Amatory Recollections of a Physician,* William Faro Inc, New York, 1932

Bell, Thomas MD, *Kalygonomia*

or *The Laws of Female Beauty,* Walpole Press, London, 1899

Bell, Q., *On Human Finery,* Hogarth Press, London, 1976

Bennett, Catherine: 'Why short men don't measure up'. *Esquire,* August 1993

Bennett, Catherine, *Esquire,* July/August 1994

Berger, John, *Ways of Seeing,* BBC & Penguin Books, 1972

Berkowitz, L. (ed.),Berscheid, E and Walster, E, *Physical Attractiveness,* Advances in Experimental Social Psychology, 7, Academic Press, New York, 1974

Berne, Eric, *Games People Play.* Penguin, 1968

Betzig, Laura, *Despotism and Differential Reproduction: A Darwinian View of History,* Hawthorne, New York, Aldine De Gruyter, 1986

Betzig, Laura and Weber, Samantha, *Polygyny in American Politics,* Politics and the Life Sciences, February, 1993

Betzig, Laura, *Roman Monogamy,* Ethology and Sociobiology, 13: 351-383 (1992)

Betzig, Laura, *Roman Polygyny,* Ethology and Sociobiology, 13: 309-349 (1992)

Betzig, Laura, *History, The Sociobiological Imagination,* ed. Mary Maxwell, Albany, 1991

Betzig, Laura, *Sex, Succession and Stratification in the First Six Civilizations,* 1993

Birtles, Jasmine (ed.), *Women on Men,* Michael O'Mara Books, London, 1994

Blacking, John (ed.), *The Anthropology of the Body,* ASA Conference on The Anthropology of the Body, Belfast, Academic Press, 1977

Block, Iwan, *Anthropological Studies in the Strange Sexual Practices of All Races In All Ages*

Keene Wallis (trans.), Anthropological Press, New York, 1933

Body Language, Sex Signals, Ideas Unlimited, Portsmouth, 1991

Bornoff, Nicholas, *Pink Samurai,* Grafton, London, 1991

Botting, Douglas, *The Amazon Voyage of the Bom Jesus dos Navegantes,* unpublished MS, 1966

Boxer, Stephen, Royal Shakespeare Company, National Theatre, *interview,* 1995

Braddock, Joseph, *The Bridal Bed,* Corgi Books, 1963

Bragg, Melvyn, *Rich: The Life of Richard Burton,* London, 1988

Brando, Marlon, with Robert Lindsay, *Brando: Songs My Mother Taught Me,* Century, 1994

Brantôme, Pierre de, *The Lives of Gallant Ladies,* 1600

Brecher, Ruth and Edward (ed.), *An Analysis of Human Sexual Response,* Panther, 1968

Brierley, J.K., *A Natural History of Man,* Heinemann, London, 1970

Brinkworth, Lisa, *Sunday Times* 2/5/93

British Medical Association, *Complete Family Health Encyclopaedia,* Dr Tony Smith (medical ed.). Dorling Kindersley, London, 1990

British Psychological Society, *Symposium on Evolutionary Theory and Human Social Behaviour,* March 1994

British Sociological Association, *Sexualities in Social Context,* BSA Conference, University of Central Lancashire, March 1994

Brook, Stephen (ed.), *The Penguin Book of Infidelities,* Viking, London, 1994

Bull, Ray and Rumsey, Nichola, *The Social Psychology of Facial Appearance,* Springer-Verlag, New York, 1988

Bull, Ray, University of Portsmouth, *interview,* 1994

Bulwer, John, *Anthropometamorphosis,* 1650

Burnham, Arthur, *interview,* 1995

Burton, Sir Richard (trans.), *Kama Sutra,* Luxor Press, London, 1966

Burton, Sir Richard (trans.), *The Perfumed Garden,* Luxor Press, London, 1966

Bush Boake Allen Ltd, *interview*

Buss, David M, *The Evolution of Desire, Strategies of Human Mating,* Basic Books, New York, 1994

Buss, David, M, *Sex Differences in Human Mate Preferences: Evolutionary Hypotheses Tested in 37 Cultures,* Behavioral and Brain Sciences, 12:1-49, 1989

Buss, David, University of Chicago, *interview,* 1994

Carruthers, Dr Malcolm, *Hormone Replacement Therapy for Men,* London 1990

Carruthers, Dr Malcolm, Andrology Centre, London, *interview,* 1994

Cashdan, Elizabeth, *'Attracting Mates: Effects of Parental Investment on Mate Attraction Strategies',* Ethology and Sociobiology 14: 1-24 (1993)

Chang, Jung, *Wild Swans,* Flamingo, London, 1993

Cinefile: Marlon Brando – Wild One, Channel 4, August, 1994

Cladel, Judith, *Auguste Rodin,* Paris, 1903

Clark, Kenneth, *The Nude,* Penguin Books, London,1985

Cleland, John, *Fanny Hill,* GP Putnam's Sons, 1963

Cohen, David, *Body Language in Relationships*, Sheldon Press, 1992

Cohen, Leonard, 'Poem', *Poems 1956-1968*, Jonathan Cape, London 1970

Comfort, Alex, *Sex in Society*, Penguin Books, Middlesex, 1964

Cook, Mark (ed.), *The Bases of Human Sexual Attraction*, Academic Press, London, 1981

Cook, Mark and Wilson, Glenn (ed.), *Love & Attraction*, International Conference on Love and Attraction, Swansea, 1977, Pergamon, Oxford, 1979

Cook, Mark and McHenry, Robert, *Sexual Attraction*, Pergamon, Oxford, 1978

Curry, Walter C., *The Middle English Ideal of Personal Beauty*, Baltimore, 1916

Dabbs, James

Daily Mail, 27/2/94

Daily Express 20/4/94

Darwin, Charles, *The Origin of the Species by Means of Natural Selection, or the Preservation of Favoured Races in the Struggle for Life*, John Murray, London, 1859

Darwin, Charles, *The Descent of Man and Selection in Relation to Sex*, Macmillan, London, 1883

Davies, David M, *Journey into the Stone Age*, 1969

Dawkins, Richard, *The Selfish Gene*, Oxford University Press, Oxford

Dodds, Dr George, *The Pheromone Foundation*, University of Warwick, 1993

Doust, J.W.L. and Huszka, L. 'Amines and aphrodisiacs in chronic schizophrenia', Journal of Nervous and Mental Disease 155 (1972), 261-4

Dove, Roja, Professeur de Parfum, Guerlain, *interview*, 1994

Downer, Lesley, *Sunday Times Magazine*, 6/11/94

Duck, Steve: *Theory and Practice of Interpersonal Attraction*, 1977

Dunbar, Robin, University College London, *interview*, 1994

Dutton, D.G. and Aron, A.P., *Some evidence for heightened sexual attraction under conditions of high anxiety*', Journal of Personality and Social Psychology 30 (1974), 510-17

Edgren, Gretchen, *The Playboy Book*, Mitchell Beazley, London, 1994

Edwards-Jones, Imogen, *Sunday Times*, 4/7/93

Egypt: Land of the Pharaohs, Time-Life, Alexandria, Va., 1992

Ekman, Paul (ed.), *Emotion in the Human Face*, Cambridge University Press, Cambridge, 1982

Elgort, Arthur, *Models Manual*, Grand Street Press, 1993

Ellis, A and Abarbanel, A., *The Encyclopedia of Sexual Behaviour, volumes 1 and 2*, Hawthorn, New York, 1961

Ellis, Havelock, *Studies in the Psychology of Sex*, New York, 1936

Ephron, Nora, *When Harry Met Sally*, 1985

Erox Corporation, *Realm*, New York, Fremont, 1993/1994

Etcoff, Nancy L., *Beauty and the Beholder*, Nature, Vol. 368, pp186-7, 17 March 1994

Evening Standard, 16/5/94

Fast, Julius, *Body Language*, Pan Books, London, 1971

Fast, Julius and Bernstein, Meredith, *Sexual Chemistry, What It Is, How To Use It*, Arrow, London, 1984

Feinstein, Sharon, *Yes! Magazine*, 16/1/94

Fellous, Collette, *Guerlain*, trans. Elizabeth Thomas, Denoel, 1989

Fennell, Tim, *Which One Would You Choose?* New Woman, September 1993

Fielding, William J, *Strange Customs of Courtship and Marriage*, Four Square Books, London, 1964

Finck, Henry T., *Romantic Love and Personal Beauty, vol. II.* New York, 1887

Fit for Fun, 11/1994, Hamburg

Flaubert, Gustave, *Flaubert in Egypt*, trans. Francis Steegmuller, The Bodley Head, 1972

Fleming, Ian, *Diamonds Are Forever*

Flügel, John Carl, *The Psychology of Clothes*, L & V Woolf, Institute of Psycho-Analysis, London, 1930

Ford, C.S. and Beach, F.A., *Patterns of Sexual Behavior*, Harper & Row, New York, 1951

Forrest, Derek William, *Francis Galton: The Life and Work of a Victorian Genius*', London, Elek, 1974

France, Louise, 'Linford Christie', *New Woman*, Sept 1993

French, Sean, *Bardot*, Pavilion Books, 1994

Freud, Sigmund, *Drei Abhandlungen zur Sexualtheorie, Three Essays on the Theory of Sexuality* trans./ed. James Strachey, Hogarth Press, London, 1962

Freud, Sigmund, *Sie Traumdeutung, The Interpretation of Dreams*, trans./ed. James Strachey, George Allen and Unwin, London, 1961

Galton, Francis, *Memories of My Life*, Methuen & Co, London, 1908

Galton, Francis, *Inquiries into Human Faculty and its*

Development, Macmillan, London, 1883

Garland, Madge, *The Changing Face of Beauty, Four Thousand Years of Beautiful Women*, Weidenfeld & Nicolson, London, 1957

Gilan, Yvonne, *interview*, 1995

Glass, Lillian, *He Says, She Says*, Piatkus, London, 1992

Goody, Jack, *The Development of the Family and Marriage in Europe*, Cambridge University Press, Cambridge, 1983

Gourmont, Rémy de, *The Nature of Love: Essay on Sexual Instinct*

Greer, Germaine, *The Female Eunuch*, Paladin, London, 1971

Grice, Julia, *What Makes a Woman Sexy*, Piatkus, London, 1988

Haire, Norman (ed.), *Encyclopaedia of Sexual Knowledge*, Francis Aldor, London, 1936

Halliday, Tim, *Survival in the Wild – Sexual Strategy*, Oxford University Press, Oxford, 1980

Halson, Bill and Penrose, *interview*, 1995

Hass, Hans, *The Human Animal*, Hodder and Stoughton, London, 1970

Hayes, Mark, Vidal Sassoon, *interview*, 1995

Hegeler, Inge and Sten, *An ABZ of Love*, David Hohnen (trans.), Neville Spearman, London, 1966

Hendrick, Susan and Hendrick, Clyde, *Romantic Love*, Sage Publications, California, 1992

Holmberg, A.R., *The Siriono*, Unpublished thesis, Yale University, 1946

Horizon: Assault on the Male, BBC2, April 1994

Mrs Humphry, *How To be Pretty Though Plain*, Truth Magazine,

London, 1899

Huston, T.L (ed.), *Foundations of Interpersonal Attraction*, Academic Press, New York, 1974

International Academy of Sex Research, *Abstracts of Twentieth Annual Meeting*, Edinburgh, July, 1994

Ionnides, Dr Andrew, Open University, *interview*, 1994

Jackson, Cindy, *interview*, 1994

Jackson, Cindy, *Consumer Report*, The Cosmetic Surgery Network

Jenkins, David, *Richard Burton - A Brother Remembered*, Century, London 1994

Jilson, Joyce, *The Fine Art of Flirting*, Grafton, London, 1990

Johnson, Robert A, *The Psychology of Romantic Love*, Arkana, London, 1936

Jones, Dylan, *Sunday Times Magazine*, 1994

Jones, Judy, *Observer*, 2/1/94

Jones, Steve, *The Language of the Genes*, London 1993

Jong, Erica, *Fear of Flying*, Panther, 1977

Jong, Erica, *Fear of Fifty*

Kahn, Elayne and Rudinfsky, David, *Love Codes, Understanding Men's Secret Body Language*, Piatkus, London, 1989

Kalma, Akko P. and de Weerth, Carolina, *The Influence of Situational Uncertainty on Females' Attraction to Two Types of Dominant Males* (draft), 1994

Kalma, Akko P. Van Houten-Pilkes, Simone and de Weerth, Carolina, *Bodily Contact Initiatives in Public: A Mate Retention Tactic?* 1994

Kenrick, Douglas T., *Evolutionary Social Psychology: From Sexual Selection To Social Cognition*, Advances in Experimental Social Psychology, Vol. 26

Kenrick, Douglas T., *Age and Human Mate Selection*, (under review) Scientific American

Kenrick, Douglas T., Neuberg, Steven L., Zierk, Kristin L. and Krones, Jacquelyn M., *Evolution and Social Cognition: Contrast Effects as a Function of Sex, Dominance, and Physical Attractiveness*, Personality and Social Psychology Bulletin, Vol. 20, No. 2, April 1994

Kern, Stephen, *Anatomy and Destiny*, 1975

Kirk-Smith, M.D., *Human Olfactory Communication*, University of Ulster

Kirk-Smith, M.D., University of Ulster, *interview*, 1994

Knapton, Ernest John, *Empress Josephine*, Cambridge, Massachusetts, 1963

Knight, Chris and Power, Camilla, *Ritual & The Origins of Symbolism*, Department of Sociology, University of East London, 1994

Lacey, Peter, *The History of the Nude in Photography*, Bantam Books, New York, 1964

Lailan, Young, *The Naked Face*, Century, London, 1993

Langlois, J.H. and Roggman, L.A.. *'Attractive Faces Are Only Average'*, Psychological Science, 1, 115-121

Lawrence, D.H., *Sex Versus Loveliness*

Lawrence, D.H., *Assorted Articles*

Lehninger, Albert L., *Principles of Biochemistry*, New York, 1982

Levi-Strauss, Claude, *Tristes Tropiques*, John and Doreen Weightmann (trans.), Penguin Books, Middlesex, 1976

Lewis, C.S., *The Four Loves*, Fontana Books, 1966

Lewis, David, *The Secret Language of Success, How to Read and Use Body Language*, Corgi, London, 1990

Lewis, David, *Loving and Loathing*, Constable, 1985

Liebowitz, Michael R., *The Chemistry of Love*, Little Brown, New York, 1983

Liggett, Arline and John, *The Tyranny of Beauty*, Gollancz, London, 1989

Liggett, John, *The Human Face*, Constable, London, 1974

Lloyd-Elliott, Martin, *The Secrets of Attraction*, Hamlyn, 1995

Low, Bobbi S., *Communication*, 1994

Lurie, Alison, *The Language of Clothes*, Hamlyn, London, 1983

Lyle, Jane, *Body Language*, Hamlyn, London, 1990

Lyle, Jane, *Understanding Body Language*, Chancellor, London, 1993

MacDougald, Duncan Jr, *Aphrodisiacs and Anaphrodisiacs; Beauty; Language and Sex; Music and Sex*, Encyclopaedia of Sex, op. cit.

MacLaine, Shirley, *Dance While You Can*

Malinowski, Bronislaw Kasper, *The Sexual Life of Savages in North-Western Melanesia*, Routledge & Sons, London, 1932

Manso, Peter, *Brando*, Weidenfeld, 1994

Marsh, Peter, *The Language of Touch*, Eye to Eye, Sidgwick & Jackson, London, 1988

Marwick, Arthur, *Beauty In History*, Thames & Hudson, London, 1988

Massey, Eric, *contribution*, 1995

Matthews, Rupert, *Body Language*, Chancellor, London, 1993

McFarland, David, *The Oxford Companion to Animal Behaviour*, Oxford University Press, Oxford, 1981

McKnight, Gerald, *The Skin Game*, Sidgwick & Jackson, London, 1989

Mead, Margaret, *Growing Up In New Guinea*, Penguin Books, London, 1954

Mead, Margaret, *Coming of Age in Samoa*, Penguin Books, London. 1954

Miller, Bill, *interview*, 1995

Milton, Sylvia, *interview*, 1995

Mitchell, Adrian, 'Celia, Celia', *For Beauty Douglas*, 1982

Mori, *Sex and the Singles*, 1993

Mori/Daily Express, *Modern Man*, 1986

Mori/Daily Express, *Sex and the British*, July, 1991

Morris, Desmond, *The Naked Ape*, Corgi Books, London,1969

Morris, Desmond, *The Human Zoo*, Jonathan Cape, London, 1969

Morris, Desmond, *Manwatching*, Jonathan Cape, London, 1977

Morris, Desmond, *Bodywatching*, Grafton, London, 1987

Morris, Desmond, *Animalwatching*, Cape, London 1990

Morris, Desmond, *Intimate Behaviour*, Vintage, London,1994

Morris, Desmond, *The Human Animal*, BBC Books, London, 1994

Muller, Julia, *The H & R Book of Perfume*, Glöss Verlag, Hamburg, 1992

Munthe, Axel, *The Story of San Michele*, London, 1929

Murray, Middleton J. (ed.), *The Journal of Katherine Mansfield*, 1954

Nash, Ogden, 'Reflection on

Ice-Breaking', 'Candy is Dandy', *Collected Works of Ogden Nash*, André Deutsch, London 1983

Neville, Richard, *Playpower*, Paladin, London, 1971

Newby, P.H., *The Egypt Story*, New York, 1985

Newcastle Journal

Nichols, Virginia, *Interview*, 1995

Nirenberg, Gerard and Calero, Henry, *How to Read a Person Like a Book*, Thorsons, London, 1980

Nourse, Alan E, *The Body*, Time-Life Books, 1969

O'Donnell, James P. *The Berlin Bunker*, J.M Dent & Sons, London, 1979

Orbach, Susie, *Fat is a Feminist Issue*, Hamlyn, Middlesex, 1979

Orth, Maureen, *Vanity Fair*, May 1993

Ovid, *The Erotic Poems, The Art of Love*, trans. Peter Green, Penguin Books, New York, 1982

Panni, Philipp, *Interview*, 1995

Parker, Andrew: *Your Genes Turn Me On*, Newcastle Journal, 13 Feb 1993

Parker, Dorothy, 'General Review of the Sex Situation', *The Collected Dorothy Parker*, Penguin Books, 1989

Partridge, James, *Changing Faces, The Challenge of Facial Disfigurement*, Penguin, Middlesex, 1990

Partridge, James, *interview*, 1994

Pasternak, Anna, *Princess In Love*, Bloomsbury, London, 1994

Paterson, Wilma and Behan, Peter, *Salmon and Women, The Feminine Angle*, Witherby, London, 1990

Patzer, Gordon L., *The Physical*

Attractiveness Phenomena, Plenum, New York, 1985

Pearsall, Ronald, *The Worm in the Bud*, Penguin Books, London, 1983

Pease, Allan, *Body Language*, Sheldon Press, 1984

Pennybaker, J.W., Dyer, M.A., Caulkins, R.S., Litowixz. D.L., Acjerman, P.L. and Anderson, D.B., *Don't the girls get prettier at closing time: A country and western application to psychology'*, Personality and Social Psychology Bulletin, 5, 122-125

Perrett, D.I., May, K.A. and Yoshikawa, S., *Facial Shape and Judgements of Female Attractiveness*, Nature, 368, pp 239-42, March 1994

Plutarch, *The Lives and Loves of the Noble Grecians and Romans*, trans. John Dryden

Postman, Neil, *Amusing Ourselves To Death*, Heinemann, London

Ratcliff, Rosemary, *Dear Worried Brown Eyes*, Robert Maxwell, London, 1969

Rees, Nigel, *A Year of Stings and Squelches*, London, 1985

Rheingold, Howard, *Virtual Reality*, Mandarin Paperbacks, London, 1992

Ridley, Matt, *The Red Queen, Sex and the Evolution of Human Nature*, Viking 1993

Roberts, Robert, *The Classic Slum*, 1971

Rossi, William A, *The Sex Life of the Foot and Shoe*, Routledge and Kegan Paul, London, 1977

Rowe, Newton A, *The Missionary Menace*, Wishart & Co., 1932

Rudofsky, Bernard, *The Unfashionable Human Body*, Hart-Davis, London, 1972

Sagan, Carl and Druyan, Ann, *Shadows of Forgotten Ancestors*, Arrow, London, 1993

Samaras, Thomas T., *The Truth About Your Height: Exploring the Myths and Realities of Human Size and its Effects on Performance*, 1994

Saxton, Martha, *Jayne Mansfield and the American 50s*, Houghton Miffin Co, Boston, 1975

Schopenhauer, Arthur, *On Women*

Seltman, Charles, *Women in Antiquity*, Pan Books, 1957

Sieghart, Mary Ann, *The Times* 9/4/94

Singh, Devendra, *Body shape and women's attractiveness. The critical role of waist-to-hip ratio*, Human Nature, Vol. 4, No. 3, pp 297-321, 1993

Singh, Devendra, *Adaptive significance of female physical attractiveness: role of waist-to-hip ratio*, Journal of Personality and Social Psychology, Vol. 65, No. 2, pp 293-307, 1993

Shakespeare, William, *Antony and Cleopatra*

Small, Meredith F., *The Evolution of Female Sexuality and Mate Selection in Humans*, Human Nature, Vol. 3, No. 2, pp. 133-156

Smart, Kate, *interview*, 1995

Smith, Anthony, *The Mind*, Hodder and Stoughton, London, 1984

Smith, Anthony, *contribution*, 1985

Sontag, Linda, *Finding the Love of Your Life*, Piccadilly, London, 1993

Sunday Times, Profile: Marlon Brando, 31/7/94

Spillane, Mary, *interview*, 1995

Steele, Valerie, *Fashion and Eroticism, Ideals of Feminine Beauty from the Victorian Era to the Jazz Age*, Oxford University Press, Oxford, 1985

Steingarten, Jeffrey, *The Sweet Smell of Sex*, Vogue, 1993

Stoddart, D Michael, *The Scented Ape*, Cambridge University Press, Cambridge, 1991

Süskind, Patrick, *Perfume. The Story of a Murderer*, Penguin Books, London, 1987

Symons, Donald, *Beauty is in the Adaptations of the Beholder: The Evolutionary Psychology of Human Female Sexual Attractivess*, University of California, Santa Barbara, 1994

The Sexual Imperative, Channel 4, July, 1994

The Shape of Evolution, Science News, Vol. 144, 1993

Taggart, ITV, Ocotber 1994

Tatler, October 1994

Tiger, Lionel and Fox, Robin, *The Imperial Animal*, Martin Secker & Warburg Ltd, London, 1972

Turner, E.S., *A History of Courting*, Pan Books, London, 1958

Twiggy, An Autobiography, London, 1975

Updike, John, *Couples*, Penguin Books, Middlesex, 1970

Veblen, Thorstein, *The Theory of the Leisure Class*, Funk & Wagnalls, New York

Voltaire, *Dictionnaire Philosophique Portatif*, 1764

Wagner, Marian, *Goddess: The Secret Lives of Marilyn Monroe*, New American Library, New York, 1986

Wainwright, Gordon R, *Body Language*, Headline, London, 1992

Wallechinsky, David, Wallace, Irving, Wallace, Amy, Wallace, Sylvia, *The Book of Lists 2*, Corgi, London, 1981

Walster, E., Aroson, E., Abrahams, D. and Rottman, L., *'Importance of physical attractiveness in dating behaviour'*, Journal of Personality and Social Psychology, 4:508-516, 1966

Warner, Rex (trans.), *Xenophon: The Persian Expedition,* Penguin Books, Middlesex, 1951

Warwick, Kevin, Professor, Department of Cybernetics, Reading University, *interview,* 1994

Waterhouse, Norman, FRCS, Wellington Hospital, London, *interview,* 1994

Watson, Dr Cynthia, *Love Potions, A Guide to Aphrodisiacs,* Optima, London, 1993

Weeks, David, *Abstracts, Edinburgh International Science Festival,* 1994

Weerth, Carolina de and Kalma, Akko P., *Female Aggression as a Response to Sexual Jealousy: A Sex Role Reversal?,* Aggressive Behavior, Vol. 19, pp 265-279 (1993)

Wilde, Oscar, *The Picture of Dorian Gray,* Collins, London, 1984

Willy A, Coester A, Fisher R, *The Practice of Sex,* Francis Aldor, London

Wilson, Glen and Nias, David, *Love's Mysteries, The Secret of Sexual Attraction,* Fontana, 1977

Without Walls, *Face Value,* Channel Four, Dec. 1994

Wolf, Annie, *The Truth About Beauty*

Wolf, Naomi, *The Beauty Myth,* Vintage, London, 1991

Woman's Journal, March 1994

Woolley, Benjamin, *Virtual Worlds,* Penguin Books, London, 1993

Wright, Robert, *The Moral Animal,* Pantheon Books, New York, 1994

Zeng, Xiao-Nong, Leyden, J.J., Lawley, H.J., Sawano, Kiyohito S., Nohara, I. and Preti, G., *'Analysis of characteristic odors from human male axillae,'* Journal of Chemical Ecology, Vol. 17, No. 7, 1991

Zeng, Xiao-Nong, Leyden, J.J., Brand, J.G., Spielman, A.I., McGinley, K.J. and Preti, George, *'An investigation of human apocrine gland secretion for axillary odor precursors',* Journal of Chemical Ecology, Vol. 18, No. 7, 1992

picture credits

Ace Photo Agency 35, 38
All Action 39, 93, 132
Douglas Botting 21, 37, 46, 90, 97, 103, 110, 138B, 166
Douglas Botting/Bush Boake Allen 160
Bruce Coleman 139, 141, 156, 169
Colorific 57, 144, 165
Colorsport 11
E.T. Archive l5, l8, 30, 45, 105, 114
Giraudon/Bridgeman Art Library 79, 88, 146
Ronald Grant 64, 84, 112, 122
Guerlain 152
Robert Harding 36, 60
Hulton Deutsch 12, 15, 61, 71, 86, 154
Kim Carlsberg/Idols 27, Denis O'Regan/Idols 102
Kobal l6, l7, 40, 47, 48, 49, 54, 62, 70, 78, 82, 85, 100, 108, 123, 163
Ray Ward/Life File 89, David Kampfner/Life File 143, Nigel Sitwell/Life File 95, Andrew Ward/Life File 134
David Fisher/London Features International 23, Nick

Elgar/London Features International 32
Niall McInerney 68, 92
Mattel UK Ltd 66
Max Factor 163
Mercedes 80
Robert Opie 33, 151
Popperfoto 65
Phil Jude/Science Photo Library 43, 59, Alfred Pasieka/Science Photo Library 58, Sydney Moulds/Science Photo Library 135T, 138T, 142, Alfred Pasieka/Science Photo Library 135B, CNRI/Science Photo Library 126, BSIP, DUCLOUX/Science Photo Library 176, Hank Morgan/Science Photo Library 177, Peter Menzel/Science Photo Library 180, Dr Ray Clark & M.R. Goff/Science Photo Library l9
Syndication International 72, 76
Telegraph Colour Library 26, 69, 96, 98, 127, 164, 172

index